THE
FIRST CHURCH OF CHRIST
SCIENTIST
AND MISCELLANY

THE
FIRST CHURCH OF CHRIST SCIENTIST
AND MISCELLANY

BY

MARY BAKER EDDY

DISCOVERER AND FOUNDER OF CHRISTIAN SCIENCE
AND AUTHOR OF SCIENCE AND HEALTH WITH
KEY TO THE SCRIPTURES

Registered U. S. Patent Office

Published by The
Trustees under the Will of Mary Baker G. Eddy
BOSTON, U.S.A.

Authorized Literature of
THE FIRST CHURCH OF CHRIST, SCIENTIST
in Boston, Massachusetts

Copyright, 1913
BY THE TRUSTEES UNDER THE WILL OF
MARY BAKER G. EDDY

*All rights reserved, including that of translation into foreign
languages, including the Scandinavian*

FOREWORD

> Lord God of Hosts, be with us yet;
> Lest we forget — lest we forget!
> — Kipling's *Recessional*

IN these stirring times of church building, when the attention of the whole world is fixed on Christian Science, when the growth and prosperity of the Cause are matters of general wonderment and frequent comment, when the right hand of fellowship is being extended to this people by other Christian denominations, when popularity threatens to supersede persecution, it is well for earnest and loyal Christian Scientists to fortify themselves against the mesmerism of personal pride and self-adulation by recalling the following historical facts: —

1. That Mary Baker Eddy discovered Christian Science in 1866, and established the Cause on a sound basis by healing the sick and reforming the sinner quickly and completely, and doing this work "without money and without price."

2. That in 1875, after nine years of arduous preliminary labor, she wrote and published the Christian Science textbook, "Science and Health with Key to the Scriptures;" that over four hundred thousand copies of this book have been sold — an unparalleled record for a work of this description; that it has healed multitudes of disease and has revealed God to well-nigh

countless numbers — facts which prove, (1) that Science and Health does not need to be interpreted to those who are earnestly seeking Truth; (2) that it is not possible to state truth absolutely in a simpler or more pleasing form.

3. That no one on earth to-day, aside from Mrs. Eddy, knows anything about Christian Science except as he has learned it from her and from her writings; and Christian Scientists are honest only as they give her full credit for this extraordinary work.

4. That Mrs. Eddy organized The First Church of Christ, Scientist, in Boston, Mass., devised its church government, originated its form of public worship, wrote its Church Manual and Tenets, and always has been and is now its guide, guardian, Leader, and wise and unerring counsellor.

5. That Mrs. Eddy founded *The Christian Science Journal* in 1883, was its first editor and for years the principal contributor to its columns; that she organized The Christian Science Publishing Society, which in 1898, with its assets valued at forty-five thousand dollars, she made over to trustees under agreement to pay all future profits to her church; that at the same time she presented to her church the property at 95 and 97 Falmouth Street, then occupied by the Publishing Society and valued at twenty-five thousand dollars, reserving for herself only a place for the publishing of her works; that she established the *Christian Science Sentinel* and authorized *Der Herold der Christian Science*, both of

which, together with *The Christian Science Journal*, are the property of the Publishing Society.

Strive it ever so hard, The Church of Christ, Scientist, can never do for its Leader what its Leader has done for this church; but its members can so protect their own thoughts that they are not unwittingly made to deprive their Leader of her rightful place as the revelator to this age of the immortal truths testified to by Jesus and the prophets.

Deeds, not words, are the sound test of love; and the helpfulness of consistent and constant right thinking — intelligent thinking untainted by the emotionalism which is largely self-glorification — is a reasonable service which all Christian Scientists can render their Leader.

— *The Christian Science Journal*, May, 1906.

CONTENTS

PART I

THE FIRST CHURCH OF CHRIST, SCIENTIST

	PAGE
Foreword	v

CHAPTER I

"Choose Ye" — Dedicatory Message, June 10, 1906.	3

CHAPTER II

The Extension of The Mother Church of Christ, Scientist: Its Inception, Construction, and Dedication

Mrs. Eddy's Message to The Mother Church, June 15, 1902	7
The Annual Meeting of The Mother Church, June 18, 1902 — Two Million Dollars Pledged	7
Greeting from the Church to Mrs. Eddy	8
Our Leader's Thanks	9
Christian Science Sentinel, May 16, 1903	10
Editorial in *Christian Science Sentinel*, May 16, 1903	11
Now and Then	12
Editorial in *Christian Science Sentinel*, January 2, 1904	14
Amendment to By-law	15
Communion, 1904	15
Extract from the Treasurer's Report, June 14, 1904	16
The Corner-stone Laid	16
Unselfish Loyalty	19
Holiday Gifts	20

CONTENTS

PAGE

THE ANNUAL MEETING, JUNE 13, 1905:
    EXTRACT FROM THE CLERK'S REPORT 22
    EXTRACT FROM THE TREASURER'S REPORT 23
    GREETING TO MRS. EDDY FROM THE ANNUAL MEETING 23
EDITORIAL IN *Christian Science Sentinel*, NOVEMBER 25, 1905 . 24
GIFTS FROM THE CHILDREN 25
CARD 25
ANNOUNCEMENT OF THE DEDICATION 26
TO THE BOARD OF DIRECTORS 26
NOTICE 27
NOTICE TO CONTRIBUTORS TO THE BUILDING FUND 27
EDITORIAL IN *Christian Science Sentinel*, JUNE 9, 1906 . . 27
COMMUNION SERVICE AND DEDICATION 29
THE ANNUAL MEETING, JUNE 12, 1906 38
    TELEGRAM TO MRS. EDDY. 44
    REPORT OF THE CLERK 47
LETTERS AND EDITORIAL 58
    EDITORIAL IN *Christian Science Sentinel*, JUNE, 1906. . 63

APPENDIX TO PART I

AS CHRONICLED BY THE NEWSPAPERS

AN ASTONISHING MOTION 65
PROGRESSIVE STEPS 65
THE FINISHING TOUCHES 66
DESCRIPTION OF THE EXTENSION. 67
AN IDEA OF THE SIZE 69
THE CHIMES 70
MAGNIFICENCE OF THE ORGAN 70
ITS ARCHITECTURE 71
UNIQUE INTERIOR 71
GATES OF BOSTON OPEN 72
CHRISTIAN SCIENTISTS HAVE ALL THE MONEY NEEDED . . 72
THE GREAT GATHERING 73
SPECIAL TRAINS COMING 73
INTERESTING AND AGREEABLE VISITORS 74
READILY ACCOMMODATED 75

CONTENTS

	PAGE
BIG CHURCH IS PAID FOR	75
GIANT TEMPLE FOR SCIENTISTS	76
DEDICATION DAY	77
CHILDREN'S SERVICE	78
ON A FAR HIGHER PEDESTAL	79
THE WEDNESDAY EVENING MEETINGS	79
EXODUS BEGINS	82

WHAT THE BOSTON EDITORS SAID:

Boston Daily Advertiser	83
Boston Herald	84
Boston Evening Record	84
Boston Post	84
Boston Herald	85
Boston Globe	86
Boston Post	86
Boston Herald	87

GENERAL EDITORIAL OPINION:

Montreal (Can.) *Gazette*	88
Concord (N. H.) *Monitor*	88
Brooklyn (N. Y.) *Eagle*	88
Denver (Col.) *News*	89
Terre Haute (Ind.) *Star*	90
Lafayette (Ind.) *Journal*	91
Springfield (Mass.) *Republican*	92
Rochester (N. Y.) *Post Express*	92
Topeka (Kan.) *Daily Capital*	93
Albany (N. Y.) *Knickerbocker*	94
Mexican Herald, City of Mexico, Mex.	95
Sandusky (Ohio) *Star-Journal*	95
Peoria (Ill.) *Journal*	96
Nebraska State Journal, Lincoln, Neb.	97
Athol (Mass.) *Transcript*	97
Portland (Ore.) *Telegram*	98
Portland (Me.) *Advertiser*	98
Denver (Col.) *Republican*	99
Bridgeport (Conn.) *Standard*	99

PART II
MISCELLANY

CHAPTER I

To the Christian World 103

CHAPTER II

The Christian Science Textbook 109

CHAPTER III
Personality

Personal Contagion 116
Letter to a Clergyman 118

CHAPTER IV
Messages to The Mother Church

Communion, January 2, 1898 121
Communion, June 4, 1899 124
Address at Annual Meeting, June 6, 1899 131
A Question Answered 133
Letter of the Pastor Emeritus, June, 1903 133
A Letter from Mrs. Eddy 134
Letter to The Mother Church 135
Card 136
Mrs. Eddy's Affidavit 137
Nota Bene 139
A Word to the Wise 139
Abolishing the Communion 140
Communion Season is Abolished 141
Mrs. Eddy's Reply 142
The Christian Science Board of Directors 142
Mrs. Eddy's Statements 143

CONTENTS

CHAPTER V

Christian Science Hall, Concord, N. H.

	PAGE
In Retrospect	145
Second Sunday Service, December 12, 1897	147
Address to the Concord Church, February, 1899	148
Message, April 19, 1899:	
Subject: "Not Matter, but Spirit"	151
First Annual Meeting, January 11, 1900	154
Easter Message, 1902	155
Annual Meeting, January 6, 1905	156

CHAPTER VI

First Church of Christ, Scientist, Concord, N. H.

Mrs. Eddy's Gift to the Concord Church	157
Corner-stone Laid at Concord	158
Message on the Occasion of the Dedication of Mrs. Eddy's Gift, July 17, 1904	159
Announcement	163
A Kindly Greeting	163
Acknowledgment of Gifts:	
To the Chicago Churches	164
To First Church of Christ, Scientist, New York	165
To The Mother Church	166
To First Church of Christ, Scientist, New London, Conn.	166
Thanksgiving Day, 1904	167
Religious Freedom	167

CHAPTER VII

Pleasant View and Concord, N. H.

Invitation to Concord, July 4, 1897	169
Visit to Concord, 1901	169
Address at Pleasant View, June, 1903	170

CONTENTS

	PAGE
VISIT TO CONCORD, 1904	171
THE DAY IN CONCORD	171
CARD OF THANKS	173
TO FIRST CONGREGATIONAL CHURCH	174
GREETINGS	175
TO FIRST CHURCH OF CHRIST, SCIENTIST, WILMINGTON, N. C.	176

CHAPTER VIII

DEDICATORY MESSAGES TO BRANCH CHURCHES

FIRST CHURCH OF CHRIST, SCIENTIST, CHICAGO, ILL.	177
FIRST CHURCH OF CHRIST, SCIENTIST, LONDON, ENGLAND	183
FIRST CHURCH OF CHRIST, SCIENTIST, BROOKLYN, N. Y.	183
FIRST CHURCH OF CHRIST, SCIENTIST, DETROIT, MICH.	183
FIRST CHURCH OF CHRIST, SCIENTIST, TORONTO, CANADA	184
WHITE MOUNTAIN CHURCH	184
FIRST CHURCH OF CHRIST, SCIENTIST, DULUTH, MINN.	186
FIRST CHURCH OF CHRIST, SCIENTIST, SALT LAKE CITY, UTAH	186
FIRST CHURCH OF CHRIST, SCIENTIST, ATLANTA, GA.	187
SECOND CHURCH OF CHRIST, SCIENTIST, CHICAGO, ILL.	191
FIRST CHURCH OF CHRIST, SCIENTIST, LOS ANGELES, CAL.	192
SECOND CHURCH OF CHRIST, SCIENTIST, MINNEAPOLIS, MINN.	193
FIRST CHURCH OF CHRIST, SCIENTIST, NEW YORK, N. Y.	193
FIRST CHURCH OF CHRIST, SCIENTIST, CLEVELAND, OHIO	195
FIRST CHURCH OF CHRIST, SCIENTIST, PITTSBURGH, PA.	196
FIRST CHURCH OF CHRIST, SCIENTIST, ST. LOUIS, MO.	196
FIRST CHURCH OF CHRIST, SCIENTIST, SAN JOSÉ, CAL.	197
FIRST CHURCH OF CHRIST, SCIENTIST, WILMINGTON, N. C.	197
FIRST CHURCH OF CHRIST, SCIENTIST, LONDON, ENGLAND	198

CHAPTER IX

LETTERS TO BRANCH CHURCHES

FIRST CHURCH OF CHRIST, SCIENTIST, PHILADELPHIA, PA.	199
FIRST CHURCH OF CHRIST, SCIENTIST, WASHINGTON, D. C.	199
FIRST CHURCH OF CHRIST, SCIENTIST, LONDON, ENGLAND	200
FIRST CHURCH OF CHRIST, SCIENTIST, NEW YORK, N. Y.	201

CONTENTS

XV

	PAGE
Second Church of Christ, Scientist, New York, N. Y.	201
First Church of Christ, Scientist, Oakland, Cal.	202
First Church of Christ, Scientist, Washington, D. C.	203
First Church of Christ, Scientist, London, England	203
First Church of Christ, Scientist, Columbus, Ohio	204
Third Church of Christ, Scientist, London, England	205
First Church of Christ, Scientist, Milwaukee, Wis.	207
A Telegram and Mrs. Eddy's Reply.	207
First Church of Christ, Scientist, Sydney, Australia	208
First Church of Christ, Scientist, Edinburgh, Scotland	208
The Committees in Conference, Chicago, Ill.	208
Comment on Letter from First Church of Christ, Scientist, Ottawa, Ontario	209

CHAPTER X

Admonition and Counsel

What Our Leader Says	210
Ways that are Vain	210
Only One Quotation	213
The Laborer and his Hire	214
The Children Contributors	216
A Correction	217
Question Answered	218
Christian Science Healing	219
Rules of Conduct	223
A Word to the Wise	223
Capitalization	225
Wherefore?	226
Significant Questions	228
Mental Digestion	229
Teaching in the Sunday School	230
Charity and Invalids	231
Lessons in the Sunday School	231
Watching *versus* Watching Out	232
Principle or Person?	233
Christian Science and China	234
Inconsistency	235

CONTENTS

	PAGE
SIGNS OF THE TIMES	235
NOTA BENE	236
TAKE NOTICE	236
TAKE NOTICE	237
TAKE NOTICE	237
PRACTITIONERS' CHARGES	237
TAKE NOTICE	237

CHAPTER XI
QUESTIONS ANSWERED

QUESTIONS AND ANSWERS	238
THE HIGHER CRITICISM	240
CLASS TEACHING	240
INSTRUCTION BY MRS. EDDY	241
MRS. EDDY'S REPLY	242
TAKE NOTICE	242

CHAPTER XII
READERS, TEACHERS, LECTURERS

THE NEW YORK CHURCHES	243
THE NOVEMBER CLASS, 1898	243
MASSACHUSETTS METAPHYSICAL COLLEGE	244
THE BOARD OF EDUCATION	246
TO A FIRST READER	247
THE CHRISTIAN SCIENCE BOARD OF LECTURESHIP	248
READERS IN CHURCH	249
WORDS FOR THE WISE	250
AFTERGLOW	250
TEACHERS OF CHRISTIAN SCIENCE	251
THE GENERAL ASSOCIATION OF TEACHERS, 1903	251
THE LONDON TEACHERS' ASSOCIATION, 1903	252
THE GENERAL ASSOCIATION OF TEACHERS, 1904	253
THE CANADIAN TEACHERS, 1904	253
STUDENTS IN THE BOARD OF EDUCATION, DECEMBER, 1904	253
THE MAY CLASS, 1905	254
THE DECEMBER CLASS, 1905	254
"ROTATION IN OFFICE"	254
MRS. EDDY'S REPLY	255

CONTENTS

CHAPTER XIII

Christmas

	PAGE
Early Chimes, December, 1898	256
Christmas, 1900	256
Christmas Gifts	257
The Significance of Christmas	259
Christmas for the Children	261
What Christmas Means to Me	261
Mrs. Eddy's Christmas Message	263

CHAPTER XIV

Contributions to Newspapers and Magazines

A Word in Defence	264
Christian Science Thanks	264
Mrs. Eddy's Response	264
Insufficient Freedom	266
Christian Science and the Times	266
Heaven	267
Prevention and Cure of Divorce	268
Harvest	269
Mrs. Eddy Describes her Human Ideal	271
Mrs. Eddy's Answer	271
Youth and Young Manhood	272
Mrs. Eddy Sends Thanks	274
Universal Fellowship	275
Mrs. Eddy's Own Denial that She is Ill	275
To Whom It May Concern	276
Politics	276

CHAPTER XV

Peace and War

Other Ways than by War	277
How Strife may be Stilled	278
The Prayer for Peace	279

	PAGE
"Hear, O Israel: The Lord our God is one Lord"	280
An Explanation	280
Practise the Golden Rule	281
Mrs. Eddy's Reply	281
Mrs. Eddy and the Peace Movement	282
Acknowledgment of Appointment as Fondateur	283
A Correction	284
To a Student	285
War	286

CHAPTER XVI

Tributes

Monument to Baron and Baroness de Hirsch	287
Tributes to Queen Victoria	289
Letter to Mrs. McKinley	290
Tribute to President McKinley	291
Power of Prayer	292
On the Death of Pope Leo XIII., July 20, 1903	294
A Tribute to the Bible	295
A Benediction	295
Hon. Clarence A. Buskirk's Lecture	296
"Hear, O Israel"	296
Miss Clara Barton	296
There is No Death	297
Mrs. Eddy's History	297

CHAPTER XVII

Answers to Criticisms

Christian Science and the Church	299
Faith in Metaphysics	301
Reply to Mark Twain	302
A Misstatement Corrected	304
A Plea for Justice	305
Reminiscences	306
Reply to McClure's Magazine	308
A Card	316

CONTENTS

CHAPTER XVIII

Authorship of Science and Health

Mrs. Eddy's Statement	317
Letters from Students	319

CHAPTER XIX

A Memorable Coincidence and Historical Facts

Mrs. Eddy's Letter	326
Miss Elizabeth Earl Jones' Letter	327
Miss Mary Hatch Harrison's Letter	329
A Card	331
Major Glover's Record as a Mason	334

CHAPTER XX

General Miscellany

The United States to Great Britain (Poem)	337
To the Public	338
Fast Day in New Hampshire, 1899	339
Spring Greeting (Poem)	341
Mrs. Eddy Talks	341
Mrs. Eddy's Successor	346
Gift of a Loving-cup	347
Fundamental Christian Science	347
Whither? (Poem)	350
A Letter from our Leader	351
Take Notice	351
Recognition of Blessings	352
Mrs. Eddy's Reply	352
Mrs. Eddy's Thanks	352
Something in a Name	353
Article XXII., Section 17	353
To Whom It May Concern	354
Extempore (Poem)	354

CONTENTS

	PAGE
MEN IN OUR RANKS	355
A PÆAN OF PRAISE	355
A STATEMENT BY MRS. EDDY	356
THE WAY OF WISDOM	356
A LETTER BY MRS. EDDY	357
TAKE NOTICE	358
A LETTER FROM MRS. EDDY	359
A LETTER BY MRS. EDDY	360
A LETTER BY MRS. EDDY	360
A TELEGRAM AND MRS. EDDY'S REPLY	361
A LETTER AND MRS. EDDY'S REPLY	362
TO THE MEMBERS OF THE CHRISTIAN SCIENTIST ASSOCIATION	363

PART I

THE FIRST CHURCH OF CHRIST SCIENTIST

THE FIRST CHURCH OF CHRIST SCIENTIST

CHAPTER I

"CHOOSE YE"

MESSAGE FROM MARY BAKER EDDY ON THE OCCASION OF THE DEDICATION OF THE EXTENSION OF THE MOTHER CHURCH OF CHRIST, SCIENTIST, JUNE 10, 1906

MY BELOVED BRETHREN: — The divine might of Truth demands well-doing in order to demonstrate truth, and this not alone in accord with human desire but with spiritual power. St. John writes: "Blessed are they that do His commandments, that they may have right to the tree of life, and may enter in through the gates into the city." The sear leaves of faith without works, scattered abroad in Zion's waste places, appeal to reformers, "Show me thy faith by thy works."

Christian Science is not a dweller apart in royal solitude; it is not a law of matter, nor a transcendentalism that heals only the sick. This Science is a law of divine Mind, a persuasive animus, an unerring impetus, an ever-present help. Its presence is felt, for it acts and acts wisely, always unfolding the highway of hope, faith, understanding. It is the higher criticism, the higher hope; and its effect on man is mainly this — that the good which has come into his life, examination compels him to think genuine, whoever did it. A Christian Scientist verifies his calling. *Choose ye!*

When, by losing his faith in matter and sin, one finds the spirit of Truth, then he practises the Golden Rule spontaneously; and obedience to this rule spiritualizes man, for the world's *nolens volens* cannot enthrall it. Lust, dishonesty, sin, disable the student; they preclude the practice or efficient teaching of Christian Science, the truth of man's being. The Scripture reads: "He that taketh not his cross, and followeth after me, is not worthy of me." On this basis, how many are following the Way-shower? We follow Truth only as we follow truly, meekly, patiently, spiritually, blessing saint and sinner with the leaven of divine Love which woman has put into Christendom and medicine.

A genuine Christian Scientist loves Protestant and Catholic, D.D. and M.D., — loves all who love God, good; and he loves his enemies. It will be found that, instead of opposing, such an individual subserves the interests of both medical faculty and Christianity, and they thrive together, learning that Mind-power is good will towards men. Thus unfolding the true metal in character, the iron in human nature rusts away; honesty and justice characterize the seeker and finder of Christian Science.

The pride of place or power is the prince of this world that hath nothing in Christ. Our great Master said: "Except ye . . . become as little children, ye shall not enter into the kingdom of heaven," — the reign of righteousness, the glory of good, healing the sick and saving the sinner. The height of my hope must remain. Glory be to Thee, Thou God most high and nigh.

Whatever is not divinely natural and demonstrably true, in ethics, philosophy, or religion, is not of God but originates in the minds of mortals. It is the Adam-dream according to the Scriptural allegory, in which man is supposed to start from dust and woman to be the outcome of man's rib, — marriage synonymous with legalized lust, and the offspring of sense the murderers of their brothers!

Wholly apart from this mortal dream, this illusion and delusion of sense, Christian Science comes to reveal man as God's image, His idea, coexistent with Him — God giving all and man having all that God gives. Whence, then, came the creation of matter, sin, and death, mortal pride and power, prestige or privilege? The First Commandment of the Hebrew Decalogue, "Thou shalt have no other gods before me," and the Golden Rule are the all-in-all of Christian Science. They are the spiritual idealism and realism which, when realized, constitute a Christian Scientist, heal the sick, reform the sinner, and rob the grave of its victory. The spiritual understanding which demonstrates Christian Science, enables the devout Scientist to worship, not an unknown God, but Him whom, understanding even in part, he continues to love more and to serve better.

Beloved, I am not with you *in propria persona* at this memorable dedication and communion season, but I am with you "in spirit and in truth," lovingly thanking your generosity and fidelity, and saying virtually what the prophet said: Continue to choose whom ye will serve.

Forgetting the Golden Rule and indulging sin, men cannot serve God; they cannot demonstrate the omnipotence of divine Mind that heals the sick and the sinner. Human will may mesmerize and mislead man; divine wisdom, never. Indulging deceit is like the defendant

6 THE FIRST CHURCH OF CHRIST, SCIENTIST

arguing for the plaintiff in favor of a decision which the defendant knows will be turned against himself.

We cannot serve two masters. Do we love God supremely? Are we honest, just, faithful? Are we true to ourselves? "God is not mocked: for whatsoever a man soweth, that shall he also reap." To abide in our unselfed better self is to be done forever with the sins of the flesh, the wrongs of human life, the tempter and temptation, the smile and deceit of damnation. When we have overcome sin in all its forms, men may revile us and despitefully use us, and we shall rejoice, "for great is [our] reward in heaven."

You have dexterously and wisely provided for The Mother Church of Christ, Scientist, a magnificent temple wherein to enter and pray. Greatly impressed and encouraged thereby, deeply do I thank you for this proof of your progress, unity, and love. The modest edifice of The Mother Church of Christ, Scientist, began with the cross; its excelsior extension is the crown. The room of your Leader remains in the beginning of this edifice, evidencing the praise of babes and the word which proceedeth out of the mouth of God. Its crowning ultimate rises to a mental monument, a superstructure high above the work of men's hands, even the outcome of their hearts, giving to the material a spiritual significance — the speed, beauty, and achievements of goodness. Methinks this church is the one edifice on earth which most prefigures self-abnegation, hope, faith; love catching a glimpse of glory.

CHAPTER II

THE EXTENSION OF THE MOTHER CHURCH OF CHRIST, SCIENTIST: ITS INCEPTION, CONSTRUCTION, AND DEDICATION

Mrs. Eddy's Message to The Mother Church, June 15, 1902

[Extract]

HERE allow me to interpolate some matters of business that ordinarily find no place in my Message. It is a privilege to acquaint communicants with the financial transactions of this church, so far as I know them, and especially before making another united effort to purchase more land and enlarge our church edifice so as to seat the large number who annually favor us with their presence on Communion Sunday.

THE ANNUAL MEETING OF THE MOTHER CHURCH, JUNE 18, 1902 — TWO MILLION DOLLARS PLEDGED

Edward A. Kimball, C.S.D., offered the following motion: —

"Recognizing the necessity for providing an auditorium for The Mother Church that will seat four or five thousand persons, and acting in behalf of ourselves and the Christian Scientists of the world, we agree to contribute any portion of two million dollars that may be necessary for this purpose."

In support of the motion, Mr. Kimball said in part:

"Our denomination is palpably outgrowing the institutional end thereof. We need to keep pace with our own growth and progress. The necessity here indicated is beyond cavil; beyond resistance in your thought."

Judge William G. Ewing, in seconding the motion, said:—

"As we have the best church in the world, and as we have the best expression of the religion of Jesus Christ, let us have the best material symbol of both of these, and in the best city in the world.

"Now I am sure that I have but expressed the universal voice of Christian Scientists, that there should be something done, and done immediately, to make reasonable accommodation for the regular business of the Christian Science church, and I believe really, with my faint knowledge of arithmetic and the relationship of figures, that a church of twenty-four thousand members should have a seating capacity of more than nine hundred, if they are all to get in."

The motion was carried unanimously.

Greeting from the Church to Mrs. Eddy

"Ten thousand Christian Scientists from throughout the world, convened in annual business meeting in Boston, send our greeting to you, whom we recognize as logically the natural and indispensable Leader of our religious denomination and its activity.

"Since the last report, in 1900, one hundred and five new churches or congregations have been added, and those previously established have had large accessions to their membership. In recognition of the necessity for providing an audience-room in The Mother Church which will seat four or five thousand persons, we have agreed to contribute any portion of two million dollars that may be needed for that purpose.

"The instinctive gratitude which not only impels the Christian to turn in loving thankfulness to his heavenly Father, but induces him to glory in every good deed and thought on the part of every man — this would be scant indeed if it did not continually move us to utter our gratitude to you and declare the depth of our affection and esteem.

"To you, who are standing in the forefront of the effort for righteous reform, we modestly renew the hope and desire that we may worthily follow with you in the way of salvation through Christ."

Our Leader's Thanks

To the Members of The Mother Church: — I am bankrupt in thanks to you, my beloved brethren, who at our last annual meeting pledged yourselves with startling grace to contribute any part of two millions of dollars towards the purchase of more land for its site, and to enlarge our church edifice in Boston. I never before felt poor in thanks, but I do now, and will draw on God for the amount I owe you, till I am satisfied with what my heart gives to balance accounts.

MARY BAKER EDDY.

PLEASANT VIEW, CONCORD, N. H.,
July 21, 1902.

[*Christian Science Sentinel*, May 16, 1903]

It is inevitable that the transforming influence of Christian Science should improve the thought, enlarge the favorable expectation, and augment the achievements of its followers. It was inevitable that this mighty impulse for good should have externalized itself, ten years ago, in an edifice for The Mother Church. It is inevitable that this same impulsion should now manifest itself in a beautiful, ample building, embodying the best of design, material, and situation.

Some money has been paid in towards the fund, and some of the churches and other organizations have taken steps in this direction, but the time is at hand, now, for this entire donation to be specifically subscribed as to amount and date of payment. No appeal has ever been made in this behalf, and it is probable that none will be made or ever be needed. It is doubtful if the Cause of Christian Science could prosper, in any particular, on the basis of fretful or reluctant sacrifice on the part of its people. Christian Scientists are not expected to contribute money against their will or as the result of importunity or entreaty on the part of some one else.

They will provide the money necessary to this end, because they recognize the importance of The Mother Church to the Cause. They realize that there must be a prosperous parent church, in order to insure the prosperity of the branch churches; indeed, they know that it is the prosperous growth of this movement which now necessitates this onward step. They know that their own individual welfare is closely interwoven with the general welfare of the Cause.

Notwithstanding the fact that as Christian Scientists we are as yet but imperfect followers of the perfect Christ, and although we may falter or stumble or loiter by the way, we know that the Leader of this movement, Mrs. Eddy, has been constantly at her post during all the storms that have surged against her for a generation. She has been the one of all the world who has encountered the full force of antagonism. We know, too, that during these years she has not tried to guide us by means of forced marches, but has waited for us to grow into readiness for each step, and we know that in all this time she has never urged upon us a step that did not result in our welfare.

A year ago she quietly alluded to the need of our Mother Church. She knew that we were ready; the response was instant, spontaneous. Later on she expressed much gratification because of prompt and liberal action, and it needs no special insight to predict that she will be cheered and encouraged to know that, having seized upon this privilege and opportunity, we have also made good the pledge.

[Editorial in *Christian Science Sentinel*, May 16, 1903]

Our readers have been informed of the purchase of the land upon which the new building will be erected, and that this land has been paid for. The location is, therefore, determined. The size of the building was decided last June, but there still remained for definite decision the amount to be expended and the date for commencing building operations. The pledge of the annual meeting was "any portion of two million dollars that may be necessary for this purpose," and this of course carried the implication that work should be commenced as soon as the money in hand justified the letting of contracts.

The spontaneous and liberal donations which enabled those having the work in charge to secure the large parcel of land adjoining The Mother Church, gives promise of the speedy accumulation of a sum sufficient to justify the decision of these remaining problems. Each person interested must remember, however, that his individual desires, both as to the amount to be expended and the date of commencing work, will be best evidenced by the liberality and promptness of his own contribution.

[Mrs. Eddy in *Christian Science Sentinel*, May 30, 1903]

Now and Then

This was an emphatic rule of St. Paul: "Behold, now is the accepted time." A lost opportunity is the greatest of losses. Whittier mourned it as what "might have been." We own no past, no future, we possess only *now*. If the reliable *now* is carelessly lost in speaking or in acting, it comes not back again. Whatever needs to be done which cannot be done now, God prepares the way for doing; while that which can be done now, but is not, increases our indebtedness to God. Faith in divine Love supplies the ever-present help and *now*, and gives the power to "act in the living present."

The dear children's good deeds are gems in the settings of manhood and womanhood. The good they desire to do, they insist upon doing now. They speculate neither on the past, present, nor future, but, taking no thought for the morrow, act in God's time.

A book by Benjamin Wills Newton, called "Thoughts on the Apocalypse," published in London, England, in 1853, was presented to me in 1903 by Mr. Marcus Holmes. This was the first that I had even heard of it. When scanning its interesting pages, my attention was arrested by the following: "The church at Jerusalem, like a sun in the centre of its system, had other churches, like so many planets, revolving around it. It was strictly a *mother* and a ruling church." According to his description, the church of Jerusalem seems to prefigure The Mother Church of Christ, Scientist, in Boston.

I understand that the members of The Mother Church, out of loving hearts, pledged to this church in Boston any part of two millions of money with which to build an ample temple dedicate to God, to Him "who forgiveth all thine iniquities; *who healeth all thy diseases;* who redeemeth thy life from destruction; who crowneth thee with lovingkindness and tender mercies; who satisfieth thy mouth with good things; so that thy youth is renewed like the eagle's," — to build a temple the spiritual spire of which will reach the stars with divine overtures, holy harmony, reverberating through all cycles of systems and spheres.

Because Christian Scientists virtually pledged this munificent sum not only to my church but to Him who returns it unto them after many days, their loving giving has been blessed. It has crystallized into a foundation for our temple, and it will continue to "prosper in the thing whereto [God, Spirit] sent it." In the *now* they brought their tithes into His storehouse. *Then*, when this bringing is consummated, God will pour them out a blessing above the song of angels, beyond the ken of mortals — a blessing that two millions of love currency will bring to be discerned in the near future as a gleam of reality; not a madness and nothing, but a sanity and something from the individual, stupendous, Godlike agency of man.

[Editorial in *Christian Science Sentinel*, January 2, 1904]

A few days ago we received a letter from a friend in another city, saying that he had just been informed — and his informant claimed to have good authority for the statement — that the entire amount required to complete The Mother Church building fund had been paid in; consequently further payments or subscriptions were not desired.

Our friend very promptly and emphatically pronounced the story a fabrication of the evil one, and he was entirely right in doing so. If the devil were really an entity, endowed with genius and inspiration, he could not have invented a more subtle lie with which to ensnare a generous and loyal people.

As a matter of fact, the building fund is not complete, but it is in such a healthy state that building operations have been commenced, and they will be carried on without interruption until the church is finished. The rapidity with which the work will be pushed forward necessitates large payments of money, and it is desirable that the contributions to the building fund keep pace with the disbursements.

[*Christian Science Sentinel*, March 5, 1904]

Amendment to By-law

Section 3 of Article XLI (XXXIV in revised edition) of the Church By-laws has been amended to read as follows:—

THE MOTHER CHURCH BUILDING. — SECTION 3. The edifice erected in 1894 for The First Church of Christ, Scientist, in Boston, Mass., shall neither be demolished nor removed from the site where it was built, without the written consent of the Pastor Emeritus, Mary Baker Eddy.

Communion, 1904

My Beloved Brethren: — My heart goes out to you as ever in daily desire that the Giver of all good transform you into His own image and likeness. Already I have said to you all that you are able to bear now, and thanking you for your gracious reception of it I close with Kate Hankey's excellent hymn, —

> I love to tell the story,
>   Of unseen things above,
> Of Jesus and his glory,
>   Of Jesus and his love.
> I love to tell the story,
>   Because I know 'tis true;
> It satisfies my longings,
>   As nothing else can do.
>
> I love to tell the story;
>   For those who know it best
> Seem hungering and thirsting
>   To hear it like the rest.
> And when, in scenes of glory,
>   I sing the NEW, NEW SONG,
> 'Twill be the OLD, OLD STORY
>   That I have loved so long.

EXTRACT FROM THE TREASURER'S REPORT, JUNE 14, 1904

The report of Mr. Stephen A. Chase, treasurer of the building fund of The Mother Church, made to the annual meeting, showed that a total of $425,893.66 had been received up to and including May 31, 1904, and that there was a balance of $226,285.73 on hand on that date, after paying out the sum of $199,607.93, which included the purchase price of the land for the site of the new building.

THE CORNER-STONE LAID

The corner-stone of the new auditorium for The Mother Church in Boston was laid Saturday, July 16, 1904, at eight o'clock in the forenoon. In addition to the members of the Christian Science Board of Directors, who have the work directly in charge, there were present on this occasion: Mr. Alfred Farlow, President of The Mother Church; Prof. Hermann S. Hering, First Reader; Mrs. Ella E. Williams, Second Reader; Mr. Charles Brigham and Mr. E. Noyes Whitcomb, respectively the architect and the builder of the new edifice.

The order of the services, which were conducted by the First Reader, was as follows: —

Scripture reading, Isaiah 28 : 16, 17,—

"Therefore thus saith the Lord God, Behold, I lay in Zion for a foundation a stone, a tried stone, a precious corner stone, a sure foundation: he that believeth shall not make haste.

"Judgment also will I lay to the line, and righteousness to the plummet: and the hail shall sweep away the

THE CORNER-STONE LAID

refuge of lies, and the waters shall overflow the hiding place."

Also, 1 Peter 2 : 1-6, —

"Wherefore laying aside all malice, and all guile, and hypocrisies, and envies, and all evil speakings,

"As newborn babes, desire the sincere milk of the word, that ye may grow thereby:

"If so be ye have tasted that the Lord is gracious.

"To whom coming, as unto a living stone, disallowed indeed of men, but chosen of God, and precious,

"Ye also, as lively stones, are built up a spiritual house, an holy priesthood, to offer up spiritual sacrifices, acceptable to God by Jesus Christ.

"Wherefore also it is contained in the scripture, Behold, I lay in Sion a chief corner stone, elect, precious: and he that believeth on him shall not be confounded."

The reading of selections from "Science and Health with Key to the Scriptures" by Mary Baker Eddy, —

Page 241, lines 13–30
" 136, " 1–5, 9–14
" 137, " 16–5
" 583, " 12–19
" 35, " 20–25

This was followed by a few moments of silent prayer and the audible repetition of the Lord's Prayer with its spiritual interpretation, as given in the Christian Science textbook, after which the following extracts from Mrs. Eddy's writings were read: —

"Hitherto, I have observed that in proportion as this church has smiled on His 'little ones,' He has blessed her. Throughout my entire connection with The Mother

Church, I have seen, that in the ratio of her love for others, hath His love been bestowed upon her; watering her waste places, and enlarging her borders.

"One thing I have greatly desired, and again earnestly request, namely, that Christian Scientists, here and elsewhere, pray daily for themselves; not verbally, nor on bended knee, but mentally, meekly, and importunately. When a hungry heart petitions the divine Father-Mother God for bread, it is not given a stone, — but more grace, obedience, and love. If this heart, humble and trustful, faithfully asks divine Love to feed it with the bread of heaven, health, holiness, it will be conformed to a fitness to receive the answer to its desire; then will flow into it the 'river of His pleasure,' the tributary of divine Love, and great growth in Christian Science will follow, — even that joy which finds one's own in another's good." (Miscellaneous Writings, p. 127.)

"Beloved brethren, the love of our loving Lord was never more manifest than in its stern condemnation of all error, wherever found. I counsel thee, rebuke and exhort one another. Love all Christian churches for the gospel's sake; and be exceedingly glad that the churches are united in purpose, if not in method, to close the war between flesh and Spirit, and to fight the good fight till God's will be witnessed and done on earth as in heaven." (Christian Science *versus* Pantheism, p. 13.)

The corner-stone was then laid by the members of the Christian Science Board of Directors. It contained the following articles: The Holy Bible; "Science and Health with Key to the Scriptures" and all other published writings of the Rev. Mary Baker Eddy, the Discoverer and Founder of Christian Science; Christian Science Hymnal; "The Mother Church;" the current numbers of *The Christian Science Journal*, *Christian Science Sentinel*, *Der Herold der Christian Science*, and the *Christian Science Quarterly*.

The ceremony concluded with the repetition of "the scientific statement of being," from Science and Health (p. 468), and the benediction, 2 Corinthians 13 : 14: "The grace of the Lord Jesus Christ, and the love of God, and the communion of the Holy Ghost, be with you all. Amen."

Unselfish Loyalty

To one of the many branch churches which contributed their local church building funds to The Mother Church building fund, Mrs. Eddy wrote as follows: —

First Church of Christ, Scientist,
    Colorado Springs, Col.

Beloved Brethren: — It is conceded that our shadows follow us in the sunlight wherever we go; but I ask for more, even this: That this dear church shall be pursued by her *substance*, the immortal fruition of her unselfed love, and that her charity, which "seeketh not her own" but another's good, shall reap richly the reward of goodness.

Those words of our holy Way-shower, vibrant through time and eternity with acknowledgment of exemplary giving, no doubt fill the memory and swell the hearts of the members of The Mother Church, because of that gift which you so sacredly bestowed towards its church building fund. These are applicable words: "Verily I say unto you, Wheresoever this gospel shall be preached throughout the whole world, this also that she hath done shall be spoken of for a memorial of her." (Mark 14 : 9.)

Gratefully yours in Christ,

MARY BAKER EDDY.

PLEASANT VIEW, CONCORD, N. H.,
September 1, 1904.

HOLIDAY GIFTS

Beloved Students: — The holidays are coming, and I trow you are awaiting on behalf of your Leader the loving liberty of their license. May I relieve you of selecting, and name your gifts to her, in advance? Send her only what God gives to His church. Bring all your tithes into His storehouse, and what you would expend for presents to her, please add to your givings to The Mother Church building fund, and let this suffice for her rich portion in due season. Send no gifts to her the ensuing season, but the evidences of glorious growth in Christian Science.

MARY BAKER EDDY.

PLEASANT VIEW, CONCORD, N. H.,
October 31, 1904.

A WORD FROM THE DIRECTORS, MAY, 1905

In view of the fact that a general attendance of the members of The Mother Church at the communion and annual meeting in Boston entails the expenditure of a large amount of money, and the further fact that it is important that the building fund of The Mother Church should be completed as early as possible, it has been decided to omit this year the usual large gathering in Boston, and to ask the members to contribute to

A WORD FROM THE DIRECTORS

the building fund the amount which they would have expended in such an event.

We all know of the loving self-sacrifices which have been made by many of the branch churches in transferring to this fund the money which had been collected for the purpose of building church homes of their own, and it will thus be seen that the course suggested will not only hasten the completion of The Mother Church, but will also advance the erection of many branch churches. We therefore feel sure that all Christian Scientists will gladly forego a visit to Boston at this time, in order to contribute more liberally to the building fund and thereby aid the progress of our Cause throughout the world.

Christian Scientists have learned from experience that divine Love more than compensates for every seeming trial and deprivation in our loyalty to Truth, and it is but right to expect that those who are willing to forego their anticipated visit this year will receive a greater blessing — "good measure, pressed down, and shaken together, and running over." The local members, who have always experienced much pleasure in welcoming their brethren from far and near, and who have anticipated much joy in meeting very many of them this year, will feel that they have been called upon to make no less sacrifice than have others; but we are confident that they too will be blessed, and that all will rejoice in the glad reunion upon the completion of the new edifice in Boston.

IRA O. KNAPP, JOSEPH ARMSTRONG,
WILLIAM B. JOHNSON, STEPHEN A. CHASE,
ARCHIBALD MCLELLAN,
The Christian Science Board of Directors.

THE ANNUAL MEETING, JUNE 13, 1905

Extract from the Clerk's Report

In the year 1902 our Leader saw the need of a larger edifice for the home of The Mother Church, one that would accommodate the constantly increasing attendance at all the services, and the large gatherings at the annual meeting; and, at the annual meeting in June, 1902, a sum of money adequate to erect such a building was pledged. Christian Scientists have contributed already for this grand and noble purpose, but let us not be unconsciously blind to the further needs of the building fund, in order to complete this great work, nor wait to be urged or to be shown the absolute necessity of giving.

Since 1866, almost forty years ago, — almost forty years in the wilderness, — our beloved Leader and teacher, Mrs. Eddy, the Founder of Christian Science, has labored for the regeneration of mankind; and time has put its seal of affirmation upon every purpose she has set in motion, and the justification of her labors is the fruit. In these years of work she has shown wisdom, faith, and a spiritual discernment of the needs of the present and of the future that is nothing less than God-bestowed.

In years to come the moral and the physical effects produced by The Mother Church, and by the advanced position taken by our Pastor Emeritus and Leader, will appear in their proper perspective. Is it not therefore the duty of all who have touched the healing hem of Christian Science, to get immediately into the proper perspective of the meaning of the erection of the new edifice of The First Church of Christ, Scientist, in Boston?

It is not necessary for us to delay our contributions in order to find out how much our neighbor has given, or to compute by the total membership of The Mother Church what amount each shall send the Treasurer. The divine Love that prompted the desire, and supplied the means to consummate the erection of the present edifice in 1894, is still with us, and will bless us so long as we follow His commands.

Extract from the Treasurer's Report

Building Fund: — Amount on hand June 1, 1905, $303,189.41; expenditures June 1, 1904 to May 31, 1905, $388,663.15; total receipts June 19, 1902 to June 1, 1905, $891,460.49.

Amount necessary to complete the sum of $2,000,000 pledged at the annual meeting, 1902, $1,108,539.51.

Greeting to Mrs. Eddy from the Annual Meeting

Beloved Teacher and Leader: — The members of your church, The Mother Church, The First Church of Christ, Scientist, in Boston, Mass., in annual business meeting assembled, send their loyal and loving greetings to you, the Discoverer and Founder of Christian Science and author of its textbook.

We rejoice greatly that the walls of our new edifice are rising, not only to faith but also to sight; that this temple, which represents the worship of Spirit, with its inseparable accompaniment, the Christ-healing, is being built in our day; and that we have the privilege of participating in the work of its erection. As the stately structure grows, and stone is laid upon stone, those who pass by are impelled to ask, What means this edifice? and they learn that the truth which Christ Jesus revealed — the truth which makes free — is to-day being proven and is ready to heal all who accept its divine ministry. We congratulate you that the building is to express in its ample auditorium something of the vastness of the truth it represents, and also to symbolize your unmeasured love for humanity, which inspires you to welcome all mankind to the privileges of this healing and saving gospel. As the walls are builded by the prayers and offerings of the thousands who have been healed through Christian Science, we know that you rejoice in the unity of thought and purpose which is thus expressed, showing that The Mother Church "fitly framed together groweth unto an holy temple in the Lord."

[Editorial in *Christian Science Sentinel*, November 25, 1905]

We are prompted to state, for the benefit of those who have inquired about the progress of the work on the extension to The Mother Church, that the erection of the building is proceeding rapidly; in fact, it is being pushed with the utmost energy, and at the present time there are no less than fifteen different trades represented. The beauty of the building, and the substantial and enduring character of its construction, have been remarked by the many visitors who have recently inspected the work, and they have gone away with the conviction that the structure is worthy of our Cause and that it will meet the needs of The Mother Church as well as this can be done by a building with a seating capacity of five thousand.

It therefore occurs to us that there could be no more appropriate time for completing the building fund than

the present Thanksgiving season; and it is suggested to our
readers that there would be great propriety in making a
special effort during the coming week to dispose fully and
finally of this feature of the demonstration.

[*Christian Science Sentinel*, March 17, 1906]

GIFTS FROM THE CHILDREN

The great interest exhibited by the children who attend
the Sunday School of The Mother Church is shown by
their contributions to the building fund. The following
figures are taken from the report of the secretary of the
Sunday School and are most gratifying:

March 1, 1903 to February 29, 1904, $621.10; March 1,
1904 to February 28, 1905, $845.96; March 1, 1905 to
February 28, 1906, $1,112.13; total, $2,579.19.

CARD

Will one and all of my dear correspondents accept this,
my answer to their fervid question: Owing to the time
consumed in travel, *et cetera*, I cannot be present *in
propria persona* at our annual communion and the dedication in June next of The Mother Church of Christ,
Scientist. But I shall be with my blessed church "in
spirit and in truth."

I have faith in the givers and in the builders of this
church edifice, — admiration for and faith in the grandeur
and sublimity of this superb superstructure, wherein all
vanity of victory disappears and the glory of divinity
appears in all its promise.

MARY BAKER EDDY.

PLEASANT VIEW, CONCORD, N. H.,
April 8, 1906.

[*Christian Science Sentinel*, April 14, 1906]

ANNOUNCEMENT OF THE DEDICATION

The Christian Science Board of Directors takes pleasure in announcing that the extension of The Mother Church will be dedicated on the date of the annual communion, Sunday, June 10, 1906.

[*Christian Science Sentinel*, April 28, 1906]

To the Board of Directors

My Beloved Students: — Your generous check of five thousand dollars, April 23, 1906, is duly received. You can imagine my gratitude and emotion at the touch of memory. Your beneficent gift is the largest sum of money that I have ever received from my church, and quite unexpected at this juncture, but not the less appreciated. My Message for June 10 is ready for you. It is too short to be printed in book form, for I thought it better to be brief on this rare occasion. This communion and dedication include enough of their own.

The enclosed notice I submit to you, and trust that you will see, as I foresee, the need of it. Now is the time to *throttle the lie* that students worship me or that I claim their homage. This historical dedication should date some special reform, and this notice is requisite to give the true animus of our church and denomination.

Lovingly yours,

Mary Baker Eddy.

Pleasant View, Concord, N. H.,
April 23, 1906.

EDITORIAL

Notice

To the Beloved Members of my Church, The Mother Church, The First Church of Christ, Scientist, in Boston: — Divine Love bids me say: Assemble not at the residence of your Pastor Emeritus at or about the time of our annual meeting and communion service, for the divine and not the human should engage our attention at this sacred season of prayer and praise.

MARY BAKER EDDY.

NOTICE TO CONTRIBUTORS TO THE BUILDING FUND

The contributors to the building fund for the extension of The Mother Church, The First Church of Christ, Scientist, in Boston, Mass., are hereby notified that sufficient funds have been received for the completion of the church building, and the friends are requested to send no more money to this fund.

STEPHEN A. CHASE,

Treasurer of the Building Fund.

BOSTON, MASS., June 2, 1906.

[Editorial in *Christian Science Sentinel*, June 9, 1906]

Christian Scientists will read with much joy and thanksgiving the announcement made by Mr. Chase in this issue of the *Sentinel* that sufficient funds have been received by him, as treasurer of the building fund, to pay all bills in connection with the extension of The Mother Church, and to most of them the fact that he has been able to make this announcement coincident with the completion of the building will be deeply significant. Our Leader has said in Science and Health (p. 494), "Divine Love always has met and always will meet every human need," and this has been proved true in the experience of many who have contributed to the building fund.

The treasurer's books will show the dollars and cents received by him, but they can give no more than a hint of the unselfish efforts, and in many instances the loving self-sacrifice, of those who have given so generously to the building of this church. Suffice it to say, however, that the giving to this fund has stimulated those gentle qualities which mark the true Christian, and its influence upon the lives of thousands has been of immense value to them.

The significance of this building is not to be found in the material structure, but in the lives of those who, under the consecrated leadership of Mrs. Eddy, and following her example, are doing the works which Jesus said should mark the lives of his followers. It stands as the visible symbol of a religion which heals the sick and reforms the sinful as our Master healed and reformed them. It proclaims to the world that Jesus' gospel was for all time and for all men; that it is as effective to-day as it was when he preached the Word of God to the multitudes of Judea and healed them of their diseases and their sins. It speaks for the successful labors of one divinely guided woman, who has brought to the world the spiritual understanding of the Scriptures, and whose ministry has revealed the one true Science and changed the whole aspect of medicine and theology.

[*Christian Science Sentinel*, June 16, 1906. Reprinted from
Boston Herald]

COMMUNION SERVICE AND DEDICATION

Five thousand people kneeling in silent communion; a stillness profound; and then, rising in unison from the vast congregation, the words of the Lord's Prayer! Such was the closing incident of the dedicatory services of the extension of The Mother Church, The First Church of Christ, Scientist, at the corner of Falmouth and Norway Streets, yesterday morning. And such was the scene repeated six times during the day.

It was a sight which no one who saw it will ever be able to forget. Many more gorgeous church pageantries have been seen in this country and in an older civilization; there have been church ceremonies that appealed more to the eye, but the impressiveness of this lay in its very simplicity; its grandeur sprang from the complete unanimity of thought and of purpose. There was something emanating from the thousands who worshipped under the dome of the great edifice whose formal opening they had gathered to observe, that appealed to and fired the imagination. A comparatively new religion launching upon a new era, assuming an altogether different status before the world!

Even the sun smiled kindly upon the dedication of the extension of The Mother Church. With a cooling breeze to temper the heat, the thousands who began to congregate about the church as early as half past five in the morning were able to wait patiently for the opening of the doors without suffering the inconveniences of an oppressive day. From that time, until the close of the evening service,

Falmouth and Norway Streets held large crowds of people, either coming from a service or awaiting admission to one. As all the services were precisely the same in every respect, nobody attended more than one, so that there were well over thirty thousand people who witnessed the opening. Not only did these include Scientists from all over the world, and nearly all the local Scientists, but many hundreds of other faiths, drawn to the church from curiosity, and from sympathy, too.

It spoke much for the devotion of the members to their faith, the character of the attendance. In those huge congregations were business men come from far distant points at personal sacrifices of no mean order; professional men, devoted women members, visitors from Australia, from India, from England, from Germany, from Switzerland, from South Africa, from Hawaii, from the coast States.

They gave generously of their means in gratitude for the epoch-making event. The six collections were large, and when the plates were returned after having been through the congregations, they were heaped high with bills, with silver, and with gold. Some of these contributions were one-hundred-dollar bills. Without ostentation and quite voluntarily the Scientists gave a sum surpassing some of the record collections secured by evangelists for the work of Christianity.

Though the church was filled for the service at half past seven, and hundreds had to be turned away, by far the largest crowd of the day applied for admission at the ten o'clock service, and it was representative of the entire body of the Christian Science church.

Before half past seven the chimes of the new church

COMMUNION SERVICE AND DEDICATION 31

began to play, first the "Communion Hymn," succeeded by the following hymns throughout the day: "The morning light is breaking;" "Shepherd, show me how to go;" "Just as I am, without one plea;" "I need Thee every hour;" "Blest Christmas morn;" "Abide with me;" "Day by day the manna fell;" "Oh, the clanging bells of time;" "Still, still with Thee;" "O'er waiting harpstrings of the mind;" Doxology.

Promptly at half past six the numerous doors of the church were thrown open and the public had its first glimpse of the great structure, the cost of which approximates two millions of dollars, contributed from over the entire world. The first impression was of vastness, then of light and cheerfulness, and when the vanguard of the thousands had been seated, expressions of surprise and of admiration were heard on every hand for the beauty and the grace of the architecture. The new home for worship that was opened by the Scientists in Boston yesterday can take a place in the front rank of the world's houses of worship, and it is no wonder that the first sight which the visitors caught of its interior should have impressed them as one of the events of their lives.

First Reader William D. McCrackan, accompanied by the Second Reader, Mrs. Laura Carey Conant, and the soloist for the services, Mrs. Hunt, was on the Readers' platform. Stepping to the front of the platform, when the congregation had taken their seats, the First Reader announced simply that they would sing Hymn 161, written by Mrs. Eddy, as the opening of the dedicatory service. And what singing it was! As though trained carefully under one leader, the great body of Scientists joined in the song of praise.

Spontaneous unanimity and repetition in unison were two of the most striking features of the services. When, after five minutes of silent communion at the end of the service, the congregation began to repeat the Lord's Prayer, they began all together, and their voices rose as one in a heartfelt appeal to the creator.

So good are the acoustic properties of the new structure that Mr. McCrackan and Mrs. Conant could be heard perfectly in every part of it, and they did not have to lift their voices above the usual platform tone.

Following the organ voluntary — Fantasie in E minor, Merkel — the order of service was as follows: —

Hymn 161, from the Hymnal. Words by the Rev. Mary Baker Eddy.[1]

Reading from the Scriptures: Deuteronomy 26 : 1, 2, 5-10 (first sentence).

Silent prayer, followed by the audible repetition of the Lord's Prayer with its spiritual interpretation as given in the Christian Science textbook.

Hymn 166, from the Hymnal.[2]

Reading of notices.

Reading of Tenets of The Mother Church.

Collection.

Solo, "Communion Hymn," words by the Rev. Mary Baker Eddy, music by William Lyman Johnson.

Reading of annual Message from the Pastor Emeritus, the Rev. Mary Baker Eddy.

Reading the specially prepared Lesson-Sermon.

After the reading of the Lesson-Sermon, silent communion, which concluded with the audible repetition of the Lord's Prayer.

[1] Hymn 306, [2] Hymn 108, in Revised Hymnal

COMMUNION SERVICE AND DEDICATION

Singing the Communion Doxology.

Reading of a despatch from the members of the church to Mrs. Eddy.

Reading of "the scientific statement of being" (Science and Health, p. 468), and the correlative Scripture, 1 John 3 : 1–3.

The benediction.

The subject of the special Lesson-Sermon was "Adam, Where Art Thou?" the Golden Text: "Search me, O God, and know my heart: try me, and know my thoughts: and see if there be any wicked way in me, and lead me in the way everlasting." (Psalms 139 : 23, 24.) The responsive reading was from Psalms 15 : 1–5; 24 : 1–6, 9, 10.

1 Lord, who shall abide in thy tabernacle? who shall dwell in thy holy hill?

2 He that walketh uprightly, and worketh righteousness, and speaketh the truth in his heart.

3 He that backbiteth not with his tongue, nor doeth evil to his neighbor, nor taketh up a reproach against his neighbor.

4 In whose eyes a vile person is contemned; but he honoreth them that fear the Lord. He that sweareth to his own hurt, and changeth not.

5 He that putteth not out his money to usury, nor taketh reward against the innocent. He that doeth these things shall never be moved.

1 The earth is the Lord's, and the fulness thereof; the world, and they that dwell therein.

2 For he hath founded it upon the seas, and established it upon the floods.

3 Who shall ascend into the hill of the Lord? or who shall stand in his holy place?

4 He that hath clean hands, and a pure heart; who hath not lifted up his soul unto vanity, nor sworn deceitfully.

5 He shall receive the blessing from the Lord, and righteousness from the God of his salvation.

6 This is the generation of them that seek him, that seek thy face, O Jacob.

9 Lift up your heads, O ye gates; even lift them up, ye everlasting doors; and the King of glory shall come in.

10 Who is this King of glory? The Lord of hosts, he is the King of glory.

The Lesson-Sermon consisted of the following citations from the Bible and "Science and Health with Key to the Scriptures" by the Rev. Mary Baker Eddy, and was read by Mr. McCrackan and Mrs. Conant: —

I

The Bible	Science and Health [1]
Genesis 3 : 9–11	224 : 22
Proverbs 8 : 1, 4, 7	559 : 8–10, 19
Mark 2 : 15–17	181 : 21–25
	307 : 31–8

II

Psalms 51 : 1–3, 6, 10, 12, 13, 17	308 : 8, 16–28 *This; Jacob*
	323 : 19–24, 28–32 *When; The effects*

[1] The Science and Health references in this lesson are according to the 1913 edition.

COMMUNION SERVICE AND DEDICATION 35

III

The Bible	Science and Health
Hebrews 11 : 1, 3, 6	297 : 20 *Faith*
Proverbs 3 : 5, 6	241 : 23–27
Job 28 : 20, 23, 28	275 : 25
1 Corinthians 14 : 20	505 : 21–28 *Understanding*
	536 : 8

IV

Psalms 86 : 15, 16	345 : 31
Matthew 9 : 2–8	337 : 10
	525 : 4
	494 : 30–2 *Our Master*
	476 : 32–4
	171 : 4

V

Mark 12 : 30, 31	9 : 17–21 *Dost thou*
John 21 : 1 (first clause), 14–17	53 : 8–11
	54 : 29–1
1 John 4 : 21	560 : 11–19, 22 *The great; Abuse*
	565 : 18–22.

VI

John 21 : 4–6, 9, 12, 13	34 : 29–29
Revelation 3 : 20	
Revelation 7 : 13, 14, 16, 17	

During the progress of each service, First Reader William D. McCrackan read to the congregation the dedicatory Message from their teacher and Leader, Mrs. Mary Baker Eddy.

The telegram from the church to Mrs. Eddy was read by Mr. Edward A. Kimball of Chicago, and the five thousand present rose as one to indicate their approval of it.

Rev. Mary Baker Eddy, *Pastor Emeritus.*

Beloved Teacher and Leader: — The members of your church have assembled at this sacred time to commune with our infinite heavenly Father and again to consecrate all that we are or hope to be to a holy Christian service that shall be acceptable unto God.

Most of us are here because we have been delivered from beds of sickness or withheld from open graves or reclaimed from vice or redeemed from obdurate sin. We have exchanged the tears of sorrow for the joy of repentance and the peace of a more righteous living, and now with blessed accord we are come, in humility, to pour out our gratitude to God and to bear witness to the abundance of salvation through His divine Christ.

At this altar, dedicated to the only true God, we who have been delivered from the depths increase the measure of our devotion to the daily life and purpose which are in the image and likeness of God.

By these stately walls; by this sheltering dome; by all the beauty of color and design, the Christian Scientists of the world, in tender affection for the cause of human weal, have fulfilled a high resolve and set up this tabernacle, which is to stand as an enduring monument, a sign of your understanding and proof that our Supreme God, through His power and law, is the natural healer

COMMUNION SERVICE AND DEDICATION 37

of all our diseases and hath ordained the way of salvation of all men from all evil. No vainglorious boast, no pride of circumstances has place within the sacred confines of this sanctuary. Naught else than the grandeur of humility and the incense of gratitude and compassionate love can acceptably ascend heavenward from this house of God.

It is from the depths of tenderest gratitude, respect, and affection that we declare again our high appreciation of all that you have done and continue to do for the everlasting advantage of this race. Through you has been revealed the verity and rule of the Christianity of Christ which has ever healed the sick. By your fidelity and the constancy of your obedience during forty years you have demonstrated this Science before the gaze of universal humanity. By reason of your spiritual achievement the Cause of Christian Science has been organized and maintained, its followers have been prospered, and the philosophy of the ages transformed. Recognizing the grand truth that God is the supreme cause of all the activities of legitimate existence, we also recognize that He has made known through your spiritual perception the substance of Christian Science, and that this church owes itself and its prosperity to the unbroken activity of your labors, which have been and will still be the pretext for our confident and favorable expectation.

We have read your annual Message to this church. We are deeply touched by its sweet entreaty, its ineffable loving-kindness, its wise counsel and admonition.

With sacred resolution do we pray that we may give heed and ponder and obey. We would be glad if our prayers, our rejoicing, and our love could recompense your long sacrifice and bestow upon you the balm of heavenly joy, but knowing that every perfect gift cometh from above, and that in God is all consolation and comfort, we rest in this satisfying assurance, while we thank you and renew the story of our love for you and for all that you are and all that you have done for us.

WILLIAM B. JOHNSON, *Clerk.*

By means of a carefully trained corps of ushers, numbering two hundred, there was no confusion in finding seats, and when all seating space had been filled no more were admitted until the next service. The church was filled for each service in about twenty minutes, and was emptied in twelve, in spite of the fact that many of the visitors showed a tendency to tarry to examine the church.

It was "children's day" at noon, for the service at half past twelve was specially reserved for them. They filled all the seats in the body of the church, and when it came to the singing, the little ones were not a whit behind their elders, their shrill trebles rising with the roll of the organ in almost perfect time. In every respect their service was the same as all the others.

There was no more impressive feature of the dedication than the silent communion. Devout Scientists said after the service that they would ever carry with them the memory of it.

THE ANNUAL MEETING, JUNE 12, 1906

The annual meeting of The First Church of Christ, Scientist, in Boston, was held in the extension of The Mother Church, Tuesday, June 12, at ten o'clock in the

THE ANNUAL MEETING, 1906

forenoon, and in order to accommodate those who could not gain admittance at that hour a second session was held at two o'clock in the afternoon. The meeting was opened by the President, Rev. William P. McKenzie, who read from the Bible and Science and Health as follows: —

The Bible	Science and Health
Isaiah 54 : 1-5, 10-15, 17	571 : 22
Revelation 19 : 1, 6-9.	574 : 3-16, 27 *The Revelator; The very*
	577 : 4.

Then followed a short silent prayer and the audible repetition of the Lord's Prayer, in which all joined. The following list of officers for the ensuing year was read by the Clerk: —

President, Willis F. Gross, C.S.B.; Treasurer, Stephen A. Chase, C.S.D.; Clerk, William B. Johnson, C.S.D.

In introducing the new President, Mr. McKenzie said:—

When I introduce the incoming President, my modest task will be ended. You will allow me, however, the privilege of saying a few words of reminder and prophecy. My thoughts revert to a former occasion, when it was my pleasant duty to preside at an annual meeting when our Pastor Emeritus, Mrs. Eddy, was present. We remember her graciousness and dignity. We recall the harmonious tones of her gentle voice. Our hearts were thrilled by her compassion, and the memory lives with us. But even more distinctly may we realize her presence with us to-day. Why? Because our own growth in love and unity enables us to comprehend better the strength and beauty of her character.

Moreover, this completed extension of The Mother Church is an evidence to us of her hospitable love. She has desired for years to have her church able to give more adequate reception to those who hunger and thirst after practical righteousness; and we are sure that now the branch churches of The Mother Church will also enlarge their hospitality, so that these seekers everywhere may be satisfied. This will imply the subsidence of criticism among workers. It may even imply that some who have been peacebreakers shall willingly enter into the blessedness of peacemakers. Nothing will be lost, however, by those who relinquish their cherished resentments, forsake animosity, and abandon their strongholds of rivalry. Through rivalries among leaders Christendom became divided into warring sects; but the demand of this age is for peacemaking, so that Christianity may more widely reassert its pristine power to bring health and a cure to pain-racked and sorrow-worn humanity. "The wisdom that is from above is first pure, then peaceable, . . . And the fruit of righteousness is sown in peace of them that make peace." "Blessed are the peacemakers: for they shall be called the children of God."

Our Leader, Mrs. Eddy, has presented to the world the ideal of Christianity, because she is an exact metaphysician. She has illustrated what the poet perceived when he said, "All's love, but all's law." She has obeyed the divine Principle, Love, without regrets and without resistance. Human sense often rebels against law, hence the proverb: *Dura lex, sed lex* (Hard is the law, nevertheless it is the law). But by her own blameless and happy life, as well as by her teachings, our Leader has induced a multitude — how great no man can number — to become gladly obedient to law, so that they think rightly or righteously.

No one can change the law of Christian metaphysics, the law of right thinking, nor in any wise alter its effects. It is a forever fact that the meek and lowly in heart are blessed and comforted by divine Love. If the proud are lonely and uncomforted, it is because they have thoughts adverse to the law of love. Pride, arrogance, and self-will are unmerciful, and so receive judgment without mercy; but the law of metaphysics says, "Blessed are the merciful," and will allow no one to escape that blessedness, howsoever far he may stray, whatsoever lawlessness of hatred he may practise and suffer from.

So we see that Christian Science makes no compromise with evil, sin, wrong, or imperfection, but maintains the perfect standard of truth and righteousness and joy. It teaches us to rise from sentimental affection which admires friends and hates enemies, into brotherly love which is just and kind to all and unable to cherish any enmity. It brings into present and hourly application what Paul termed "the law of the Spirit of life in Christ Jesus," and shows man that his real estate is one of blessedness. Why should any one postpone his legitimate joy, and disregard his lawful inheritance, which is "incorruptible and undefiled"? Our Leader and teacher not only discovered Christian Science, but through long years of consecration has obeyed its every demand, for our sakes as well as for her own; and we begin to understand how illimitable is the Love which supports such selfless devotion, we begin to comprehend the "beauty of holiness," and to be truly grateful to her who has depicted its form and comeliness. We have found it true that "she openeth her mouth with wisdom; and in her tongue is the law of kindness."

It is my pleasure to introduce to you a faithful follower of this Leader as the President for the coming year, Willis F. Gross, C.S.B., one who has for many years "witnessed a good confession" in the practice of Christian Science. You are no doubt already acquainted with him as one of the helpful contributors to our periodicals, so that any further words of mine are unnecessary.

Mr. Gross, on assuming office, said: —

Beloved Friends: — Most unexpectedly to me came the call to serve you in this capacity, and I desire to improve this opportunity to express my thanks for the honor conferred upon me. With a heart filled with gratitude for the countless blessings which have come into my life through Christian Science, I shall endeavor to perform this service to the best of my ability.

It affords me great pleasure to welcome you to our first annual meeting held in the extension of The Mother Church. I shall not attempt to speak of the deep significance of this momentous occasion. I realize that only as infinite good unfolds in each individual consciousness can we begin to comprehend, even in small degree, how great is the work that has been inaugurated by our beloved Leader, how faithful is her allegiance to God, how untiring are her efforts, and how successful she is in the performance of her daily tasks.

"With a mighty hand, and with an outstretched arm" were the children of Israel delivered from the bondage of the Egyptians, but this deliverance did not put them in possession of the promised land. An unknown wilderness was before them, and that wilderness must be conquered. The law was given that they might know what was required of them, that they might have a definite rule of action whereby to order aright the affairs of daily life. Obedience to the demands of the law revealed the God of their fathers, and they learned to know Him. During their sojourn in the wilderness they suffered defeats and met with disappointments, but they learned from experience and finally became willingly obedient to the voice of their leader. The crossing of the Jordan brought them into the promised land, and this experience was almost as marvellous as had been the passage of the Red Sea forty years before. In obedience to the command of Joshua, twelve stones taken from the midst of the river were set up on the other side for a memorial. In future generations when it was asked, "What mean ye by these stones?" it was told them: Israel came over this Jordan on dry ground.

Forty years ago the Science of Christian healing was revealed to our beloved Leader, the Rev. Mary Baker Eddy. A few years later she gave us our textbook, "Science and Health with Key to the Scriptures." Obedience to the teachings of this book has brought us to this hour. We have learned from experience, and to-day we rejoice that we have found in Christian Science that which heals and saves.

The world looks with wonder upon this grand achievement, — the completion and dedication of our magnificent temple, — and many are asking, "What mean ye by these stones?" The answer is, The way out of the wilderness of human beliefs has been revealed. Through the understanding of God as an ever-present help, the sick are being healed, the shackles of sin are being broken, heavy burdens are being laid down, tears are being wiped away, and Israel is going up to possess the promised land of eternal, harmonious existence.

Friends, our progress may be fast or it may be slow, but one thing is certain, it will be sure, if we are obedient to the loving counsel of our ever faithful Leader. The Christ is here, has come to individual consciousness; and the faithful disciple rejoices in prophecy fulfilled, "Lo, I am with you alway, even unto the end of the world."

Telegram to Mrs. Eddy

Judge Septimus J. Hanna then advanced to the front of the platform, read the following despatch, and moved that it be forwarded at once to our Leader, Mrs. Eddy. The motion was carried unanimously by a rising vote.

The despatch was as follows: —

To the Rev. Mary Baker Eddy,
    Pleasant View, Concord, N. H.

Beloved Teacher and Leader: — The members of The Mother Church, The First Church of Christ, Scientist, in Boston, Mass., in annual meeting assembled, hereby convey to you their sincere greetings and their deep love.

They desire to express their continued loyalty to your teachings, their unshaken confidence in the unerring wisdom of your leadership, and their confident assurance that strict and intelligent recognition of and obedience to the comprehensive means by you provided for the furtherance of our Cause, will result in its perpetuity as well as in the ultimate regeneration of its adherents and of mankind.

We are witnessing with joy and gratitude the significant events associated with this, one of the greatest and most important gatherings of Christian Scientists in the annals of our history. Yet the upwards of thirty thousand who are physically present at the dedication represent only a small part of the entire body who are of us and with us in the animus and spirit of our movement.

The great temple is finished! That which you have long prophetically seen has been accomplished. The magnificent edifice stands a fitting monument of your obedience and fidelity to the divine Principle revealed to you in that momentous hour when purblind mortal sense declared you to be *in extremis*. You followed unswervingly the guidance of Him who went before you by day in a pillar of cloud to lead you in the way, and by night in a pillar of fire to give you light, and the results of such following have been marvellous beyond human ken. As clearly as in retrospect we see the earlier leading, we now discern the fulfilment of the later prophecy, that "He took not away the pillar of cloud by day, nor the pillar of fire by night," for each advancing step has logically followed the preceding one.

The great temple is finished! This massive pile of New Hampshire granite and Bedford stone, rising to a height of two hundred and twenty-four feet, one foot loftier than the Bunker Hill monument, stands a material type of Truth's permanence. In solid foundation, in symmetrical arches, in generous hallways, in commodious foyer and broad stairways, in exquisite and expansive auditorium, and in towering, overshadowing dome, the great structure stands, silently but eloquently beckoning us on towards a higher and more spiritual plane of living, for we know that without this spiritual significance it were but a passing dream.

In the best sense it stands in prophetic verity of the primary declaration of this church in its original organization; namely, "To organize a church designed to commemorate the word and works of our Master, which should reinstate primitive Christianity and its lost element of healing." (Church Manual, p. 17.) To rise to the demands of this early pronouncement is the work of true Christian Scientists.

To preach the gospel and heal the sick on the Christ-basis is the essential requirement of a reinstated Christianity. Only as we pledge ourselves anew to this demand, and then fulfil the pledge in righteous living, are we faithful, obedient, deserving disciples.

On this solemn occasion, and in the presence of this assembled host, we do hereby pledge ourselves to a deeper consecration, a more sincere and Christly love of God and our brother, and a more implicit obedience to the sacred teachings of the Bible and our textbook, as well as to the all-inclusive instructions and admonitions of our Church Manual in its spiritual import, that we may indeed reach "unto the city of the living God, the heavenly Jerusalem, and to an innumerable company of angels, to the general assembly and church of the firstborn."

WILLIAM B. JOHNSON, *Clerk*.

BOSTON, MASS., June 12, 1906.

Report of the Clerk

Beloved Brethren of The First Church of Christ, Scientist, in Boston, Mass.: — It seems meet at this time, when thousands of Christian Scientists have gathered here from all parts of the world, many of whom have not had the means of knowing the steps by which this church has reached its present growth, to present in this report a few of the stages of its progress, as gleaned from the pages of its history.

After a work has been established, has grown to great magnitude, and people the world over have been touched by its influence for good, it is with joy that those who have labored unceasingly for the work look back to the picturesque, interesting, and epoch-marking stages of its growth, and recall memories of trials, progress, and victories that are precious each and all. To-day we look back over the years that have passed since the inception of this great Cause, and we cannot help being touched by each landmark of progress that showed a forward effort into the well-earned joy that is with us now. For a Cause that has rooted itself in so many distant lands, and inspired so many of different races and tongues into the demonstration of the knowledge of God, the years that have passed since Mrs. Eddy founded her first church seem but a short time. And this little church, God's word in the wilderness of dogma and creed, opened an era of Christian worship founded on the commands of Jesus: "Go ye into all the world, and preach the gospel to every creature. . . . And these signs shall follow them that believe; In my name shall they cast out devils; they shall speak with new tongues; they shall take up ser-

48 THE FIRST CHURCH OF CHRIST, SCIENTIST

pents; and if they drink any deadly thing, it shall not hurt them; they shall lay hands on the sick, and they shall recover."

Not until nineteen centuries had passed was there one ready to receive the inspiration, to restore to human consciousness the stone that had been rejected, and which Mrs. Eddy made "the head of the corner" of The Church of Christ, Scientist.

With the reading of her textbook, "Science and Health with Key to the Scriptures," Mrs. Eddy insisted that her students make, every day, a prayerful study of the Bible, and obtain the spiritual understanding of its promises. Upon this she founded the future growth of her church, and twenty-six years later the following splendid appreciation of her efforts appeared in the *Methodist Review* from the pen of the late Frederick Lawrence Knowles: —

"Mrs. Eddy . . . in her insistence upon the constant daily reading of the Bible and her own writings, . . . has given to her disciples a means of spiritual development which . . . will certainly build such truth as they do gain into the marrow of their characters. The scorn of the gross and sensual, and the subordination of merely material to spiritual values, together with the discouragement of care and worry, are all forces that make for righteousness. And they are burned indelibly upon the mind of the neophyte every day through its reading. The intellects of these people are not drugged by scandal, drowned in frivolity, or paralyzed by sentimental fiction. . . . They feed the higher nature through the mind, and I am bound as an observer of them to say, in all fairness, that the result is already manifest in their faces, their conversation,

THE ANNUAL MEETING, 1906

and their bearing, both in public and private. What wonder that when these smiling people say, 'Come thou with us, and we will do thee good,' the hitherto half-persuaded one is wholly drawn over, as by an irresistible attraction. The religious body which can direct, and control, in no arbitrary sense, but through sane counsel, the reading of its membership, stands a great chance of sweeping the world within a generation."

The charter of this little church was obtained August 23, 1879, and in the same month the members extended a unanimous invitation to Mrs. Eddy to become its pastor. At a meeting of those who were interested in forming the church, Mrs. Eddy was appointed on the committee to formulate the rules and by-laws, also the tenets and church covenant. The first business meeting of the church was held August 16, 1879, in Charlestown, Mass., for the purpose of electing officers. August 22 the Clerk, by instructions received at the previous meeting, sent an invitation to Mrs. Eddy to become pastor of the church. August 27 the church held a meeting, with Mrs. Eddy in the chair. An interesting record of this meeting reads: "The minutes of the previous meeting were read and approved. Then Mrs. Eddy proceeded to instruct those present as to their duties in the Church of Christ, giving some useful hints as to the mode of conducting the church."

At a meeting held October 19, 1879, it was unanimously voted that "Dr. and Mrs. Eddy merited the thanks of the society for their devoted labors in the cause of Truth," and at the annual meeting, December 1 of the same year, it was voted to instruct the Clerk to call Mrs. Eddy to the pastorate of the church, and at this meeting Mrs. Eddy accepted the call. The first meeting of this little church for deliberation before a Communion Sabbath was held at the home of the pastor, Mrs. Eddy, January 2, 1880.

Most of those present had left their former church homes, in which they had labored faithfully and ardently, and had united themselves into a little band of prayerful workers. As the Pilgrims felt the strangeness of their new home, the vast gloom of the mysterious forests, and knew not the trials before them, so this little band of pioneers, guided by their dauntless Leader and teacher, starting out on their labors against the currents of dogma, creed, sickness, and sin, must have felt a peculiar sense of isolation, for their records state, "The tone of this meeting for deliberation before Communion Sabbath was rather sorrowful;" but as they turned steadfastly from the mortal side, and looked towards the spiritual, as the records further relate, "yet there was a feeling of trust in the great Father, of Love prevailing over the apparently discouraging outlook of the Church of Christ." The Communion Sunday, however, brought fresh courage to the earnest band, and the records contain these simple but suggestive words, — "Sunday, January 4, 1880. The church celebrated her Communion Sabbath as a church, and it was a very inspiring season to us all, and two new members were added to the church." This was indeed the little church in the wilderness, and few knew of its teachings, but those few saw the grandeur of its work and were willing to labor for the Cause.

The record of May 23, 1880, more than twenty-six years ago, states: "Our pastor, Mrs. Eddy, preached her farewell sermon to the church. The business committee met after the services to call a general meeting of the church

THE ANNUAL MEETING, 1906

to devise means to pay our pastor, so as to keep her with us, as there is no one in the world who could take her place in teaching us the Science of Life." May 26 of the same year the following resolutions were passed: "That the members of the Church of Christ, and all others now interested in said church, do most sincerely regret that our pastor, Mrs. Eddy, feels it her duty to tender her resignation, and while we feel that she has not met with the support that she should have reason to expect, we venture to hope she will remain with us. That it would be a serious blow to her Cause to have the public services discontinued at a time when there is such an interest manifested on the part of the people, and we know of no one who is so able as she to lead us to the higher understanding of Christianity, whereby to heal the sick and reform the sinner. It was moved to instruct the Clerk to have our pastor remain with us for a few Sundays if not permanently."

At a meeting of the church, December 15, 1880, an invitation was extended to Mrs. Eddy to accept the pastorate for the ensuing year; but, as the records state, "she gave no definite answer, believing that it was for the interest of the Cause, and her duty, to go into new fields to teach and preach."

An interesting record relative to this very early work of the church, and its appreciation of Mrs. Eddy's tireless labors, is that of July 20, 1881, which reads, "That we, the members of The Church of Christ, Scientist, tender to our beloved pastor, Mrs. Eddy, the heartfelt thanks and gratitude shared by all who have attended the services, in appreciation of her earnest endeavors, her arduous labors, and successful instructions to heal the sick, and reform the sinner, by metaphysical truth or Christian Science, during the past year. Resolved: That while she had many obstacles to overcome, many mental hardships to endure, she has borne them bravely, blessing them that curse her, loving them that despitefully use her, thereby giving in her Christian example, as well as her instructions, the highest type of womanhood, or the love that heals. And while we sincerely acknowledge our indebtedness to her, and to God, for these blessings, we, each and all, will make greater efforts more faithfully to sustain her in her work. Resolved: That while we realize the rapid growth, and welcome the fact of the spreading world wide of this great truth, that Mind, Truth, Life, and Love, as taught and expressed by our pastor, does heal the sick, and, when understood, does bring out the perfection of all things, we also realize we must use more energy and unselfish labor to establish these our Master's commands and our pastor's teachings, namely, heal the sick, and preach the gospel, and love our neighbor as ourselves."

Eighteen years ago, the Rev. James Henry Wiggin, who was not a Christian Scientist, wrote as follows: "Whatever is to be Mrs. Eddy's future reputation, time will show. Little cares she, if only through her work Truth may be glorified. More than once, in her earnestness, she has reached her bottom dollar, but the interest of the world to hear her word has always filled her coffers anew. Within a few months she has made sacrifices from which most authors would have shrunk, to insure the moral rightness of her book." This statement "Phare Pleigh" [the *nom de plume* of the Rev. James Henry Wiggin] makes out of his own peculiar knowledge of the circumstances. "Day after day flew by, and weeks lengthened into months; from every quarter came important missives of inquiry and mercantile reproach; hundreds of dollars were sunk into a bottomless sea of corrections; yet not until the authoress was satisfied that her duty was wholly done, would she allow printer and binder to send forth her book to the world." This book has now reached its four hundredth edition, each of one thousand copies.

On September 8, 1882, it was voted that the church hold its meetings of worship in the parlors of Mrs. Eddy's home, 569 Columbus Avenue, Boston. The services were held there until November, 1883, and then in the Hawthorne Rooms, at No. 3 Park Street, the seating capacity of which place was about two hundred and twenty-five. At a meeting October 22, 1883, the church voted to wait upon Mrs. Eddy, to ascertain if she would preach for the society for ten dollars a Sunday, which invitation she accepted. After establishing itself as a church in the Hawthorne Rooms, the number of attendants steadily increased. The pulpit was supplied by Mrs. Eddy, when she could give the time to preach, and by her students and by clergymen of different denominations, among whom was the Rev. A. P. Peabody, D.D., of Cambridge, Mass.

The annual report of the business committee of the church, for the year ending December 7, 1885, contains some very interesting statements, among which is this: "There was a steadily increasing interest in Christian Science among the people, even though the continuity of thought must have been very much broken by having so many different ones address them on the subject. When our pastor preached for us it was found that the

Hawthorne Rooms were inadequate for the occasion, hundreds going away who could not obtain entrance; those present enduring the inconvenience that comes from crowding, for the sake of the eternal truth she taught them." The *Boston Traveler* contained the following item: "The Church of Christ, Scientist, had their meeting Easter Sunday at Hawthorne Rooms, which were crowded one hour before the service commenced, and half an hour before the arrival of the pastor, the Rev. Mary Baker Eddy, the tide of men and women was turned from the door with the information, 'No more standing-room.'"

On February 8, 1885, communion was held at Odd Fellows Hall, and there were present about eight hundred people. At this time the Hawthorne Rooms, which had been regarded as the church home, were outgrown. During the summer vacation, different places were considered, but no place suitable could be found that was available, and the Sunday services were postponed. There was an expectation that some place would be obtained, but the desire for services was so great that the Hawthorne Rooms were again secured. A record of this period reads, "It should be here stated that from the first of September to our opening, crowds had besieged the doors at the Hawthorne Rooms, Sunday after Sunday." On October 18, 1885, the rooms were opened and a large congregation was present. It was then concluded to engage Chickering Hall on Tremont Street. In the previous consideration of places for meeting it had been decided that this hall was too large, as it seated four hundred and sixty-four. The first Sunday service held in Chickering Hall was on October 25, 1885. Mrs. Eddy preached at this service

THE ANNUAL MEETING, 1906

and the hall was crowded. This date is memorable as the one upon which the Sunday School was formed.

Meanwhile it was felt that the church needed a place of its own, and efforts were made to obtain by purchase some building, or church, in a suitable location. Several places were considered, but were not satisfactory; yet the thought of obtaining a church edifice, although given up for a time, was not forgotten. In the mean time, not only was the attendance rapidly growing in this church in Chickering Hall, but the Cause itself was spreading over the land. September 1, 1892, Mrs. Eddy gave the plot of ground on which The Mother Church now stands. On the twenty-third day of September, 1892, twelve of the members of the church met, and, upon Mrs. Eddy's counsel, reorganized the church, and named it The First Church of Christ, Scientist. This effort of Mrs. Eddy was an inspiration to Christian Scientists, and plans were made for a church home.

In the mean time Sunday services were held in Chickering Hall, and continued there until March, 1894, and during the last year the hall was crowded to overflowing. In March, however, the church was obliged to seek other quarters, as Chickering Hall was to be remodelled. At this time the church removed to Copley Hall on Clarendon Street, which had a seating capacity of six hundred and twenty-five, and in that place Sunday services were held until The Mother Church edifice was ready for occupancy, December 30, 1894. During the months that the congregation worshipped in Copley Hall there was a steady increase in attendance.

Twelve years ago the twenty-first of last month, the corner-stone of The Mother Church edifice was laid, and at that time it was thought the seating capacity would be adequate for years to come. Attendance at the Sunday service gradually increased, until every seat was filled and many stood in the aisles, and in consequence two services were held, morning and afternoon, the latter a repetition of the morning service. The date of the inauguration of two Sunday services was April 26, 1896. It was soon evident that even this provision was inadequate to meet the need, and it was found necessary to organize branch churches in such suburbs of Boston as would relieve the overcrowded condition of The Mother Church; therefore three branch churches were organized, one in each of the following named places: Cambridge, Chelsea, and Roxbury.

For a while it seemed that there would be ample room for growth of attendance in The Mother Church, but notwithstanding the relief that the organization of branch churches had given, the number of attendants increased faster than ever. From the time that the three foregoing named churches were established, the membership and the attendance at them and at The Mother Church steadily grew, and more branch churches were established in other suburbs, members of which had formerly been attendants at The Mother Church. In the spring of 1905 the overcrowded condition of the morning service showed that still further provision must be made, as many were obliged to leave the church for the reason that there was not even standing-room. Therefore, beginning October 1, 1905, three services were held each Sunday, the second and third being repetitions of the first service.

This continued growth, this continued overcrowding, proved the need of a larger edifice. Our communion ser-

THE ANNUAL MEETING, 1906

vices and annual meetings were overcrowded in The Mother Church, they were overcrowded in Tremont Temple, in Symphony Hall, and in the Mechanics Building, and the need was felt of an auditorium that would be of great seating capacity, and one that would have the sacred atmosphere of a church home.

In Mrs. Eddy's Message to the church in 1902 she suggested the need of a larger church edifice, and at the annual meeting of the same year the church voted to raise any part of two millions of dollars for the purpose of building a suitable edifice. The labor of clearing the land was begun in October, 1903, and the corner-stone was laid July 16, 1904.

The first annual meeting of the church was held in Chickering Hall, October 3, 1893, and the membership at that date was 1,545. The membership of this church to-day is 40,011. The number of candidates admitted June 5 of this year is the largest in the history of the church and numbers 4,889, which is 2,194 more than the hitherto largest admission, that of June, 1903. The total number admitted during the last year is 6,181. The total number of branch churches advertised in *The Christian Science Journal* of this June is 682, 614 of which show a membership of 41,944. The number of societies advertised in the *Journal* is 267.

Shortly before the dedication of The Mother Church in 1895, the *Boston Evening Transcript* said: "Wonders will never cease. Here is a church whose Treasurer has sent out word that no sums except those already subscribed can be received. The Christian Scientists have a faith of the mustard-seed variety. What a pity some of our practical Christian folk have not a faith approximate to that of these impractical Christian Scientists."

The fact that a notice was published in the *Christian Science Sentinel* of last Saturday that no more funds are needed to complete the extension of The Mother Church, proves the truth of the axiom, "History repeats itself." These are the evidences of the magnificent growth of this Cause, and are sufficient refutation of the statements that have been made that "Christian Science is dying out."

The majesty and the dignity of this church edifice not only shows the growth of this Cause, but proclaims the trust, the willingness of those who have contributed to the erection of these mighty walls.

This magnificent structure, this fitting testimonial in stone, speaks more than words can picture of the love and gratitude of a great multitude that has been healed and purified through the labor and sacrifice of our revered Leader and teacher, Mary Baker Eddy, the one through whom God has revealed a demonstrable way of salvation. May her example inspire us to follow her in preaching, "The kingdom of heaven is at hand," by healing the sick and reforming the sinful, and, as she has done, verifying Jesus' words, "Lo, I am with you alway."

LETTERS AND EDITORIAL

Mrs. Mary Baker Eddy,
    Pleasant View, Concord, N. H.

My Dear Teacher: — Of the many thousands who attended the dedicatory services at the Christian Science church last Sunday it is doubtful if there was one so deeply

LETTERS AND EDITORIAL

impressed with the grandeur and magnitude of your work as was the writer, whom you will recall as a member of your *first* class in Lynn, Mass., nearly forty years ago. When you told us that the truth you expounded was the little leaven that should leaven the whole lump, we thought this might be true in some far distant day beyond our mortal vision. It was above conception that in less than forty years a new system of faith and worship, as well as of healing, should number its adherents by the hundreds of thousands and its tenets be accepted wholly or in part by nearly every religious and scientific body in the civilized world.

Seated in the gallery of that magnificent temple, which has been reared by you, gazing across that sea of heads, listening again to your words explaining the Scriptures, my mind was carried back to that first public meeting in the little hall on Market Street, Lynn, where you preached to a handful of people that would scarce fill a couple of pews in this grand amphitheatre; and as I heard the sonorous tones of the powerful organ and the mighty chorus of five thousand voices, I thought of the little melodeon on which my wife played, and of my own feeble attempts to lead the singing.

In years gone by I have been asked, "Did Mrs. Eddy really write Science and Health? Some say she did not." My answer has invariably been, "Send those who say she did not to me. I heard her talk it before it was ever written. I read it in manuscript before it was ever printed." Now my testimony is not needed. No human being in this generation has accomplished such a work or been so thoroughly endorsed or so completely vindicated. It is marvellous beyond all imagining to one who knew of your early struggles. I have been solicited by many of your followers to say something about the early history of Christian Science. I have replied that if Mrs. Eddy thought it wise to instruct them on the subject she would doubtless do so.

Possibly you may remember the words of my uncle, the good old deacon of the First Congregational Church of Lynn, when told that I had studied with you. "My boy, you will be ruined for life; it is the work of the devil." He only expressed the thought of all the Christian(?) people at that time. What a change in the Christian world! "The stone which the builders rejected" has become the corner-stone of this wonderful temple of "wisdom, Truth, and Love." (Science and Health, p. 495.) I have yet the little Bible which you gave me as a reward for the best paper on the spiritual significance of the first chapter of Genesis. It has this inscription on the fly-leaf in your handwriting, "With all thy getting get understanding."

Respectfully and faithfully yours,

S. P. BANCROFT.

CAMBRIDGE, MASS., June 12, 1906.

MRS. MARY BAKER EDDY,
    Pleasant View, Concord, N. H.

Dear Leader and Guide: — Now that the great event, the dedication of our new church building, is over, may I ask a little of your time to tell you of the interesting part I had to perform in this wonderful consummation. On the twenty-fifth of last March I was asked by one of the Directors if I would care to do a little watching

LETTERS AND EDITORIAL

at the church. I gladly answered in the affirmative, and have been in the building part of every night since that time. To watch the transformation has been very interesting indeed, and the lessons I have learned of the power of divine Mind to remove human obstructions have been very precious. At first I thought that, since it seemed impossible for the building to be completed before the end of summer, the communion would likely be postponed until that time. Then came the announcement that the services would be held in the new extension on June 10. I saw at once that somebody had to wake up. I fought hard with the evidence of mortal sense for a time; but after a while, in the night, as I was climbing over stones and planks and plaster, I raised my eyes, and the conviction that the work would be accomplished came to me so clearly, I said aloud, "Why, there is no fear; this house will be ready for the service, June 10." I bowed my head before the might of divine Love, and never more did I have any doubt.

One feature about the work interested me. I noticed that as soon as the workmen began to admit that the work could be done, everything seemed to move as by magic; the human mind was giving its consent. This taught me that I should be willing to let God work. I have often stood under the great dome, in the dark stillness of the night, and thought, "What cannot God do?" (Science and Health, p. 135.)

As I discovered the many intricate problems which must necessarily present themselves in such an immense undertaking, I appreciated as never before the faithful, earnest work of our noble Board of Directors. With unflinching faith and unfailing fidelity they have stood at the breastworks in the battle, and won the reward, "Well done, good and faithful servant; . . . enter thou into the joy of thy lord."

But what of this magnificent structure? Whence did it come? To me it is the result of the love that trembled in one human heart when it whispered: "Dear God, may I not take this precious truth and give it to my brothers and sisters?" How can we ever thank God enough for such an one, — ever thank you enough for your unselfed love. May the glory which crowns the completion of this structure shed its brightest beams on your pathway, and fill your heart with the joy of Love's victory.

Your sincere follower,
JAMES J. ROME.
BOSTON, MASS., June 30, 1906.

REV. MARY BAKER EDDY,
 Pleasant View, Concord, N. H.

Beloved Leader and Teacher: — We, the Directors of your church, send you loving greetings and congratulations upon the completion of the magnificent extension of The Mother Church of Christ, Scientist, and we again express our thankful appreciation of your wise counsel, timely instruction, and words of encouragement when they were so much needed.

We acknowledge with many thanks the valuable services rendered to this Board by the members of the business committee, who were ever ready to assist us in every way possible; also the services of other members of the church, who gave freely of their time and efforts when there was urgent need of both.

We do not forget that it was through you we were enabled to secure the services of Mr. Whitcomb as builder in the early days of the construction of the church, and of Mr. Beman in an advisory capacity in the later days; for this, and for their valuable services, we are grateful.

Lovingly and gratefully your students,

THE CHRISTIAN SCIENCE BOARD OF DIRECTORS,
By WILLIAM B. JOHNSON, *Secretary*.

BOSTON, MASS., July 10, 1906.

[Editorial in *Christian Science Sentinel*, June 23, 1906]

Our annual communion and the dedication of the extension of The Mother Church are over, and this happy and holy experience has become a part of our expanding consciousness of Truth, to abide with us and enable us better to work out the purposes of divine Love. It was scarcely possible to repress a feeling of exultation as friend met friend at every turn with words of rejoicing; and even the greetings and congratulations of those not of our faith seemed to say that all the world was in some degree sharing in our joy. But within our sacred edifice there came a deeper feeling, a feeling of awe and of reverence beyond words, — a new sense of the magnitude of Christian Science, this revelation of divinity which has come to the present age. Grandly does our temple symbolize this revelation, in its purity, stateliness, and vastness; but even more impressive than this was the presence of the thousands who had come, as the Master predicted, "from the east, and from the west, and from the north, and from the south," to tell by their presence that they had been healed by Christ, Truth, and had found the kingdom of God.

As one thought upon the significance of the occasion, the achievements of our beloved Leader and her relation to the experiences of the hour took on a larger and truer meaning. The glories of the realm of infinite Mind, revealed to us through her spiritual attainments and her years of toil, encompassed us, and hearts were thrilled with tender gratitude and love for all that she has done. If to-day we feel a pardonable pride in being known as Christian Scientists, it is because our Leader has made the name an honored one before the world.

In her dedicatory Message to The Mother Church, Mrs. Eddy says, "The First Commandment of the Hebrew Decalogue, 'Thou shalt have no other gods before me,' and the Golden Rule are the all-in-all of Christian Science." In all her writings, through all the years of her leadership, she has been teaching her followers both by precept and example how to obey this commandment and rule, and her success in so doing is what constitutes the high standing of Christian Science before the world. Fearlessly does she warn all her followers against the indulgence of the sins which would prevent the realization of ideal manhood — the reign of the Christ — and now it is ours to address ourselves with renewed faith and love to the high and holy task of overcoming all that is unlike God, and thus prove our worthiness to be "living stones" in the universal temple of Spirit, and worthy members of The Mother Church before men.

APPENDIX TO PART I
AS CHRONICLED BY THE NEWSPAPERS

[*Boston Journal*, June 19, 1902]

AN ASTONISHING MOTION

Assembled in the largest church business meeting ever held in Boston — perhaps the largest ever held in the United States — the members of The First Church of Christ, Scientist, Boston, The Mother Church of the denomination, voted yesterday afternoon to raise any part of two million dollars that might be needed to build in this city a church edifice capable of seating between four and five thousand persons. This astonishing motion was passed with both unanimity and assurance. It was not even talked over, beyond two brief explanations why the building was needed. Learning that a big church was required, the money to provide it was pledged with the readiness and despatch of an ordinary mortal passing out a nickel for carfare.

[*Boston Globe*, April, 1903]

PROGRESSIVE STEPS

The last parcel in the block bounded by Falmouth, Norway, and St. Paul Streets, in the shape of a triangle, has passed to the ownership of the Christian Science church, the deed being taken by Ira O. Knapp *et al.*, trustees. The purchase of this parcel, which is known as the Hotel Brookline, a four-story brick building also in the shape of a triangle, gives to the above society the ownership of the entire block.

During the past two weeks considerable activity has been going on in property on these streets, no less than ten estates having been conveyed by deed to the Christian Science church, and now comes the purchase of the last parcel on St. Paul Street by the above society, which gives them the ownership of the entire block.

Just what use the society will make of the property has not been stated, but it is said that a number of changes will be made that will enable the church to expand, and to do so it was necessary to have this property. No block is so well situated for church purposes as this one, being in a fine part of the city.

[*Boston Post*, June 6, 1906]

THE FINISHING TOUCHES

Artisans and artists are working night and day and craftsmen are hurrying on with their work to make the spacious and elegant edifice complete for the elaborate observances of Sunday, when six services will be held, and when the words of Mary Baker Eddy will come from her beautiful home, Pleasant View, in Concord, N. H., welcoming her children and giving her blessing to the structure.

The services of Sunday will mark an epoch in the history of Christian Science. Since the discovery by Mrs. Eddy, many beautiful houses of worship have been erected, but never before has such a grand church been built as that

AS CHRONICLED BY THE NEWSPAPERS

which raises its dome above the city at the corner of Falmouth and Norway Streets.

[Boston Post]

DESCRIPTION OF THE EXTENSION

Extension of The Mother Church

Cost	$2,000,000
Shape, triangular	220x220x236 ft.
Height	224 ft.
Area of site	40,000 sq. ft.
Seating capacity	5,000
Checking facilities	3,000 garments

Notable Dates in Christian Science

Christian Science discovered	1866
First church organized	1879
First church erected	1894
Corner-stone of cathedral laid	1904
Cathedral to be dedicated	1906

Two million dollars was set aside for the building of this addition to The First Church of Christ, Scientist, and the money was used in giving Boston an edifice that is a marvel of architectural beauty. But one church in the country exceeds it in seating capacity, and, while vaster sums of money were spent in other instances, never was a more artistic effect reached.

This new temple, begun nearly two years ago, will in its simple grandeur surpass any church edifice erected in this city. Notwithstanding its enormous size, it is so proportionately built that its massiveness is unnoticed in the graceful outlines.

Built in the Italian Renaissance style, the interior of this church is carried out with the end in view of impressing the audiences with the beauty and strength of the design. The great auditorium, with its high-domed ceiling, supported on four arches springing from the tops of great stone piers, contains about one mile and a half of pews.

The dome surmounting the building is more than twice the size of the dome on the State House, having a diameter of eighty-two feet and a height of fifty-one feet.

The top of the dome is two hundred and twenty-four feet above the street, and reaches an altitude twenty-nine feet higher than that of the State House.

The old church at the corner of Falmouth and Norway Streets, with a seating capacity of twelve hundred, built twelve years ago, will remain as it was, and Mrs. Eddy's famous room will be undisturbed.

The Readers' platform is of a beautiful foreign marble, and the color scheme for all the auditorium is of a warm gray, to harmonize with the Bedford stone which enters so largely into the interior finish.

The great organ is placed back of the Readers' platform and above the Readers' special rooms. It has an architectural stone screen and contributes not a little to the imposing effect of the interior.

Bedford stone and marble form the interior finish, with elaborate plaster work for the great arches and ceilings. The floors of the first story are of marble.

There are twelve exits and seven broad marble stairways, the latter framed of iron and finished with bronze, marble, and Bedford stone.

Bronze is used in the lighting fixtures, and the pews and principal woodwork are of mahogany.

AS CHRONICLED BY THE NEWSPAPERS

The church is unusually well lighted, and one of the extraordinary features is the eight bronze chains, each suspending seventy-two lamps, each lamp of thirty-two candle-power.

Where ceiling or roof and side walls come together no sharp angles are visible, such meetings presenting an oval and dome appearance and forming a gently curved and panelled surface, whereon are placed inscriptions illustrative of the faith of Christian Science.

Two large marble plates with Scripture quotations are also placed on the two sides of the organ.

Everywhere within the building where conditions permitted it pure white marble was used, and the hammer and chisel of the sculptor added magnificent carvings to the rich beauty of the interior.

The auditorium contains seven galleries, two on either side and three at the back, yet not a single pillar or post anywhere in the vast space interrupts the view of the platform from any seat.

Another unusual feature is the foyer, where five thousand people can freely move. Adjoining this foyer are the Sunday School and the administration offices, while in the basement is a cloak-room of the capacity of three thousand wraps.

[Boston Globe]

AN IDEA OF THE SIZE

If one would get an idea of the size of this building and the manner in which the dome seems to dominate the entire city, the best point of view is on top of the tower in Mt. Auburn cemetery in Cambridge, some four miles away. From this point the building and dome can be seen in their relation to the city itself, and it certainly looks imposing.

One thing is certain: for a religion which has been organized only thirty years, and which erected its first church only twelve years ago, Christian Science has more fine church edifices to its credit in the same time than any other denomination in the world, and they are all paid for.

[Boston Evening Transcript]

THE CHIMES

The chimes for the new Christian Science temple are worthy of the dome. The effect on all within earshot is quite remarkable. They say that workingmen stopped in the street and stood in silent admiration while the chimes were being tested the other day. Millet's "Angelus" had living reproductions on every corner in the neighborhood.

[Boston Post]

MAGNIFICENCE OF THE ORGAN

The new church is replete with rare bits of art, chosen from the works of both ancient and modern masters, but there is nothing more wonderful than the organ which has been installed. Nowhere in the world is there a more beautiful, more musical, or more capable instrument. In reality it is a combination of six organs, with four manuals, seventy-two stops, nineteen couplers, nineteen adjustable combination pistons, three balanced swells, a grand crescendo pedal, seven combination pedals, and forty-five hundred and thirty-eight pipes, the largest of which is thirty-two feet long. Attached to the organ is a set of cathedral chimes, stationed in one of the towers, and some of the most intricate discoveries of organ builders enable the organist to produce the most beautiful effects by means of the bells. There is also a solo organ attached.

[*Boston Journal*]

ITS ARCHITECTURE

There is no need of fussing about the underlying spirit that built the Christian Science cathedral. We can all agree that it is a stunning piece of architecture and a great adornment to the city.

[*Boston Globe*]

UNIQUE INTERIOR

When these people enter this new cathedral or temple which has been in process of construction, they will find themselves in one of the most imposing church edifices in the country — yes, in the world. For in its interior architecture it is different from any other church in the world. In fact, nearly all the traditions of church interior architecture have been set aside in this temple, for here are neither nave, aisles, nor transept — just one vast auditorium which will seat exactly five thousand and twelve people on floor and galleries, and seat them comfortably. And what is more, every person seated in the auditorium, either on floor or galleries, can see and hear the two Readers who conduct the services on the platform in front of the great organ.

This was the aim and object of the architect: to construct an auditorium that would seat five thousand people, each of whom could see the Readers, and with such nicely adjusted acoustic properties that each person could hear what was said. To do this it was necessary to set aside the traditions of interior church architecture.

[*Boston Post*]

GATES OF BOSTON OPEN

The gates of Boston are open wide in welcome to nobility. Never before has the city been more frequented by members of the titled aristocracy of the old world than it is now. From all the centres of Europe there are streaming into town lords and ladies who come to attend the dedication of the new church for Christian Scientists.

[*Boston Globe*]

CHRISTIAN SCIENTISTS HAVE ALL THE MONEY NEEDED

"Please do not send us any more money — we have enough!"

Briefly that is the notice which Stephen A. Chase, treasurer of the building fund of the new Christian Science temple, sent forth to the thirty thousand or more Christian Scientists who have come to Boston to attend the dedication exercises, and also through the *Christian Science Sentinel* to members of the church all over the world.

This means that nearly two million dollars has been subscribed for the new building, and that every cent of it was paid in before the work was actually completed.

That is the way the Christian Scientists began when they erected the first church in Boston twelve years ago

AS CHRONICLED BY THE NEWSPAPERS

—The Mother Church. Then it was found necessary to issue a similar notice or order, and even to return more than ten thousand dollars which had been oversubscribed. They have erected dozens of churches all over this country and in other countries since that time, but it is claimed that very few of them owe a cent.

If you ask a Christian Scientist how they do it, the reply will be in the form of a quotation from Science and Health (p. 494), "Divine Love always has met and always will meet every human need."

[*Boston Globe*]

THE GREAT GATHERING

Christian Scientists are flocking from all over the world to Boston to-day, as they have been for several days past and will be for several days to come, to attend the June meetings of The Mother Church and the dedication of the new temple.

The headquarters was thrown open to visitors this forenoon in Horticultural Hall, corner of Huntington and Massachusetts Avenues. It is in charge of G. D. Robertson, and here the visitors will receive all information concerning rooms and board, hotels, railroads, *etc.* There is here also a post-office to which all mail may be directed, and telegraph and telephone service.

[*Boston Evening Transcript*]

SPECIAL TRAINS COMING

Special trains and extra sections of trains are due to arrive in Boston to-night, bearing the first instalments of the crowds of Christian Scientists from the central and western sections of this country. Those from abroad and from the far West to a large degree are already in Boston. From now until Saturday night the inrush will be from the sections within two or three days' ride, and no doubt the night trains of Saturday will bring considerable numbers of belated church members from New York and elsewhere who will arrive in this city just about in time for the first Sunday service.

[Boston Evening Transcript]

INTERESTING AND AGREEABLE VISITORS

The Christian Scientists are here in force, and they are very interesting and agreeable visitors, even to those who are unable to accompany them in their triumph of mind over matter. Boston is indebted to them for one of the finest architectural achievements in this or any other city, and other denominations might profit by their example of paying for their church before dedicating it. It is a monument to the sincerity of their faith; and the pride and satisfaction that is not only evident from their addresses but reflected in their faces, is justifiable. They are an intelligent and a happy appearing body, and even if those outside are unable to believe that they have escaped from the bondage of the material world, it would be idle to attempt to deny them the satisfaction that springs from a belief in such emancipation. Our present relations with them are as the guests of the city, and as such they are welcome.

Within two weeks we have had here the representatives of the two poles of healing, the material and the mental, and each is interesting, one for its hopefulness and the other for its novelty. Whatever opinions we may entertain of the value of the latter, we cannot well withhold our respectful acknowledgment of its enthusiasm, its energy, and its faith in its fundamentals. Its votaries are certainly holding the centre of the stage this week.

[Boston Globe]

READILY ACCOMMODATED

Yesterday was a busy day at the headquarters of the Christian Scientists in Horticultural Hall. They poured into the city from every direction and most of them headed straight for Horticultural Hall, where they were assigned rooms in hotels or lodging-houses, if they had not already been provided for. So perfect have been all the preliminary arrangements for the handling of a great number of visitors that there has not been the slightest hitch in the matter of securing accommodations. And if there was it would not make much difference, for these people would take it all very good-naturedly. They do not get excited over trifles. They are very patient and good-natured. Crowded as the hall was yesterday, and warm as the day was, there was not the slightest evidence of temper, no matter how far they had travelled or what discomforts they might have endured in their travels.

[Boston Evening Transcript]

BIG CHURCH IS PAID FOR

According to the custom of the Christian Scientists, the big addition to The Mother Church will be dedicated to-morrow free from debt. No church has ever yet been dedicated by this denomination with any part of the expense of its construction remaining unprovided for, and it went without saying that the same practice would be followed with this new two-million-dollar edifice, the largest of them all. Up to within ten days the notices that more money was needed had been in circulation, and new contributions were constantly being received; but on June 2 it became evident to the Board of Directors that enough money was on hand to provide for the entire cost of the building, and the formal announcement was made that no more contributions to the building fund were needed. That it was received with rejoicing by the thousands of church members and their friends only feebly expresses the gratification.

A similar decision was reached and published at the time of the dedication of The Mother Church in 1895, all of which goes to show the earnestness and loyalty which Christian Scientists manifest in the support of their church work, and which enables them to dedicate their churches free of debt without exception. The estimated cost of the extension of The Mother Church was pledged by the members assembled in their annual church meeting in Boston, in 1902, and all contributions have been voluntary.

[*New York Herald*]

GIANT TEMPLE FOR SCIENTISTS

There will be dedicated in Boston to-morrow the first great monument to Christian Science, the new two-million-dollar cathedral erected by the devotees of a religion which twenty-seven years ago was founded in Boston by Mrs. Mary Baker Eddy with a membership of twenty-six persons.

The new structure, which is now completed, has for

months been the cynosure of all eyes because of its great size, beautiful architecture, and the novelty of the cult which it represents. This temple is one of the largest in the world. It has a seating capacity of over five thousand. In this respect it leads the Auditorium of Chicago. Beside it the dome of the Massachusetts State House, which is the leading landmark of Boston, pales into insignificance, as its dimensions are only half as great.

From all over the world Christian Scientists are rapidly gathering in this city to participate in the most notable feature in the life of their cult. From beyond the Rockies, from Canada, from Great Britain, and practically every civilized country, daily trainloads of pilgrims are pouring into Boston, and it is estimated that not less than twenty-five thousand visitors will participate in the dedication.

[New York World]

DEDICATION DAY

Over the heads of a multitude which began to gather at daybreak and which filled the streets leading to the magnificent temple of the Christian Science church, there pealed from the chimes a first hymn of thanksgiving at six o'clock this morning. It was dedication day, and Christian Scientists from all quarters of the globe were present to participate in the occasion.

It was estimated that nearly forty thousand believers had gathered in Boston. Word was conveyed to them that the temple would open its doors absolutely free of debt, every penny of the two million dollars required to build the imposing edifice in the Back Bay district having been secured by voluntary subscription.

78 THE FIRST CHURCH OF CHRIST, SCIENTIST

The seating capacity of the temple is five thousand, and in order that all might participate in the dedication, six services, identical in character, were held during the morning, afternoon, and evening.

The worshippers saw an imposing structure of gray stone with a massive dome rising to a height of two hundred and twenty-four feet and visible from every quarter of the city. The multitude passed through the twelve entrances beneath a series of arches in the several façades. They looked upon an interior done in soft gray with decorative carvings peculiarly rich and impressive. The seating is accomplished in a semi-circular sweep of mahogany pews and in triple galleries.

The offertory taken at the beginning of the services found every basket piled high with bank-notes, everybody contributing, and none proffering small change.

At the close of the Lesson-Sermon, and in accordance with the custom of the Christian Science church, the entire congregation knelt in silent communion, followed by the audible repetition of the Lord's Prayer. One of the remarkable features of the services was the congregation singing in perfect unison. The acoustic properties of the temple, in spite of its vast interior, were found to be perfect.

[*Boston Globe*]

CHILDREN'S SERVICE

No mere words can convey the peculiar impressiveness of the half past twelve service; the little children, awed by the grandeur of the great room in which they were seated, drinking in every word of the exercises and apparently understanding all they heard, joining with their shrill voices in the singing and responsive reading, and then, at the last, kneeling for silent communion before the pews, in absolute stillness, their eyes closed and their solemn little faces turned upward.

[*Norfolk* (Neb.) *Tribune*]

ON A FAR HIGHER PEDESTAL

To those who seem to see no good in Christian Science, it must stagger their faith not a little to read the account of the dedication of the vast temple located in the heart of the city of Boston, the supposed fountain of knowledge and seat of learning of America; the spectacle of thirty thousand people assembling to gain admission to the temple shows an enthusiasm for Christian Science seldom witnessed anywhere in the world on any occasion; and this occurred in staid old Boston, and the fact was heralded in flaming headlines in the leading newspapers of the world. According to the despatches, that assembly was not a gathering of "the vulgar throng;" the intelligence and wisdom of the country were there. There certainly must be something more than a fad in Christian Science, which was placed upon a far higher pedestal by that demonstration than it ever occupied before.

[*Boston Herald*]

THE WEDNESDAY EVENING MEETINGS

Quietly, without a trace of fanaticism, making their remarkable statements with a simplicity which sprang from the conviction that they would be believed, scores of Christian Scientists told of cures from diseases, physical and mental, at the testimony meetings that marked the close of their visit to Boston; cures that carried one back to the age of miracles. To hear prosperous, contented men and women, people of substance and of standing, earnestly assure thousands of auditors that they had been cured of blindness, of consumption in its advanced stages, of heart disease, of cancer; that they had felt no pain when having broken bones set; that when wasted unto death they had been made whole, constituted a severe tax upon frail human credulity, yet they were believed.

Meetings were held in the extension of The Mother Church, in the extension vestry, in the old auditorium of The Mother Church, in The Mother Church vestry, Horticultural Hall (Exhibition Hall), Horticultural Hall (Lecture Hall), Jordan Hall, Potter Hall, Howe and Woolson Halls, Chickering Hall.

At each of the meetings the introductory services were identical, consisting of hymns, an appropriate reading from the Bible, and selections from "Science and Health with Key to the Scriptures" by Mrs. Mary Baker Eddy.

Fifteen thousand Scientists crowded into the auditorium of the extension of The Mother Church, into the old church, into Horticultural Hall, Jordan Hall, Potter Hall, Woolson Hall, and Chickering Hall, and it took ten meetings to accommodate the great throngs who wanted to give testimony or who wanted to hear it. And when these places had all been filled, there were many hundreds waiting vainly in the streets. A few were upon the scene as early as three o'clock in the afternoon to secure seats in the main body of the church, where the largest meeting was held, and long before seven the auditorium was comfortably filled.

AS CHRONICLED BY THE NEWSPAPERS

Upon entering The Mother Church one was immediately struck with the air of well-being and of prosperity of the great congregation. The Scientists fairly radiate good nature and healthy satisfaction with life. No pessimistic faces there! So ingrained is this good nature, so complete this self-abnegation, that at the very height of fervor, when bursting with a desire to testify to the benefits and the healing power of the faith, one of them would pause and laughingly give precedence to another who had been the first to catch the Reader's eye.

When Mr. McCrackan announced at the main meeting that they were ready to receive testimony, up leaped half a dozen Scientists. They had been told to name, before beginning, the places where they lived. "Indianapolis!" "Des Moines!" "Glasgow!" "Cuba!" "Dresden!" "Peoria!" they cried. No more cosmopolitan audience ever sat in Boston.

Those who poured out their debts of gratitude for ills cured, for hearts lifted up, spoke simply and gratefully, but occasionally the voices would ring out in a way there was no mistaking. In those people was the depth of sincerity, and, when they sang, the volume of holy song rose tingling to the great dome, swelling as one voice. It was a practical demonstration of the Scientist claims, a fitting close to a memorable week.

If an attempt were made to give any account of the marvellous cures narrated at the meetings of the Scientists, or wherever two or more of them are met together, it would be impossible to convey a conception of the fervor of belief with which each tells his or her experience. These are tales of people of standing and of substance, professional men, hard-headed shrewd business men. Yet they all have the same stories of their conversion, either through a cure to themselves or to one near and dear to them.

[*Boston Herald*]

EXODUS BEGINS

For a while this morning it looked as though all the Christian Scientists who have been crowding Boston the last week were trying to get away at the same time. Hotels, boarding-houses, and private houses were disgorging trunks and smaller articles of baggage so fast that it was a matter of wonder where there could be secured express wagons enough to accommodate the demand.

At the dedicatory services of The Mother Church extension on Sunday, and at the sessions of the annual meeting, Tuesday, it was the pride of the Church Directors that the edifice was emptied of its crowds in something like ten minutes. It would seem that this ability to get away when the entertainment is over is a distinguishing characteristic of Christian Scientists, for at noon to-day [June 14] the indications were that Boston would be emptied of its twenty thousand and more visitors by midnight to-night.

Transportation facilities at the two stations were taxed to the utmost from early morning, and trains pulled out of the city in double sections.

Although the Scientists came to Boston in such numbers and are departing with such remarkable expedition, their going will not be noticeable to the residents of Boston, except perhaps those living in the streets leading directly to Horticultural Hall. This fact will be due to the custom Christian Scientists have of never going about labelled. Ordinarily the holding of a great convention is patent to every one residing in the convention city. Up at Horticultural Hall the one hundred and fifty members of the local arrangement committee wore tiny white, unmarked buttons, for their own self-identification, otherwise there has been no flaunting of badges or insignia of any kind. Christian Scientists frequently wear a small pin, but this is usually hidden away in the laces of the women's frocks, and the men go entirely unadorned.

Therefore, with the exception of the street-car men and policemen, who will doubtless have fewer questions as to locality to answer, and the hotel and restaurant keepers, who will have time to rest and sleep, the public at large will scarcely realize that the Scientists have gone.

WHAT THE BOSTON EDITORS SAID

[Boston Daily Advertiser]

The meeting of the Christian Scientists in this city naturally takes on a tone of deserved satisfaction, in view of the announcement, which has just been made, that the two million dollars needed for the construction of the new temple has been raised even before the building itself has been completed.

The thirty thousand visitors have other evidences of the strength and growth of their organization, which has made steady gains in recent years. But of this particular example of the readiness of the members to bear each his or her share of the necessary expense of church work, the facts speak more plainly than mere assertion could. Nothing is more of a drag on a church than a heavy debt, the interest on which calls for practically all the resources of the institution. Many a clergyman can testify from his own experience how a "church debt" cramps and retards and holds back work that would otherwise be done. It is a rule in some denominations that a church edifice may not be formally dedicated until it be wholly free from debt. And the experience of many generations has affirmed its wisdom.

[*Boston Herald*]

Boston is the Mecca for Christian Scientists all over the world. The new temple is something to be proud of. Its stately cupola is a fitting crown for the other architectural efforts in that section of the Back Bay.

[*Boston Evening Record*]

Boston is near to another great demonstration of the growth of the Christian Science idea in numbers, wealth, vigor, and faithful adherence. It is a remarkable story which the gathering here tells. Its very magnitude and the cheerful optimism and energy of its followers impress even the man who cannot reconcile himself to the methods and tenets of the sect. Its hold and development are most notable.

[*Boston Post*]

The gathering of Christian Scientists for the dedication of the beautiful structure on Falmouth Street, which is to take place on Sunday, is notable in many ways. It is remarkable in the character of the assembling membership, in its widely international range, and in the significance of the occasion.

The growth of this cult is the marvel of the age. Thirty years ago it was comparatively unknown; one church and a mere handful of members measured its vogue. To-day its adherents number probably a million, its churches have risen by hundreds, and its congregations meet in Europe and in the antipodes, as from the Atlantic to the Pacific on this continent.

One does not need to accept the doctrines of Mrs. Eddy to recognize the fact that this wonderful woman is a world power. This is conclusive; it is conspicuously manifest. And here in Boston the zeal and enthusiasm of the followers of this creed have been manifested in the building of a church structure which will hold place among the architectural beauties of the country.

[*Boston Herald*]

Another glory for Boston, another "landmark" set in the illustrious list for future generations to reverence and admire! The Science church has become the great centre of attraction, not merely for its thousands of worshippers, but for a multitude of strangers to whom this historic city is the Mecca of their love and duty. Last Sunday it was entirely credible that the spirit of faith and brotherhood rested on this structure, which is absolutely unique in its symmetrical and appropriate design. Aside from every other consideration, this church, with its noble dome of pure gray tint, forming one of the few perfect sky-lines in an American city, is doubly welcomed. Henceforth the greeting of admiring eyes, too often unaccustomed to fine architectural effects, will be constant and sincere.

As Boston has ever loved its golden State House dome, so will it now find pleasure in this new symbol, brooding elevation, guarding as it were, embracing as it may be, the hosts of a new religion.

[Boston Globe]

Thousands of Christian Scientists have been pouring into Boston in the past few days to be present at the dedication yesterday of their new two-million-dollar church, and to take part in the subsequent ceremonies and exercises. Not only was every cent of the estimated cost contributed before the actual work was completed, but the treasurer of the building fund of the great temple appealed to his brethren to give no more money, since he had enough. This must be regarded as an extraordinary achievement, and one which indicates plainly enough the generosity of the devotion that the Christian Scientists maintain towards their church.

[Boston Post]

The dedication of the edifice of the Christian Scientists on the Back Bay has proved one of the most interesting and in some of its aspects the most notable of such occasions.

The attendance at the ceremonies yesterday was remarkable, probably unprecedented, as regards numbers. Not even the great size of the auditorium could accommodate the throng of participants. At each of the identical services, repeated at intervals from early morning until the evening, the attendance was greater than the building could contain. And the transportation facilities of the town have been strained to their utmost to care for the multitudes going and coming.

The temporary increase of the population of Boston has been apparent to the most casual observer. And so, we think, must be the characteristics of this crowd of visitors. It is a pleasant, congenial, quietly happy, well-to-do, intellectual, and cheerfully contented multitude that has invaded the town. There are among them visitors of title and distinction, but one does not notice these unless they are pointed out. The impression created is that of a great gathering of people we like to know and like to have here.

We congratulate these comfortable acquaintances upon the fact that they have their costly church fully paid for, and we feel that Boston is to be congratulated upon the acquisition of an edifice so handsome architecturally.

[Boston Herald]

I do not think I have ever seen more cheerful looking groups of people than I have met in Boston during the past few days. Their happy faces would make sunshine on the grayest day. If Christian Science gives such serene, beautiful expressions, it would not be a bad thing if all the world turned to the new religion. There is one thing about it: it is certainly imbued with the spirit of unselfishness and helpfulness, and, whatever one's special creed may be, there is nothing antagonistic to it in this doctrine of health, happiness, and in the cheerful doing of good.

GENERAL EDITORIAL OPINION

[Montreal (Can.) Gazette]

Twenty thousand Christian Scientists have assembled at Boston to attend the opening of their great new temple. Christian Science, as now before this continent, is the development of a short lifetime. It shows strength in all parts, and among classes above the average in intelligence.

[Concord (N. H.) Monitor]

The dedication, Sunday, in Boston, of the new Mother Church of the Christian Science faith was a ceremonial of far more than usual ecclesiastic significance. The edifice itself is so rich in the architectural symbolisms of aspiration and faith, its proportions are so large, and its accommodations are so wide, that its dedication abounds in remarkable external manifestations which must arrest public attention. But externals constitute the smallest feature of the Christian Science faith, and this beautiful temple, striking as are its beauties, is only a slight and material development in evidence of that beauty and serenity of faith, life, and love which finds its temple in the heart of all that increasing host who have found the truths of Christian Science to be a marvellous revelation given to this generation by a noble and devoted woman, to whom they rightfully turn with respect and affection.

[Brooklyn (N. Y.) Eagle]

The stoutest enemies of Christian Science will confess at least an æsthetic debt to that great and growing cult, which is implied in the building of a great church in Boston. This church is one of the largest and seemliest in America, and in its size, if not in its aspect, it may be held to symbolize that faith which is so much a faith that all facts inhospitable to it are deemed by its professors not to exist at all. The building is of light stone, with a dome over two hundred and twenty feet high, a chime of bells, and one of the largest organs in the world. The architect has joined lightness and grace to solidity, and the edifice needs only an open space about it, such as one finds in the English cathedrals, to achieve its extreme of beauty. A sect that leaves such a monument has not lived in vain.

A remarkable thing in this building is that, although it cost two million dollars, it is not blanketed with debts and mortgages. Everything, even to the flagstones in front of it, is paid for, and subscriptions are not solicited. Here is an occasion for joy that marks it as different from almost all other of the Christian churches, where petitions for money are almost as constant as petitions for divine mercy.

[Denver (Col.) News]

The dedication of the new Mother Church of the Christian Scientists in Boston is not a matter of interest to that city alone, but to the nation; not to the nation alone, but to the world; not to this time alone, but to history.

The growth of this form of religious faith has been one of the marvels of the last quarter century. It is, in some respects, the greatest religious phenomenon of all history. That a woman should found a religious movement of international sway; that its followers should number many thousands during her lifetime; that hundreds of great buildings should be filled at every meeting Sundays or on week-days with devout worshippers, wooed by no eloquence of orator or magnetic ritual, — all these things are new, utterly new, in the history of religious expression.

Unaccountable? Hardly so. Whatever else it is, this faith is real and is given very real tests. Thousands upon thousands believe that it has cured them of diseases many and diverse. All the passionate love for life with which nature endows the children of men, grips hold of their faith and insures fidelity in pain or death for self or dear ones. But, while health-seeking is the door to this gospel for many, it is not the only source of appeal. A faith which teaches that hate is atheism, that discord is poisonous, that gloom is sin, has a mission that can be readily grasped by sick or well.

The world is enormously richer for this reincarnation of the old, old gospel of "on earth peace, good will toward men."

[*Terre Haute* (Ind.) *Star*]

The dedication of The Mother Church of Christian Science at Boston, with its paid-up cost of two million dollars and its tremendous outpouring of eager communicants from all over the civilized world, is an event of impressiveness and momentous significance. The historic place of Mrs. Eddy as the Founder of a great denomination can no longer be questioned, and the sources of her power and following can be readily apprehended. Prominent among these is the denomination's peculiar department of healing, the efficacy of which to some extent is established beyond cavil. The immense membership of the body is proof positive that it supplies these persons, most of whom were already nominal Christians, something they did not find in other communions. It affords refutation of the notion that spiritual and mystic mediation has been drowned out in this so-called commercial age. The Christian Scientists set a good example to other denominations in requiring their church edifices to be fully paid for before they are dedicated. It is to be said for Christian Science that no person's spiritual aspirations were ever deadened or his moral standards debased through its agency. Its communicants are cheerful and shed sunshine about them — no insignificant element in true Christianity.

[*Lafayette* (Ind.) *Journal*]

The dedication of a Christian Science temple at Boston serves to call attention to one of the most remarkable religious movements that this country or any other country has ever known. It has not been very many years since Christian Science was announced as a discovery of Mary Baker Eddy of Concord, N. H. The few thousand persons who followed Mrs. Eddy during the first years of her preaching were the objects of much ridicule, but despite the obstacles put in the way the church has continued to grow. Its growth in numbers is remarkable, but even stranger is its increase in wealth. The temple which has just been dedicated at Boston cost two million dollars, and is one of the finest places of worship in the world, at least it is the largest in New England. This Mother Church is absolutely free from debt. After but a few years, Christian Science has congregations in every important town and city of the United States. Of course the new idea will never have determined its real position in the doctrines of the world until it has stood the test of time. But its beginning has been impressive, and that large numbers of intelligent men and women should be converted to it makes it appear that Science cannot be brushed aside by ridicule alone.

[*Springfield* (Mass.) *Republican*]

The prodigious convention of Christian Scientists in Boston is a portent worthy of perhaps even more interest than it has evoked in that city, where a new temple to Isis and Osiris would be hardly more than a day's wonder. With the swift growth of the new faith the public has in a general way been familiar; it is but a few years ago that the astonishing revelation was made that since 1890 its following had increased from an insignificant number to hundreds of thousands, a rate at which every other sect in the country would soon be left behind. But mere statistics give a feeble impression in comparison with so huge and concrete a demonstration as the dedication of this vast temple. The statistics have been ridiculed by the hostile as mere guesswork, but one cannot sneer away the two-million-dollar stone edifice or the thirty thousand worshippers who entered its portals Sunday.

[*Rochester* (N. Y.) *Post Express*]

There are two things to be said in favor of Christian Science. Its growth has been wonderfully rapid, and due apparently to nothing save the desire in the human heart for some such comfort as it promises. Christian Scientists, as a class, so far as the writer knows them, are happy, gentle, and virtuous. They are multiplying without efforts at proselytizing; they are in no wise at war with society; and they have little of the spirit of bigotry. The dedication of their great church in Boston is a material evidence of their prosperity; and it may be said that if their opinions seem visionary, there is nothing in them to attract any class save the moderately well-to-do, the intelligent, and the well-behaved. It has been said cynically that a religion prospers according to the pledges which it holds out to its votaries; and though Christian Science promises nothing in the way of gratifying the passions or attaining dominion over others, yet it has rare lures for weary hearts, — physical health and spiritual peace.

[*Topeka* (Kan.) *Daily Capital*]

Those of us who do not accept the doctrine of Christian Science are possibly too prone to approach it in a spirit of levity, too often disposed to touch upon it with the tongue of facetiousness. Too often we see only its ridiculous phases, attaching meanwhile no importance to the saneness and common sense which underlie many of the practices in its name. And many of us have missed entirely its tremendous growth and the part it has come to play in the economy of our social and religious life.

To those of us who have overlooked these essentials of its hold upon the public, certain statistics brought to light by the great meeting of the church now being held in Boston will come in the nature of a revelation. In 1890 the faith had but an insignificant following. To-day its adherents number hundreds of thousands, and if the growth continues in like proportion through another decade every other sect will be left behind in the race for numerical supremacy. The figures given out by the church itself have been ridiculed by the hostile as mere guesswork, but some of the evidence appears in the concrete and cannot be combated. "One cannot sneer away the two-million-dollar stone edifice or the thirty thousand worshippers who entered its portals Sunday," says the *Springfield Republican*. Neither can we overlook the steady, consistent growth of the sect in every community in which it has found a foothold. In the adherence of its converts to the faith, and in the absence of dissent among them in the interpretation of its tenets, there is also much to convince the skeptic.

[*Albany* (N. Y.) *Knickerbocker*]

The remarkable growth and the apparent permanency of Christian Science were noted in the recent dedication in Boston of the magnificent new temple of the cult. When the doors were opened to the public, the structure was free from debt. While the dedicatory services were being held at different hours of the day, forty thousand Christian Scientists from every State in the Union and from many foreign countries were in attendance.

Although Mrs. Eddy, the Founder of Christian Science, was not in attendance, she sent greetings in which she declared that the "crowning ultimate" of the church "rises to a mental monument, a superstructure high above the work of men's hands, even the outcome of their hearts, giving to the material a spiritual significance — the speed, beauty, and achievements of goodness."

But a few years ago, men there were who predicted that

Christian Science would soon be included among the cults which flourish for a time like a green bay-tree, and are then forgotten. Those predictions have not been verified. The church which has been built upon the tenets first presented by Mrs. Eddy is being constantly strengthened by members who represent the intelligence of many communities in different parts of the world.

[*Mexican Herald*, City of Mexico, Mex.]

The dedication of the magnificent Christian Science church in Boston has brought that cheerful and prosperous body of believers before the press gallery of commentators. They have built a huge church, which has cost them about two million dollars, and it has a dome which rivals that of the famous old Massachusetts State House. During the great assembly of forty thousand Christian Scientists in Boston they were described in the newspapers of the Hub as a contented and well-dressed body of people.

The faith of these people is certainly great. They go about telling of miracles performed in this twentieth century when "advanced" clergymen of other denominations are avowing their disbelief in the miraculous.

The higher critics and the men of science may think they can banish faith in the supernatural, but no religion of growth and vitality exists without faith in the things unseen.

[*Sandusky* (Ohio) *Star-Journal*]

It is doubtful if, since the days of the primitive Christians, there has been such a wonderful demonstration of religious faith and enlightened zeal as that exhibited at

Boston, Sunday, when forty thousand Christian Scientists from all parts of the world assembled to participate in the dedication of the extension of The Mother Church of that denomination. These people were of the highest order of intelligence, many of them prominent figures in the social and business world, and none of them afflicted with the slightest trace of fanaticism. The gathering can in no sense, save one, be compared with those of Mecca and the Hindu shrines, where fanaticism dominates everything else. The one point of resemblance is that the Christian Scientists are thoroughly in earnest and take joy in attesting their faith in the creed of the church of their choice. It is a faith based upon reason, and reached only through intelligent and unbiased study and comparison with other creeds.

A remarkable feature, perhaps the most remarkable, of the gathering was the generosity of its adherents towards their church. The building they were in Boston to dedicate cost approximately two million dollars. Members were invited to contribute what they could to pay for it. The money was sent in such quantities that before the day set for the dedication arrived the fund was full to overflowing and the members were asked to quit giving.

[*Peoria* (Ill.) *Journal*]

It is the custom to sneer at Christian Science, but it is evident that the cult will soon be beyond the sneering point. The dedication of what is known as The Mother Church extension in Boston, the other day, was attended by people from all parts of the United States. And they were people of intelligence.

The fact is that Christian Science just goes a little

beyond what almost every one is inclined to admit. The best physicians now admit the power of mind over matter. They believe that firm faith on the part of a sick person, for instance, will go far towards making the patient well. These same physicians, however, ridicule the idea of a patient getting well without the use of medicine. It has yet to be shown that of the sick who abjure medicine a larger proportion have died than among those who were medically treated. The *Journal* has kept no books on the subject, and is not a Christian Scientist, but believes that if the figures could be given they might show that the Scientists have a little the advantage so far as this goes.

[*Nebraska State Journal*, Lincoln, Neb.]

Zion's Herald, a rather bitter critic of Mrs. Eddy and her cult, speaks of "the audacious, stupendous, inexplicable faith of this well-dressed, good-looking, eminently respectable, evidently wealthy congregation in their teacher and her utterances." The opening of the new Mother Church of the Christian Science faith at Boston has opened the eyes of the country anew to the growth of the new church and the zeal of its membership.

[*Athol* (Mass.) *Transcript*]

The Christian Scientists who descended upon Boston to the number of forty thousand last week to dedicate the new temple, just built at a cost of two million dollars, have mostly departed, but Boston has not yet recovered from the effects produced by that stupendous gathering. The incidents witnessed during the week were calculated to impress the most determined skeptic. Forty thousand people truly make up a mighty host, but these, it is declared, are but a twentieth of the Christian Science army in this country to-day, and this is the wonderful growth of less than a score of years. Christian Science may be anything that its foes try to prove it to be, but that magnificent church, holding five thousand people, dedicated free from debt, and the centre of an enthusiasm and reverence of worship such as religious annals hardly parallel in modern times, is a tangible reality, and critics who seek the light must have done with scoffs and jeers if they would deal with the phenomenon with any effect.

[*Portland* (Ore.) *Telegram*]

The last issue of the *Christian Science Sentinel* contains a rather remarkable announcement to the effect that friends were requested to send no more money for the building of the church which was recently dedicated at Boston. This structure cost about two million dollars, and all of the funds required to build it were raised in a little less than three years. It was dedicated absolutely free of debt, and no member of the church anywhere, in this country or elsewhere, was asked to contribute a dollar. Contributions were entirely voluntary. No resort was had to any of the latter-day methods of raising money. The record is one of which any church might well be proud.

[*Portland* (Me.) *Advertiser*]

The erection in Boston of the two-million-dollar church of the Christian Scientists and its dedication free from debt has been a wonderful achievement, but as our contemporary, the *Boston Times*, comments, it is but one of the marvellous, great, and really good things that this sect is doing. It says: "A faith which is able to raise its believers above the suffering of petty ills; a religion that makes the merry heart that doeth good like a medicine, not a necessity, but a pleasure and an essential; a cult able to promote its faith with so great an aggregation of good and beneficial works, is welcomed within our midst and bidden Godspeed."

[*Denver* (Col.) *Republican*]

Christian Scientists are a remarkably optimistic body of people, and it must be said in their behalf that they are enthusiasts whenever their form of religion is concerned. They have recently built a splendid cathedral in Boston, seating five thousand people, at a cost of two million dollars, and when it was dedicated there was not a cent of indebtedness left. Thirty thousand of the faith, coming from all parts of the world, attended the dedicatory exercises, and the press reports state that the contribution baskets when passed around were literally stuffed and jammed with money.

Less than a generation ago there was not a Christian Science church in the land. To-day there are hundreds of such churches. The denomination has grown with a rapidity that is startling, and the end is not yet.

[*Bridgeport* (Conn.) *Standard*]

Facts and figures are stubborn things, and ignore them as we may their existence points out their meaning and leaves no choice but the acceptance of them at their face value. The recent dedication of a Christian Science temple in Boston has inevitably brought out in connection with the event some of the facts and figures belonging to it, which are as remarkable in their aggregate as they are unmistakable in their trend. The temple recently dedicated at Boston cost about two million dollars and is therefore the property of no poverty-stricken sect. On the Sunday of the dedication, thirty thousand worshippers were present in the building, coming from all, or nearly all, parts of the country, and representing a vast number of the followers of the cult.

It is only twenty-five years, or thereabout, since the Christian Science sect made its appearance as a distinctive organization among religious bodies, but its members are numbered by thousands to-day, and they are very generally of a class who are reputable, intelligent, and who think for themselves.

PART II
MISCELLANY

MISCELLANY

CHAPTER I

TO THE CHRISTIAN WORLD

IN the midst of the imperfect, perfection is reluctantly seen and acknowledged. Because Science is unimpeachable, it summons the severest conflicts of the ages and waits on God.

The faith and works demanded of man in our textbooks, the Bible and "Science and Health with Key to the Scriptures," and the proof of the practicality of this faith and these works, show conclusively that Christian Science is indeed Science, — the Science of Christ, the Science of God and man, of the creator and creation. In every age and at its every appearing, Science, until understood, has been persecuted and maligned. Infinite perfection is unfolded as man attains the stature of man in Christ Jesus by means of the Science which Jesus taught and practised. Alluding to this divine method, the Psalmist said: "Why do the heathen rage, and the people imagine a vain thing?"

I have set forth Christian Science and its application to the treatment of disease just as I have discovered them. I have demonstrated through Mind the effects of Truth on the health, longevity, and morals of men; and I have found nothing in ancient or in modern systems on which to found my own, except the teachings and demonstrations of our great Master and the lives of prophets and apostles. The Bible has been my only authority. I have had no other guide in the strait and narrow way of Truth.

Jewish pagans thought that the learned St. Paul, the Mars' Hill orator, the canonized saint, was a "pestilent fellow," but to-day all sorts of institutions flourish under the name of this "pestilent fellow." That epithet points a moral. Of old the Pharisees said of the great master of metaphysics, "He stirreth up the people." Because they could find no fault in him, they vented their hatred of Jesus in opprobrious terms. But what would be thought to-day of a man that should call St. Paul a "pest," and what will be thought to-morrow of him who shall call a Christian Scientist a "pest"? Again, what shall be said of him who says that the Saviour of men, the healer of men, the Christ, the Truth, "stirreth up the people"?

It is of the utmost concern to the world that men suspend judgment and sentence on the pioneers of Christianity till they know of what and of whom these pioneers speak. A person's ignorance of Christian Science is a sufficient reason for his silence on the subject, but what can atone for the vulgar denunciation of that of which a man knows absolutely nothing?

On November 21, 1898, in my class on Christian Science were many professional men and women of the highest talents, scholarship, and character in this or any other country. What was it that brought together this class to learn of her who, thirty years ago, was met with the anathema spoken of in Scripture: "Blessed are ye, when men shall revile you, and persecute you, and shall say all manner of evil against you falsely, for my sake"? It was the healing of the sick, the saving of sinners, the works

TO THE CHRISTIAN WORLD

even more than the words of Christ, Truth, which had of a verity stirred the people to search the Scriptures and to find in them man's only medicine for mind and body. This Æsculapius, defined Christianly and demonstrated scientifically, is the divine Principle whose rules demonstrated prove one's faith by his works.

After my discovery of Christian Science, I healed consumption in its last stages, a case which the M.D.'s, by verdict of the stethoscope and the schools, declared incurable because the lungs were mostly consumed. I healed malignant diphtheria and carious bones that could be dented by the finger, saving the limbs when the surgeon's instruments were lying on the table ready for their amputation. I have healed at one visit a cancer that had eaten the flesh of the neck and exposed the jugular vein so that it stood out like a cord. I have physically restored sight to the blind, hearing to the deaf, speech to the dumb, and have made the lame walk.

About the year 1869, I was wired to attend the patient of a distinguished M.D., the late Dr. Davis of Manchester, N. H. The patient was pronounced dying of pneumonia, and was breathing at intervals in agony. Her physician, who stood by her bedside, declared that she could not live. On seeing her immediately restored by me without material aid, he asked earnestly if I had a work describing my system of healing. When answered in the negative, he urged me immediately to write a book which should explain to the world my curative system of metaphysics. In the ranks of the M.D.'s are noble men and women, and I love them; but they must refrain from persecuting and misrepresenting a system of medicine which from personal experience I have proved to be more certain and curative in functional and organic diseases than any material method. I admonish Christian Scientists either to speak charitably of all mankind or to keep silent, for love fulfils divine law and without this proof of love mental practice were profitless.

The list of cases healed by me could be made to include hopeless organic diseases of almost every kind. I name those mentioned above simply to show the folly of believing that the immutable laws of omnipotent Mind have not power over and above matter in every mode and form, and the folly of the cognate declaration that Christian Science is limited to imaginary diseases! On the contrary, Christian Science has healed cases that I assert it would have been impossible for the surgeon or *materia medica* to cure. Without Mind, man and the universe would collapse; the winds would weary, and the world stand still. It is already proved that Christian Science rests on the basis of fixed Principle, and overcomes the evidence of diseased sensation. Human mentality, expressed in disease, sin, and death, in tempest and in flood, the divine Mind calms and limits with a word.

In what sense is the Christian Scientist a "pest"? Is it because he minds his own business more than does the average man, is not a brawler, an alcohol drinker, a tobacco user, a profane swearer, an adulterer, a fornicator, nor a dishonest politician or business man? Or is it because he is the very antipode of all these? In what sense is the Christian Scientist a charlatan? Is it because he heals the sick without drugs?

Our great Exemplar, the Nazarene Prophet, healed through Mind, and commanded his followers to do likewise. The prophets and apostles and the Christians in the first century healed the sick as a token of their Christianity. Has Christianity improved upon its earlier records, or has it retrograded? Compare the lives of its professors with those of its followers at the beginning of the Christian era, and you have the correct answer.

As a pertinent illustration of the general subject under discussion, I will cite a modern phase of medical practice, namely, the homœopathic system, to which the old school has become reconciled. Here I speak from experience. In homœopathy, the one thousandth attenuations and the same triturations of medicine have not an iota of the drug left in them, and the lower attenuations have so little that a vial full of the pellets can be swallowed without harm and without appreciable effect. Yet the homœopathist administers half a dozen or less of these same globules, and he tells you, and you believe him, that with these pellets he heals the sick. The diminishing of the drug does not disprove the efficiency of the homœopathic system. It enhances its efficiency, for it identifies this system with mind, not matter, and places it nearer the grooves of omnipotence. O petty scorner of the infinite, wouldst thou mock God's miracles or scatter the shade of one who "shall abide under the shadow of the Almighty"? If, as Scripture declares, God made all that was made, then whatever is entitled to a classification as truth or science must be comprised in a knowledge or understanding of God, for there can be nothing beyond illimitable divinity.

The homœopathist handles in his practice and heals the most violent stages of organic and inflammatory diseases, stops decomposition, removes enteritis, gastritis, hyperæmia, pneumonia, diphtheria, and ossification — the effects of calcareous salts formed by carbonate and sulphate of lime; and the homœopathic physician succeeds as well in healing his cases without drugs as does the allopath who depends upon drugs. Then is mind or matter the intelligent cause in pathology? If matter, I challenge matter to act apart from mind; and if mind, I have proved beyond cavil that the action of the divine Mind is salutary and potent in proportion as it is seen to act apart from matter. Hence our Master's saying, "The flesh profiteth nothing." The difference between metaphysics in homœopathy and metaphysics in Christian Science consists in this forcible fact: the former enlists faith in the pharmacy of the human mind, and the latter couples faith with spiritual understanding and is based on the law of divine Mind. Christian Science recognizes that this Mind is the only lawgiver, omnipotent, infinite, All. Hence the divine Mind is the sovereign appeal, and there is nothing in the divine Mind to attenuate. The more of this Mind the better for both physician and patient.

Ignorance, slang, and malice touch not the hem of the garment of Christian Scientists, for if they did once touch it, they would be destroyed. To be stoned for that which our Master designated as his best work, saying, "For which of those works do ye stone me," is to make known the best work of a Christian Scientist.

Finally, beloved brethren in Christ, the words of the New York press — "Mrs. Eddy not shaken" — are valid. I remain steadfast in St. Paul's faith, and will close with his own words: "Christ is the head of the church: and he is the saviour of the body."

CHAPTER II

THE CHRISTIAN SCIENCE TEXTBOOK

MATTER is but the subjective state of mortal mind. Matter has no more substance and reality in our day-dreams than it has in our night-dreams. All the way mortals are experiencing the Adam-dream of mind in matter, the dream which is mortal and God-condemned and which is not the spiritual fact of being. When this scientific classification is understood, we shall have one Mind, one God, and we shall obey the commandment, "Love thy neighbor as thyself."

If nineteen hundred years ago Christ taught his followers to heal the sick, he is to-day teaching them the same heavenly lesson. Christ is "the same yesterday, and to-day, and forever." "God is Love," the ever-operative divine Principle (or Person, if you please) whose person is not corporeal, not finite. This infinite Person we know not of by the hearing of the ear, yet we may sometimes say with Job, "But now mine eye [spiritual sense] seeth Thee."

God is one because God is All. Therefore there can be but one God, one Christ. We are individually but specks in His universe, the reflex images of this divine Life, Truth, and Love, in whom "we live, and move, and have our being." Divine metaphysics is not to be scoffed at; it is Truth with us, God "manifest in the flesh," not alone by miracle and parable, but by proof;

it is the divine nature of God, which belongs not to a dispensation now ended, but is ever present, casting out evils, healing the sick, and raising the dead — resurrecting individuals buried above-ground in material sense.

At the present time this Bethlehem star looks down upon the long night of materialism, — material religion, material medicine, a material world; and it shines as of yore, though it "shineth in darkness; and the darkness comprehended it not." But the day will dawn and the daystar will appear, lighting the gloom, guiding the steps of progress from molecule and mortals outward and upward in the scale of being.

Hidden electrical forces annihilating time and space, wireless telegraphy, navigation of the air; in fact, all the *et cetera* of mortal mind pressing to the front, remind me of my early dreams of flying in airy space, buoyant with liberty and the luxury of thought let loose, rising higher and forever higher in the boundless blue. And what of reality, if waking to bodily sensation is real and if bodily sensation makes us captives? The night thought, methinks, should unfold in part the facts of day, and open the prison doors and solve the blind problem of matter. The night thought should show us that even mortals can mount higher in the altitude of being. Mounting higher, mortals will cease to be mortal. Christ will have "led captivity captive," and immortality will have been brought to light.

Robert Ingersoll's attempt to convict the Scriptures of inconsistency made his life an abject failure. Happily, the misquoting of "Science and Health with Key to the Scriptures," or quoting sentences or paragraphs torn from their necessary contexts, may serve to call attention to that book, and thus reveal truths which otherwise the reader would not have sought. Surely "the wrath of man shall praise Thee."

The nature and truth of Christian Science cannot be destroyed by false psychics, crude theories or modes of metaphysics. Our master Metaphysician, the Galilean Prophet, had much the same class of minds to deal with as we have in our time. They disputed his teachings on practically the same grounds as are now assumed by many doctors and lawyers, but he swept away their illogical syllogisms as chaff is separated from the wheat. The genuine Christian Scientist will tell you that he has found the physical and spiritual status of a perfect life through his textbook.

The textbook of Christian Science maintains primitive Christianity, shows how to demonstrate it, and throughout is logical in premise and in conclusion. Can Scientists adhere to it, establish their practice of healing on its basis, become successful healers and models of good morals, and yet the book itself be absurd and unscientific? Is not the tree known by its fruit? Did Jesus mistake his mission and unwittingly misguide his followers? Were the apostles absurd and unscientific in adhering to his premise and proving that his conclusion was logical and divine?

"The scientific statement of being" (Science and Health, p. 468) may irritate a certain class of professionals who fail to understand it, and they may pronounce it absurd, ambiguous, unscientific. But that Christian Science is valid, simple, real, and self-evident, thousands upon thousands attest with their individual demonstrations. They have themselves been healed and have healed others by means of the Principle of Christian Science. Science has always been first met with denunciations. A fiction or a false philosophy flourishes for a time where Science gains no hearing. The followers of the Master in the early Christian centuries did just what he enjoined and what Christian Science makes practical today to those who abide in its teachings and build on its chief corner-stone. Our religious denominations interpret the Scriptures to fit a doctrine, but the doctrines taught by divine Science are founded squarely and only on the Scriptures.

"Science and Health with Key to the Scriptures" is not inconsistent in a single instance with its logical premise and conclusion, and ninety-nine out of every hundred of its readers — honest, intelligent, and scholarly — will tell you this. The earnest student of this book, understanding it, demonstrates in some degree the truth of its statements, and knows that it contains a Science which is demonstrable when understood, and which is fully understood when demonstrated. That Christian Scientists, because of their uniformly pure morals and noble lives, are better representatives of Christian Science than the textbook itself, is not in accordance with the Scriptures. The tree is known by its fruit. The student of this book will tell you that his higher life is the result of his conscientious study of Science and Health in connection with the Bible.

A book that through the good it does has won its way into the palaces of emperors and kings, into the home of the President of the United States, into the chief cities and the best families in our own and in foreign lands, a book which lies beside the Bible in hundreds of pulpits and in thousands of homes, which heals the sick and reclaims sinners in court and in cottage, is not less the evangel of Christian Science than is he who practises the teachings of this book or he who studies it and thereby is healed of disease. Can such a book be ambiguous, self-contradictory, or unprofitable to mankind?

St. Paul was a follower but not an immediate disciple of our Lord, and Paul declares the truth of the complete system of Christian Science in these brief sentences: "There is therefore now no condemnation to them which are in Christ Jesus, who walk not after the flesh, but after the Spirit. For the law of the Spirit of life in Christ Jesus hath made me free from the law of sin and death." Was it profane for St. Paul to aspire to this knowledge of Christ and its demonstration, healing sin and sickness, because he was not a disciple of the personal Jesus? Nay, verily. Neither is it presumptuous or unscriptural or vain for another, a suckling in the arms of divine Love, to perfect His praise.

A child will demonstrate Christian Science and have a clear perception of it. Then, is Christian Science a cold, dull abstraction, or is that unscientific which all around us is demonstrated on a fixed Principle and a given rule, — when, in proportion as this Principle and rule are understood, men are found casting out the evils of mortal thought, healing the sick, and uplifting human consciousness to a more spiritual life and love? The signs of the times emphasize the answer to this in the rapid and steady advancement of this Science among the scholarly and titled, the deep thinkers, the truly great men and women of this age. In the words of the Master, "Can ye not discern the signs of the times?"

Christian Science teaches: Owe no man; be temperate; abstain from alcohol and tobacco; be honest, just, and pure; cast out evil and heal the sick; in short, Do unto others as ye would have others do to you.

Has one Christian Scientist yet reached the maximum of these teachings? And if not, why point the people to the lives of Christian Scientists and decry the book which has moulded their lives? Simply because the treasures of this textbook are not yet uncovered to the gaze of many men, the beauty of holiness is not yet won.

My first writings on Christian Science began with notes on the Scriptures. I consulted no other authors and read no other book but the Bible for about three years. What I wrote had a strange coincidence or relationship with the light of revelation and solar light. I could not write these notes after sunset. All thoughts in the line of Scriptural interpretation would leave me until the rising of the sun. Then the influx of divine interpretation would pour in upon my spiritual sense as gloriously as the sunlight on the material senses. It was not myself, but the divine power of Truth and Love, infinitely above me, which dictated "Science and Health with Key to the Scriptures." I have been learning the higher meaning of this book since writing it.

Is it too much to say that this book is leavening the whole lump of human thought? You can trace its teachings in each step of mental and spiritual progress, from pulpit and press, in religion and ethics, and find these progressive steps either written or indicated in the book. It has mounted thought on the swift and mighty chariot of divine Love, which to-day is circling the whole world.

I should blush to write of "Science and Health with Key to the Scriptures" as I have, were it of human origin, and were I, apart from God, its author. But, as I was only a scribe echoing the harmonies of heaven in divine metaphysics, I cannot be super-modest in my estimate of the Christian Science textbook.

CHAPTER III

PERSONALITY

Personal Contagion

AT a time of contagious disease, Christian Scientists endeavor to rise in consciousness to the true sense of the omnipotence of Life, Truth, and Love, and this great fact in Christian Science realized will stop a contagion.

In time of religious or scientific prosperity, certain individuals are inclined to cling to the personality of its leader. This state of mind is sickly; it is a contagion — a mental malady, which must be met and overcome. Why? Because it would dethrone the First Commandment, Thou shalt have one God.

If God is one and God is Person, then Person is infinite; and there is no personal worship, for God is divine Principle, Love. Hence the sin, the danger and darkness of personal contagion.

Forgetting divine Principle brings on this contagion. Its symptoms are based upon personal sight or sense. Declaring the truth regarding an individual or leader, rendering praise to whom praise is due, is not a symptom of this contagious malady, but persistent pursuit of his or her person is.

Every loss in grace and growth spiritual, since time began, has come from injustice and personal contagion. Had the ages helped their leaders to, and let them alone

Copyright, 1909, by Mary Baker Eddy.

in, God's glory, the world would not have lost the Science of Christianity.

"What went ye out for to see?" A person, or a Principle? Whichever it be, determines the right or the wrong of this following. A personal motive gratified by sense will leave one "a reed shaken with the wind," whereas helping a leader in God's direction, and giving this leader time and retirement to pursue the infinite ascent, — the comprehending of the divine order and consciousness in Science, — will break one's own dream of personal sense, heal disease, and make one a Christian Scientist.

Is not the old question still rampant? "When saw we thee a stranger, and took thee in? or naked, and clothed thee? Or when saw we thee sick, or in prison, and came unto thee?" But when may we see you, to get some good out of your personality?

"In the beginning was the Word, and the Word was with God, and the Word was God" (St. John). This great truth of God's impersonality and individuality and of man in His image and likeness, individual, but not personal, is the foundation of Christian Science. There was never a religion or philosophy lost to the centuries except by sinking its divine Principle in personality. May all Christian Scientists ponder this fact, and give their talents and loving hearts free scope only in the right direction!

I left Boston in the height of prosperity to *retreat* from the *world*, and to seek the one divine Person, whereby and wherein to show others the footsteps from sense to Soul. To give me this opportunity is all that I ask of mankind.

My soul thanks the loyal, royal natures of the beloved members of my church who cheerfully obey God and steadily go on promoting the true Principle of Christian Science. Only the disobedient spread personal contagion, and any imaginary benefit they receive is the effect of self-mesmerism, wherein the remedy is worse than the disease.

Letter to a Clergyman

My Dear Sir: — I beg to thank you for your most excellent letter. It is an outpouring of goodness and greatness with which you honor me.

In a call upon my person, you would not see me, for spiritual sense demands and commands us; hence I seek to be "absent from the body," and such circumstances embarrass the higher criticism.

The Scripture reads: "Blessed are they that have not seen, and yet have believed." A saving faith comes not of a person, but of Truth's presence and power. Soul, not sense, receives and gives it. One's voluntary withdrawal from society, from furnishing the demands upon the finite to supply the blessings of the infinite, — something impossible in the Science of God and credited only by human belief, by a material and not by the spiritual sense of man, — should come from conscience.

The doctrine of Buddha, which rests on a heathen basis for its Nirvana, represents not the divinity of Christian Science, in which Truth, or Christ, finds its paradise in Spirit, in the consciousness of heaven within us — health, harmony, holiness, entirely apart from limitations, which would dwarf individuality in personality and couple evil

LETTER TO A CLERGYMAN

with good. It is convenient for history to record limitations and to regard evil as real, but it is impossible in Science to believe this, or on such a basis to demonstrate the divine Principle of that which is real, harmonious, and eternal — that which is based on one infinite God, and man, His idea, image, and likeness.

In Science, we learn that man is not absorbed in the divine nature, but is absolved by it. Man is free from the flesh and is individual in consciousness — in Mind, not in matter. Think not that Christian Science tends towards Buddhism or any other "ism." *Per contra,* Christian Science destroys such tendency. Mary of old wept because she *stooped down* and looked into the sepulchre — looked for the person, instead of the Principle that reveals Christ. The Mary of to-day looks up for Christ, away from the supposedly crucified to the ascended Christ, to the Truth that "healeth all thy diseases" and gives dominion over all the earth. The doubting disciple could not identify Christ spiritually, but he could materially. He turned to the person, to the prints of the nails, to prove Christ, whereas the discharged evidence of material sense gave the real proof of his Saviour, the veritable Christ, Truth, which destroys the false sense with the evidence of Soul, immortality, eternal Life without beginning or end of days.

Should I give myself the pleasant pastime of seeing your personal self, or give you the opportunity of seeing mine, you would not see me thus, for I am not there. I have risen to look and wait and watch and pray for the spirit of Truth that leadeth away from person — from body to Soul, even to the true image and likeness of God. St. John found Christ, Truth, in the Word which *is* God. We look for the sainted Revelator in his writings, and there we find him. Those who look for me in person, or elsewhere than in my writings, lose me instead of find me. I hope and trust that you and I may meet in truth and know each other there, and know as we are known of God.

Accept my gratitude for the chance you give me to answer your excellent letter. Forgive, if it needs forgiveness, my honest position. Bear with me the burden of discovery and share with me the bliss of seeing the risen Christ, God's spiritual idea that takes away all sin, disease, and death, and gives to soul its native freedom.

CHAPTER IV

MESSAGES TO THE MOTHER CHURCH

Communion, January 2, 1898

My Beloved Brethren: — I have suggested a change in the time for holding our semi-annual church meetings, in order to separate these sessions from the excitement and commotion of the season's holidays.

In metaphysics we learn that the strength of peace and of suffering is sublime, a true, tried mental conviction that is neither tremulous nor relapsing. This strength is like the ocean, able to carry navies, yet yielding to the touch of a finger. This peace is spiritual; never selfish, stony, nor stormy, but generous, reliable, helpful, and always at hand.

Peace, like plain dealing, is somewhat out of fashion. Yet peace is desirable, and plain dealing is a jewel as beautiful as the gems that adorn the Christmas ring presented to me by my students in 1897. Few blemishes can be found in a true character, for it is always a diamond of the first water; but external gentility and good humor may be used to disguise internal vulgarity and villainy. No deformity exists in honesty, and no vulgarity in kindness. Christian Science, however, adds to these graces, and reflects the divine likeness.

Self-denial is practical, and is not only polite to all but is pleasant to those who practise it. If one would follow the advice that one gratuitously bestows on others, this would create for one's self and for the world a destiny more grand than can issue from the brain of a dreamer.

That glory only is imperishable which is fixed in one's own moral make-up.

Sin is like a dock root. To cut off the top of a plant does no good; the roots must be eradicated or the plant will continue to grow. Now I am done with homilies and, you may add, with tedious prosaics.

On the fifth of July last, my church tempted me tenderly to be proud! The deportment of its dear members was such as to command respect everywhere. It called forth flattering comment and created surprise in our good city of Concord.

Beloved brethren, another Christmas has come and gone. Has it enabled us to know more of the healing Christ that saves from sickness and sin? Are we still searching diligently to find where the young child lies, and are we satisfied to know that our sense of Truth is not demoralized, finitized, cribbed, or cradled, but has risen to grasp the spiritual idea unenvironed by materiality? Can we say with the angels to-day: "He is risen; he is not here: behold the place where they laid him"? Yes, the real Christian Scientist can say his Christ is risen and is not the material Christ of creeds, but is Truth, even as Jesus declared; and the sense of Truth of the real Christian Scientist is spiritualized to behold this Christ, Truth, again healing the sick and saving sinners. The mission of our Master was to all mankind, and included the very hearts that rejected it — that refused to see the power of Truth in healing.

Our unity and progress are proverbial, and this church's gifts to me are beyond comparison — they have become a wonder! To me, however, love is the greater marvel, so I must continue to prize love even more than the gifts which would express it. The great guerdon of divine Love, which moves the hearts of men to goodness and greatness, will reward these givers, and this encourages me to continue to urge the perfect model for your acceptance as the ultimate of Christian Science.

To-day in Concord, N. H., we have a modest hall in one of the finest localities in the city, — a reading-room and nine other rooms in the same building. "Tell it not in Gath"! I had the property bought by the courtesy of another person to be rid of the care and responsibility of purchasing it, and furnished him the money to pay for it. The original cost of the estate was fourteen thousand dollars. With the repairs and other necessary expenses the amount is now about twenty thousand dollars. Ere long I will see you in this hall, *Deo volente;* but my outdoor accommodations at Pleasant View are bigger than the indoor. My little hall, which holds a trifle over two hundred people, is less sufficient to receive a church of ten thousand members than were the "five loaves and two fishes" to feed the multitude; but the true Christian Scientist is not frightened at miracles, and ofttimes small beginnings have large endings.

Seeing that we have to attain to the ministry of righteousness in all things, we must not overlook small things in goodness or in badness, for "trifles make perfection," and "the little foxes . . . spoil the vines."

As a peculiar people whose God is All-in-all, let us say with St. Paul: "We faint not; but have renounced the hidden things of dishonesty, not walking in craftiness, nor handling the word of God deceitfully; but by manifestation of the truth commending ourselves to every man's conscience."

Communion, June 4, 1899

My Beloved Brethren: — Looking on this annual assemblage of human consciousness, — health, harmony, growth, grandeur, and achievement, garlanded with glad faces, willing hands, and warm hearts, — who would say to-day, "What a fond fool is hope"? The fruition of friendship, the world's arms outstretched to us, heart meeting heart across continents and oceans, bloodless sieges and tearless triumphs, the "well done" already yours, and the undone waiting only your swift hands, — these are enough to make this hour glad. What more abounds and abides in the hearts of these hearers and speakers, pen may not tell.

Nature reflects man and art pencils him, but it remains for Science to reveal man to man; and between these lines of thought is written in luminous letters, O man, what art thou? Where art thou? Whence and whither? And what shall the answer be? Expressive silence, or with finger pointing upward, — Thither! Then produce thy records, time-table, log, traveller's companion, *et cetera*, and prove fairly the facts relating to the thitherward, — the rate of speed, the means of travel, and the number *en route*. Now what have you learned? The mystery of godliness — God made "manifest in the flesh," seen of men, and spiritually understood; and the mystery of iniquity — how to separate the tares from the wheat, that they consume in their own fires and no longer kindle altars for human sacrifice. Have you learned to conquer sin, false affections, motives, and aims, — to be not only sayers but doers of the law?

Brethren, our annual meeting is a grave guardian. It requires you to report progress, to refresh memory, to rejuvenate the branches and to vivify the buds, to bend upward the tendrils and to incline the vine towards the parent trunk. You come from feeding your flocks, big with promise; and you come with the sling of Israel's chosen one to meet the Goliaths.

I have only to dip my pen in my heart to say, All honor to the members of our Board of Lectureship connected with The Mother Church. Loyal to the divine Principle they so ably vindicate, they earn their laurels. History will record their words, and their works will follow them. When reading their lectures, I have felt the touch of the spirit of the Mars' Hill orator, which always thrills the soul.

The members of the Board of Education, under the auspices of the Massachusetts Metaphysical College, have acquitted themselves nobly. The students in my last class in 1898 are stars in my crown of rejoicing.

We are deeply grateful that the church militant is looking into the subject of Christian Science, for Zion must put on her beautiful garments — her bridal robes. The hour is come; the bride (Word) is adorned, and lo, the bridegroom cometh! Are our lamps trimmed and burning?

The doom of the Babylonish woman, referred to in Revelation, is being fulfilled. This woman, "drunken with the blood of the saints, and with the blood of the martyrs of Jesus," "drunk with the wine of her fornication," would enter even the church, — the body of Christ, Truth; and, retaining the heart of the harlot and the purpose of the destroying angel, would pour wormwood into the waters — the disturbed human mind — to drown the strong swimmer struggling for the shore, — aiming for Truth, — and if possible, to poison such as drink of the living water. But the recording angel, standing with "right foot upon the sea, and his left foot on the earth," has in his hand a book open (ready to be read), which uncovers and kills this mystery of iniquity and interprets the mystery of godliness, — how the first is finished and the second is no longer a mystery or a miracle, but a marvel, casting out evil and healing the sick. And a voice was heard, saying, "Come out of her, my people" (hearken not to her lies), "that ye receive not of her plagues. For her sins have reached unto heaven, and God hath remembered her iniquities . . . double unto her double according to her works: in the cup which she hath filled fill to her double . . . for she saith in her heart, I . . . am no widow, . . . Therefore shall her plagues come in one day, death, and mourning, and famine; . . . for strong is the Lord God who judgeth her." That which the Revelator saw in spiritual vision will be accomplished. The Babylonish woman is fallen, and who should mourn over the widowhood of lust, of her that "is become the habitation of devils, and the hold of every foul spirit, and a cage of every unclean . . . bird"?

One thing is eternally here; it reigns supreme to-day, to-morrow, forever. We need it in our homes, at our firesides, on our altars, for with it win we the race of the centuries. We have it only as we live it. This is that needful one thing — divine Science, whereby thought is *spiritualized,* reaching outward and upward to Science in Christianity, Science in medicine, in physics, and in metaphysics.

Happy are the people whose God is All-in-all, who ask only to be judged according to their works, who live to love. We thank the Giver of all good for the marvellous speed of the chariot-wheels of Truth and for the steadfast, calm coherence in the ranks of Christian Science.

On comparison, it will be found that Christian Science possesses more of Christ's teachings and example than all other religions since the first century. Comparing our scientific system of metaphysical therapeutics with *materia medica,* we find that divine metaphysics completely overshadows and overwhelms *materia medica,* even as Aaron's rod swallowed up the rods of the magicians of Egypt. I deliberately declare that when I was in practice, out of one hundred cases I healed ninety-nine to the ten of *materia medica.*

We should thank God for persecution and for prosecution, if from these ensue a purer Protestantism and monotheism for the latter days of the nineteenth century. A siege of the combined centuries, culminating in fierce attack, cannot demolish our strongholds. The forts of Christian Science, garrisoned by God's chosen ones, can never surrender. Unlike Russia's armament, ours is not costly as men count cost, but it is rich beyond price, staunch and indestructible on land or sea; it is not curtailed in peace, surrendered in conquest, nor laid down at the feet of progress through the hands of omnipotence. And why? Because it is "on earth peace, good will toward men," — a cover and a defence adapted to all men, all nations, all times, climes, and races. I cannot quench my desire to say this; and words are not vain when the depth of desire can find no other outlet to liberty.

"Therefore . . . let us go on unto perfection; not laying again the foundation of repentance from dead works." (Hebrews 6: 1.)

A coroner's inquest, a board of health, or class legislation is less than the Constitution of the United States, and infinitely less than God's benign government, which is "no respecter of persons." Truth crushed to earth springs spontaneously upward, and whispers to the breeze man's inalienable birthright — *Liberty*. "Where the Spirit of the Lord is, there is liberty." God is everywhere. No crown nor sceptre nor rulers rampant can quench the vital heritage of freedom — man's right to adopt a religion, to employ a physician, to live or to die according to the dictates of his own rational conscience and enlightened understanding. Men cannot punish a man for suicide; God does that.

Christian Scientists abide by the laws of God and the laws of the land; and, following the command of the Master, they go into all the world, preaching the gospel and healing the sick. Therefore be wise and harmless, for without the former the latter were impracticable. A lack of wisdom betrays Truth into the hands of evil as effectually as does a subtle conspirator; the motive is not as wicked, but the result is as injurious. Return not evil for evil, but "overcome evil with good." Then, whatever the shaft aimed at you or your practice may be, it will fall powerless, and God will reward your enemies according to their works. Watch, and pray daily that evil suggestions, in whatever guise, take no root in your thought nor bear fruit. Ofttimes examine yourselves, and

see if there be found anywhere a deterrent of Truth and
Love, and "hold fast that which is good."

I reluctantly foresee great danger threatening our nation, — imperialism, monopoly, and a lax system of religion. But the spirit of humanity, ethics, and Christianity sown broadcast — all concomitants of Christian Science — is taking strong hold of the public thought throughout our beloved country and in foreign lands, and is tending to counteract the trend of mad ambition.

There is no night but in God's frown; there is no day but in His smile. The oracular skies, the verdant earth — bird, brook, blossom, breeze, and balm — are richly fraught with divine reflection. They come at Love's call. The nod of Spirit is nature's natal.

And how is man, seen through the lens of Spirit, enlarged, and how counterpoised his origin from dust, and how he presses to his original, never severed from Spirit! O ye who leap disdainfully from this rock of ages, return and plant thy steps in Christ, Truth, "the stone which the builders rejected"! Then will angels administer grace, do thy errands, and be thy dearest allies. The divine law gives to man health and life everlasting — gives a soul to Soul, a present harmony wherein the good man's heart takes hold on heaven, and whose feet can never be moved. These are His green pastures beside still waters, where faith mounts upward, expatiates, strengthens, and exults.

Lean not too much on your Leader. Trust God to direct your steps. Accept my counsel and teachings only as they include the spirit and the letter of the Ten Commandments, the Beatitudes, and the teachings and example of Christ Jesus. Refrain from public controversy; correct the false with the true — then leave the latter to propagate. Watch and guard your own thoughts against evil suggestions and against malicious mental malpractice, wholly disloyal to the teachings of Christian Science. This hidden method of committing crime — socially, physically, and morally — will ere long be unearthed and punished as it deserves. The effort of disloyal students to blacken me and to keep my works from public recognition — students seeking only public notoriety, whom I have assisted pecuniarily and striven to uplift morally — has been made too many times and has failed too often for me to fear it. The spirit of Truth is the lever which elevates mankind. I have neither the time nor the inclination to be continually pursuing a lie — the one evil or the evil one. Therefore I ask the help of others in this matter, and I ask that according to the Scriptures my students reprove, rebuke, and exhort. A lie left to itself is not so soon destroyed as it is with the help of truth-telling. Truth never falters nor fails; it is our faith that fails.

All published quotations from my works must have the author's name added to them. Quotation-marks are not sufficient. Borrowing from my copyrighted works, without credit, is inadmissible. But I need not say this to the loyal Christian Scientist — to him who keeps the commandments. "Science and Health with Key to the Scriptures" has an enormous strain put upon it, being used as a companion to the Bible in all your public ministrations, as teacher and as the embodiment and substance of the truth that is taught; hence my request, that you borrow little else from it, should seem reasonable.

Beloved, that which purifies the affections also strengthens them, removes fear, subdues sin, and endues with divine power; that which refines character at the same time humbles, exalts, and commands a man, and obedience gives him courage, devotion, and attainment. For this hour, for this period, for spiritual sacrament, sacrifice, and ascension, we unite in giving thanks. For the body of Christ, for the life that we commemorate and would emulate, for the bread of heaven whereof if a man eat "he shall live forever," for the cup red with loving restitution, redemption, and inspiration, we give thanks. The signet of the great heart, given to me in a little symbol, seals the covenant of everlasting love. May apostate praise return to its first love, above the symbol seize the spirit, speak the "new tongue" — and may thought soar and Soul be.

Address at Annual Meeting, June 6, 1899

My Beloved Brethren: — I hope I shall not be found disorderly, but I wish to say briefly that this meeting is very joyous to me. Where God is we can meet, and where God is we can never part. There is something suggestive to me in this hour of the latter days of the nineteenth century, fulfilling much of the divine law and the gospel. The divine law has said to us: "Bring ye all the tithes into the storehouse, that there may be meat in mine house, and prove me now herewith, saith the Lord of hosts, if I will not open you the windows of heaven, and pour you out a blessing, that there shall not be room enough to receive it."

There is with us at this hour this great, great blessing; and may I say with the consciousness of Mind that the fulfilment of divine Love in our lives is the demand of this hour — the special demand. We begin with the law as just announced, "Prove me now herewith, . . . if I will not open you the windows of heaven, and pour you out a blessing," and we go to the Gospels, and there we hear: "In the world ye shall have tribulation; but be of good cheer; I have overcome the world."

The Christian Scientist knows that spiritual faith and understanding pass through the waters of Meribah here — bitter waters; but he also knows they embark for infinity and anchor in omnipotence.

Oh, may this hour be prolific, and at this time and in every heart may there come this benediction: Thou hast no longer to appeal to human strength, to strive with agony; I am thy deliverer. "Of His own will begat He us with the word of truth." Divine Love has strengthened the hand and encouraged the heart of every member of this large church. Oh, may these rich blessings continue and be increased! Divine Love hath opened the gate Beautiful to us, where we may see God and live, see good in good, — God all, one, — one Mind and that divine; where we may love our neighbor as ourselves, and bless our enemies.

Divine Love will also rebuke and destroy disease, and destroy the belief of life in matter. It will waken the dreamer — the sinner, dreaming of pleasure in sin; the sick, dreaming of suffering matter; the slothful, satisfied to sleep and dream. Divine Love is our only physician, and never loses a case. It binds up the broken-hearted; heals the poor body, whose whole head is sick and whose whole heart is faint; comforts such as mourn, wipes away the unavailing, tired tear, brings back the wanderer to the Father's house in which are many mansions, many welcomes, many pardons for the penitent.

Ofttimes I think of this in the great light of the present, the might and light of the present fulfilment. So shall all earth's children at last come to acknowledge God, and be one; inhabit His holy hill, the God-crowned summit of divine Science; the church militant rise to the church triumphant, and Zion be glorified.

A Question Answered

My beloved church will not receive a Message from me this summer, for my annual Message is swallowed up in sundries already given out. These crumbs and monads will feed the hungry, and the fragments gathered therefrom should waken the sleeper, — "dead in trespasses and sins," — set the captive sense free from self's sordid sequela; and one more round of old Sol give birth to the sowing of Solomon.

MARY BAKER EDDY.

PLEASANT VIEW, CONCORD, N. H.,
    May 11, 1903.

Letter of the Pastor Emeritus, June, 1903

My Beloved Brethren: — I have a secret to tell you and a question to ask. Do you know how much I love you and the nature of this love? No: then my sacred secret is incommunicable, and we live apart. But, yes: and this inmost something becomes articulate, and my book is not all you know of me. But your knowledge with its magnitude of meaning uncovers my life, even as your heart has discovered it. The spiritual bespeaks our temporal history. Difficulty, abnegation, constant battle against the world, the flesh, and evil, tell my long-kept secret — evidence a heart wholly in protest and unutterable in love.

The unprecedented progress of Christian Science is proverbial, and we cannot be too grateful nor too humble for this, inasmuch as our daily lives serve to enhance or to stay its glory. To triumph in truth, to keep the faith individually and collectively, conflicting elements must be mastered. Defeat need not follow victory. Joy over good achievements and work well done should not be eclipsed by some lost opportunity, some imperative demand not yet met.

Truth, Life, and Love will never lose their claim on us. And here let me add: —

> Truth happifies life in the hamlet or town;
> Life lessens all pride — its pomp and its frown —
> Love comes to our tears like a soft summer shower,
> To beautify, bless, and inspire man's power.

A Letter from Mrs. Eddy

At the Wednesday evening meeting of April 3, 1907, in The First Church of Christ, Scientist, in Boston, the First Reader, Mr. William D. McCrackan, read the following letter from Mrs. Eddy. In announcing this letter, he said: —

"Permission has been secured from our beloved Leader to read you a letter from her to me. This letter is in Mrs. Eddy's own handwriting, with which I have been familiar for several years, and it shows her usual mental and physical vigor."

MRS. EDDY'S LETTER

Beloved Student: — The wise man has said, "When I was a child, I spake as a child, I understood as a child, I thought as a child: but when I became a man, I put away childish things." That this passage of Scripture and its concluding declaration may be applied to old age, is a solace.

Perhaps you already know that I have heretofore personally attended to my secular affairs, — to my income, investments, deposits, expenditures, and to my employees. But the increasing demands upon my time and labor, and my yearning for more peace in my advancing years, have caused me to select a Board of Trustees to take the charge of my property; namely, the Hon. Henry M. Baker, Mr. Archibald McLellan, and Mr. Josiah E. Fernald.

As you are the First Reader of my church in Boston, of about forty thousand members, I inform you of this, the aforesaid transaction.

Lovingly yours in Christ,
MARY BAKER EDDY.

PLEASANT VIEW, CONCORD, N. H.,
March 22, 1907.

LETTER TO THE MOTHER CHURCH

THE FIRST CHURCH OF CHRIST, SCIENTIST, BOSTON, MASS.

My Beloved Church: — Your love and fidelity cheer my advancing years. As Christian Scientists you understand the Scripture, "Fret not thyself because of evildoers;" also you spiritually and scientifically understand that God is divine Love, omnipotent, omnipresent, infinite; hence it is enough for you and me to know that our "Redeemer liveth" and intercedeth for us.

At this period my demonstration of Christian Science cannot be fully understood, theoretically; therefore it is best explained by its fruits, and by the life of our Lord as depicted in the chapter Atonement and Eucharist, in "Science and Health with Key to the Scriptures."

MARY BAKER EDDY.

PLEASANT VIEW, CONCORD, N. H.,
April 2, 1907.

CARD

I am pleased to say that the following members constitute the Board of Trustees who own my property: —

1. The Hon. Henry M. Baker, who won a suit at law in Washington, D. C., for which it is alleged he was paid the highest fee ever received by a native of New Hampshire.

2. Archibald McLellan, editor-in-chief of the Christian Science periodicals, circulating in the five grand divisions of our globe; also in Canada, Australia, *etc*.

3. Josiah E. Fernald, justice of the peace and president of the National State Capital Bank, Concord, N. H.

To my aforesaid Trustees I have committed the hard earnings of my pen, — the fruits of honest toil, the labor that is known by its fruits, — benefiting the human race; and I have so done that I may have more peace, and time for spiritual thought and the higher criticism.

MARY BAKER EDDY.

PLEASANT VIEW, CONCORD, N. H.,
April 3, 1907.

Mrs. Eddy's Affidavit

The following affidavit, in the form of a letter from Mrs. Eddy to Judge Robert N. Chamberlin of the Superior Court, was filed in the office of the Clerk of the Court, Saturday, May 18. The *Boston Globe*, referring to this document, speaks of it as, "in the main, an example of crisp, clear, plain-speaking English." The entire letter is in Mrs. Eddy's own handwriting and is characteristic in both substance and penmanship: —

Hon. Judge Chamberlin, Concord, N. H.

Respected Sir: — It is over forty years that I have attended personally to my secular affairs, to my income, investments, deposits, expenditures, and to my employees. I have personally selected all my investments, except in one or two instances, and have paid for the same.

The increasing demands upon my time, labors, and thought, and yearning for more peace and to have my property and affairs carefully taken care of for the persons and purposes I have designated by my last will, influenced me to select a Board of Trustees to take charge of my property; namely, the Hon. Henry M. Baker, Mr. Archibald McLellan, Mr. Josiah E. Fernald. I had contemplated doing this before the present proceedings were brought or I knew aught about them, and I had consulted Lawyer Streeter about the method.

I selected said Trustees because I had implicit confidence in each one of them as to honesty and business capacity. No person influenced me to make this selection. I find myself able to select the Trustees I need without the help of others. I gave them my property to take care of because I wanted it protected and myself relieved of the burden of doing this. They have agreed with me to take care of my property and I consider this agreement a great benefit to me already.

This suit was brought without my knowledge and is being carried on contrary to my wishes. I feel that it is not for my benefit in any way, but for my injury, and I know it was not needed to protect my person or property. The present proceedings test my trust in divine Love. My personal reputation is assailed and some of my students and trusted personal friends are cruelly, unjustly, and wrongfully accused.

Mr. Calvin A. Frye and other students often ask me to receive persons whom I desire to see but decline to receive solely because I find that I cannot "serve two masters." I cannot be a Christian Scientist except I leave all for Christ.

Trusting that I have not exceeded the bounds of propriety in the statements herein made by me,

I remain most respectfully yours,

MARY BAKER EDDY.

PLEASANT VIEW, CONCORD, N. H.,
May 16, 1907.

STATE OF NEW HAMPSHIRE, Merrimack, ss.

On this sixteenth day of May, 1907, personally appeared Mary Baker Eddy and made oath that the statements contained in the annexed letter directed to Honorable Judge Chamberlin and dated May 16, 1907, are true.

Before me: ALLEN HOLLIS,
Justice of the Peace.

Nota Bene

Beloved Students: — Rest assured that your Leader is living, loving, acting, enjoying. She is neither dead nor plucked up by the roots, but she is keenly alive to the reality of living, and safely, soulfully founded upon the rock, Christ Jesus, even the spiritual idea of Life, with its abounding, increasing, advancing footsteps of progress, primeval faith, hope, love.

Like the verdure and evergreen that flourish when trampled upon, the Christian Scientist thrives in adversity; his is a life-lease of hope, home, heaven; his idea is nearing the Way, the Truth, and the Life, when misrepresented, belied, and trodden upon. Justice, honesty, cannot be abjured; their vitality involves Life, — calm, irresistible, eternal.

A Word to the Wise

My Beloved Brethren: — When I asked you to dispense with the Executive Members' meeting, the purpose of my request was sacred. It was to turn your sense of worship from the material to the spiritual, the personal to the impersonal, the denominational to the doctrinal, yea, from the human to the divine.

Already you have advanced from the audible to the inaudible prayer; from the material to the spiritual communion; from drugs to Deity; and you have been greatly recompensed. Rejoice and be exceedingly glad, for so doth the divine Love redeem your body from disease; your being from sensuality; your soul from sense; your life from death.

Of this abounding and abiding spiritual understanding the prophet Isaiah said, "And I will bring the blind by a way that they knew not; I will lead them in paths that they have not known: I will make darkness light before them, and crooked things straight. These things will I do unto them, and not forsake them."

MARY BAKER EDDY.

CHESTNUT HILL, MASS.

[Boston Globe]

ABOLISHING THE COMMUNION

In a letter addressed to Christian Scientists the Rev. Mary Baker Eddy explains that dropping the annual communion service of The First Church of Christ, Scientist, in Boston, need not debar distant members from attending occasionally The Mother Church. The following is Mrs. Eddy's letter: —

Beloved Christian Scientists: — Take courage. God is leading you onward and upward. Relinquishing a material form of communion advances it spiritually. The material form is a "Suffer it to be so now," and is abandoned so soon as God's Way-shower, Christ, points the advanced step. This instructs us how to be abased and how to abound.

Dropping the communion of The Mother Church does not prevent its distant members from occasionally attending this church.

MARY BAKER EDDY.

CHESTNUT HILL, MASS.,
      June 21, 1908.

[*Boston Globe*]

Communion Season is Abolished

The general communion service of the Christian Science denomination, held annually in The First Church of Christ, Scientist, in this city, has been abolished by order of Mrs. Mary Baker Eddy. The services attended last Sunday [June 14] by ten thousand persons were thus the last to be held. Of late years members of the church outside of Boston have not been encouraged to attend the communion seasons except on the triennial gatherings, the next of which would have been held next year.

The announcement in regard to the services was made last night [June 21] by Alfred Farlow of the publication committee as follows: —

The First Church of Christ, Scientist, in Boston, has taken steps to abolish its famous communion seasons. In former years, the annual communion season of the Boston church has offered an occasion for the gathering of vast multitudes of Christian Scientists from all parts of the world. According to the following statement, which Mrs. Eddy has just given out to the press, these gatherings will be discontinued: —

"The house of The Mother Church seats only five thousand people, and its membership includes forty-eight thousand communicants, hence the following: —

"The branch churches continue their communion seasons, but there shall be no more communion season in The Mother Church that has blossomed into spiritual beauty, communion universal and divine. 'For who hath known the mind of the Lord, that he may instruct him? But we have the mind of Christ.' (1 Corinthians, 2 : 16.)"

[Mrs. Eddy has only abolished the disappointment of communicants who come long distances and then find no seats in The Mother Church. — EDITOR *Sentinel*.]

MRS. EDDY'S REPLY

JUDGE CLIFFORD P. SMITH, LL.B., C.S.B.,
   First Reader, The Mother Church, Boston, Mass.

Beloved Christian Scientist: — Accept my thanks for your approval of abolishing the communion season of The Mother Church. I sought God's guidance in doing it, but the most important events are criticized.

The Mother Church communion season was literally a communion of branch church communicants which might in time lose its sacredness and merge into a meeting for greetings. My beloved brethren may some time learn this and rejoice with me, as they so often have done, over a step higher in their passage from sense to Soul.

Most truly yours,
MARY BAKER EDDY.

BOX G, BROOKLINE, MASS.,
   June 24, 1908.

THE CHRISTIAN SCIENCE BOARD OF DIRECTORS

Beloved Students: — I thank you for your kind invitation to be present at the annual meeting of The Mother Church on June 7, 1909. I will attend the meeting, but not *in propria persona*. Watch and pray that God directs your meetings and your lives, and your Leader will then be sure that they are blessed in their results.

Lovingly yours,

MARY BAKER EDDY.

BROOKLINE, MASS.,
June 5, 1909.

MRS. EDDY'S STATEMENTS

To Whom It May Concern: — I have the pleasure to report to one and all of my beloved friends and followers that I exist in the flesh, and am seen daily by the members of my household and by those with whom I have appointments.

Above all this fustian of either denying or asserting the personality and presence of Mary Baker Eddy, stands the eternal fact of Christian Science and the honest history of its Discoverer and Founder. It is self-evident that the discoverer of an eternal truth cannot be a temporal fraud.

The Cause of Christian Science is prospering throughout the world and stands forever as an eternal and demonstrable Science, and I do not regard this attack upon me as a trial, for when these things cease to bless they will cease to occur.

"And we know that all things work together for good to them that love God, to them who are the called according to His purpose. . . . What shall we then say to these things? If God be for us, who can be against us?"

MARY BAKER EDDY.

CHESTNUT HILL, MASS.,
June 7, 1909.

Mrs. Eddy also sent the following letter to the members of her church in Concord, N. H.: —

FIRST CHURCH OF CHRIST, SCIENTIST, CONCORD, N. H.

My Beloved Brethren: — Give yourselves no fear and spare not a moment's thought to lies afloat that I am sick, helpless, or an invalid. The public report that I am in either of the aforesaid conditions is utterly false.

With love, ever yours,
MARY BAKER EDDY.

BOX G, BROOKLINE, MASS.,
June 7, 1909.

CHAPTER V

CHRISTIAN SCIENCE HALL, CONCORD, N. H.

In Retrospect

MY DEAR EDITORS:—You are by this time acquainted with the small item that in October, 1897, I proposed to one of Concord's best builders the plan for Christian Science Hall in Concord, N. H. He drew the plan, showed it to me, and I accepted it. From that time, October 29, 1897, until the remodelling of the house was finished, I inspected the work every day, suggested the details outside and inside from the foundations to the tower, and saw them carried out. One day the carpenters' foreman said to me: "I want to be let off for a few days. I do not feel able to keep about. I am feeling an old ailment my mother had." I healed him on the spot. He remained at work, and the next morning said to Mr. George H. Moore of Concord, "I am as well as I ever was."

Within the past year and two months, I have worked even harder than usual, but I cannot go upon the platform and still be at home attending to the machinery which keeps the wheels revolving. This well-known fact makes me the servant of the race — and gladly thus, if in this way I can serve equally my friends and my enemies.

In explanation of my dedicatory letter to the Chicago church (see page 177), I will say: It is understood by all Christians that Jesus spoke the truth. He said: "They shall take up serpents; and if they drink any deadly thing, it shall not hurt them." I believe this saying because I understand it, but its verity has not been acknowledged since the third century.

The statement in my letter to the church in Chicago, in substance as follows, has been quoted and criticized: "If wisdom lengthens my sum of years to fourscore, I may then be even younger than now."

Few believe this saying. Few believe that Christian Science contains infinitely more than has been demonstrated, or that the altitude of its highest propositions has not yet been reached. The heights of the great Nazarene's sayings are not fully scaled. Yet his immortal words and my poor prophecy, if they are true at all, are as true to-day as they will be to-morrow. I am convinced of the absolute truth of his sayings and of their present application to mankind, and I am equally sure that what I wrote is true, although it has not been demonstrated in this age.

Christian Scientists hold as a vital point that the beliefs of mortals tip the scale of being, morally and physically, either in the right or in the wrong direction. Therefore a Christian Scientist never mentally or audibly takes the side of sin, disease, or death. Others who take the side of error do it ignorantly or maliciously. The Christian Scientist voices the harmonious and eternal, and nothing else. He lays his whole weight of thought, tongue, and pen in the divine scale of being — for health and holiness.

SECOND SUNDAY SERVICE, DECEMBER 12, 1897

Friends and Brethren: — There are moments when at the touch of memory the past comes forth like a pageant and the present is prophetic. Over a half century ago, between the morning and afternoon services of the First Congregational Church, the grand old elm on North State Street flung its foliage in kindly shelter over my childhood's Sunday noons. And now, at this distant day, I have provided for you a modest hall, in which to assemble as a sort of Christian Science kindergarten for teaching the "new tongue" of the gospel with "signs following," of which St. Mark prophesies.

May this little sanctum be preserved sacred to the memory of this pure purpose, and subserve it. Let the Bible and the Christian Science textbook preach the gospel which heals the sick and enlightens the people's sense of Christian Science. This ministry, reaching the physical, moral, and spiritual needs of humanity, will, in the name of Almighty God, speak the truth that to-day, as in olden time, is found able to heal both sin and disease.

I have purchased a pleasant place for you, and prepared for your use work-rooms and a little hall, which are already dedicated to Christ's service, since Christian Scientists never stop ceremoniously to dedicate halls. I shall be with you personally very seldom. I have a work to do that, in the words of our Master, "ye know not of." From the interior of Africa to the utmost parts of the earth, the sick and the heavenly homesick or hungry hearts are calling on me for help, and I am helping them. You have less need of me than have they, and you must not expect me further to do your pioneer work in this city. Faithfully and more than ever persistently, you are now, through the providence of God, called to do your part wisely and to let your faith be known by your works. All that we ask of any people is to judge our doctrine by its fruits. May the good folk of Concord have this opportunity, and may the God of all grace, truth, and love be and abide with you henceforth.

ADDRESS TO THE CONCORD CHURCH, FEBRUARY, 1899

My Beloved Brethren: — In the annals of our denomination this church becomes historic, having completed its organization February 22 — Washington's birthday. Memorable date, all unthought of till the day had passed! Then we beheld the omen, — religious liberty, — the Father of the universe and the father of our nation in concurrence.

To-day, with the large membership of seventy-four communicants, you have met to praise God. I, as usual at home and alone, am with you in spirit, joining in your rejoicing, and my heart is asking: What are the angels saying or singing of this dear little flock, and what is each heart in this house repeating, and what is being recorded of this meeting as with the pen of an angel?

Bear in mind always that Christianity is not alone a gift, but that it is a growth Christward; it is not a creed or dogma,— a philosophical phantasm,— nor the opinions of a sect struggling to gain power over contending sects and scourging the sect in advance of it. Christianity is the summons of divine Love for man to be Christlike— to emulate the words and the works of our great Master.

To attain to these works, men must know somewhat of the divine Principle of Jesus' life-work, and must prove their knowledge by doing as he bade: "Go, and do thou likewise."

We know Principle only through Science. The Principle of Christ is divine Love, resistless Life and Truth. Then the Science of the Principle must be Christlike, or Christian Science. More than regal is the majesty of the meekness of the Christ-principle; and its might is the ever-flowing tides of truth that sweep the universe, create and govern it; and its radiant stores of knowledge are the mysteries of exhaustless being. Seek ye these till you make their treasures yours.

When a young man vainly boasted, "I am wise, for I have conversed with many wise men," Epictetus made answer, "And I with many rich men, but I am not rich." The richest blessings are obtained by labor. A vessel full must be emptied before it can be refilled. Lawyers may know too much of human law to have a clear perception of divine justice, and divines be too deeply read in scholastic theology to appreciate or to demonstrate Christian charity. Losing the comprehensive in the technical, the Principle in its accessories, cause in effect, and faith in sight, we lose the Science of Christianity, — a predicament quite like that of the man who could not see London for its houses.

Clouds parsimonious of rain, that swing in the sky with dumb thunderbolts, are seen and forgotten in the same hour; while those with a mighty rush, which waken the stagnant waters and solicit every root and every leaf with the treasures of rain, ask no praising. Remember, thou canst be brought into no condition, be it ever so severe, where Love has not been before thee and where its tender lesson is not awaiting thee. Therefore despair not nor murmur, for that which seeketh to save, to heal, and to deliver, will guide thee, if thou seekest this guidance.

Pliny gives the following description of the character of true greatness: "Doing what deserves to be written, and writing what deserves to be read; and rendering the world happier and better for having lived in it." Strive thou for the joy and crown of such a pilgrimage — the service of such a mission.

A heart touched and hallowed by one chord of Christian Science, can accomplish the full scale; but this heart must be honest and in earnest and never weary of struggling to be perfect — to reflect the divine Life, Truth, and Love.

Stand by the limpid lake, sleeping amid willowy banks dyed with emerald. See therein the mirrored sky and the moon ablaze with her mild glory. This will stir your heart. Then, in speechless prayer, ask God to enable you to reflect God, to become His own image and likeness, even the calm, clear, radiant reflection of Christ's glory, healing the sick, bringing the sinner to repentance, and raising the spiritually dead in trespasses and sins to life in God. Jesus said: "If ye abide in me, and my words abide in you, ye shall ask what ye will, and it shall be done unto you."

Beloved in Christ, what our Master said unto his disciples, when he sent them forth to heal the sick and preach the gospel, I say unto you: "Be ye therefore wise as serpents, and harmless as doves." Then, if the wisdom you manifest causes Christendom or the disclaimer against God to call this "a subtle fraud," "let your peace return to you."

I am patient with the newspaper wares and the present schoolboy epithets and attacks of a portion of Christendom:

(1) Because I sympathize with their ignorance of Christian Science:

(2) Because I know that no Christian can or does understand this Science and not love it:

(3) Because these attacks afford opportunity for explaining Christian Science:

(4) Because it is written: "The wrath of man shall praise Thee: the remainder of wrath shalt Thou restrain."

Rest assured that the injustice done by press and pulpit to this denomination of Christians will cease, when it no longer blesses this denomination. "This I know; for God is for me" (Psalms). And in the words of St. Paul, "If God be for us, who can be against us?"

> "Pass ye the proud fane by,
>   The vaulted aisles by flaunting folly trod,
> And 'neath the temple of uplifted sky —
>   Go forth, and worship God."

MESSAGE, APRIL 19, 1899

SUBJECT: "NOT MATTER, BUT SPIRIT"

My Beloved Brethren: — We learn from the Scriptures that the Baalites or sun-worshippers failed to look "through nature up to nature's God," thus missing the discovery of all cause and effect. They were content to look no higher than the symbol. This departure from Spirit, this worshipping of matter in the name of nature, was idolatry then and is idolatry now. When human thought discerned its idolatrous tendencies, it took a step higher; but it immediately turned to another form of idolatry, and, worshipping person instead of Principle, anchored its faith in troubled waters. At that period, the touch of Jesus' robe and the handkerchief of St. Paul were supposed to heal the sick, and our Master declared, "Thy faith hath made thee whole." The medicine-man, far lower in the scale of thought, said, "My material tonic has strengthened you." By reposing faith in man and in matter, the human race has not yet reached the understanding of God, the conception of Spirit and its all-power.

The restoration of pure Christianity rests solely on spiritual understanding, spiritual worship, spiritual power. Ask thyself, Do I enter by the door and worship only Spirit and spiritually, or do I climb up some other way? Do I understand God as Love, the divine Principle of all that really is, the infinite good, than which there is none else and in whom is all? Unless this be so, the blind is leading the blind, and both will stumble into doubt and darkness, even as the ages have shown. To-day, if ye would hear His voice, listen to His Word and serve no other gods. Then the divine Principle of good, that we call God, will be found an ever-present help in all things, and Christian Science will be understood. It will also be seen that this God demands all our faith and love; that matter, man, or woman can never heal you nor pardon a single sin; while God, the divine Principle of nature and man, when understood and demonstrated, is found to be the remote, predisposing, and present cause of all that is rightly done.

I have the sweet satisfaction of sending to you weekly flowers that my skilful florist has coaxed into loveliness despite our winter snows. Also I hear that the loving hearts and hands of the Christian Scientists in Concord send these floral offerings in my name to the sick and suffering. Now, if these kind hearts will only do this in Christ's name, the power of Truth and Love will fulfil the law in righteousness. The healing and the gospel ministry of my students in Concord have come to fulfil the whole law. Unto "the angel of the church in Philadelphia," the church of brotherly love, "these things saith He that is holy."

To-day our great Master would say to the aged gentleman healed from the day my flowers visited his bedside: Thy faith hath healed thee. The flowers were imbued and associated with no intrinsic healing qualities from my poor personality. The scientific, healing faith is a saving faith; it keeps steadfastly the great and first commandment, "Thou shalt have no other gods before me" — no other than the spiritual help of divine Love. Faith in aught else misguides the understanding, ignores the power of God, and, in the words of St. Paul, appeals to an unknown power "whom therefore ye ignorantly worship." This trembling and blind faith, in the past as in the present, seeks personality for support, unmindful of the divine law of Love, which can be understood, the Principle of which works intelligently as the divine Mind, not as matter, casting out evil and healing the sick.

Christian Science healing is "the Spirit and the bride," — the Word and the wedding of this Word to all human thought and action, — that says: Come, and I will give thee rest, peace, health, holiness. The sweet flowers should be to us His apostles, pointing away from matter and man up to the one source, divine Life and Love, in whom is all salvation from sin, disease, and death. The Science of all healing is based on Mind — the power of Truth over error. It is not the person who gives the drug nor the drug itself that heals, but it is the law of Life understood by the practitioner as transcending the law of death.

I shall scarcely venture to send flowers to this little hall if they can be made to infringe the divine law of Love even in thought. Send flowers and all things fair and comforting to the dear sick, but remember it is not he who gives the flowers that confers the blessing, but "my Spirit, saith the Lord;" for "in Him was life," and that life "was the light of men."

First Annual Meeting, January 11, 1900

My Beloved Brethren: — At this, your first annual meeting, permit me to congratulate this little church in our city, weaving the new-old vesture in which to appear and to clothe the human race. Carlyle wrote: "Wouldst thou plant for eternity? Then plant into the deep infinite faculties of man. If the poor toil that we have food, must not the high and glorious toil for him in return that we have light, freedom, immortality?" I agree with him; and in our era of the world I welcome the means and methods, light and truth, emanating from the pulpit and press. Altogether it makes the church militant, embodied in a visible communion, the foreshadowing of the church triumphant. Communing heart with heart, mind with mind, soul with soul, wherein and whereby we are looking heavenward, is not looking nor gravitating earthward, take it in whatever sense you may. Such communing uplifts man's being; it makes healing the sick and reforming the sinner a mutual aid society, which is effective here and now.

May this dear little church, nestled so near my heart and native hills, be steadfast in Christ, always abounding in love and good works, having unfaltering faith in the prophecies, promises, and proofs of Holy Writ. May this church have one God, one Christ, and that one the God and Saviour whom the Scriptures declare. May it catch the early trumpet-call, take step with the twentieth century, leave behind those things that are behind, lay down the low laurels of vainglory, and, pressing forward in the onward march of Truth, run in joy, health, holiness, the race set before it, till, home at last, it finds the full fruition of its faith, hope, and prayer.

Easter Message, 1902

Beloved Brethren: — May this glad Easter morn find the members of this dear church having a pure peace, a fresh joy, a clear vision of heaven here, — heaven within us, — and an awakened sense of the risen Christ. May long lines of light span the horizon of their hope and brighten their faith with a dawn that knows no twilight and no night. May those who discourse music to-day, sing as the angels heaven's symphonies that come to earth.

May the dear Sunday School children always be gathering Easter lilies of love with happy hearts and ripening goodness. To-day may they find some sweet scents and beautiful blossoms in their Leader's love, which she sends to them this glad morn in the flowers and the cross from Pleasant View, smiling upon them.

Annual Meeting, January 6, 1905

Beloved Brethren: — You will accept my gratitude for your dear letter, and allow me to reply in words of the Scripture: "I know whom I have believed, and am persuaded that He is able" — "able to do exceeding abundantly above all that we ask or think," "able to make all grace abound toward you; that ye, always having all sufficiency in all things, may abound to every good work," "able to keep that which I have committed unto Him against that day."

When Jesus directed his disciples to prepare for the material passover, which spiritually speaking is the passover from sense to Soul, he bade them say to the goodman of the house: "The Master saith unto thee, Where is the guestchamber, where I shall eat the passover with my disciples? and he shall show you a large upper room furnished: there make ready."

In obedience to this command may these communicants come with the upper chambers of thought prepared for the reception of Truth — with hope, faith, and love ready to partake of the bread that cometh down from heaven, and to "drink of his blood" — to receive into their affections and lives the inspiration which giveth victory over sin, disease, and death.

CHAPTER VI

FIRST CHURCH OF CHRIST, SCIENTIST, CONCORD, N. H.

[*Concord* (N. H.) *Monitor*]

MRS. EDDY'S GIFT TO THE CONCORD CHURCH

"BELOVED TEACHER AND LEADER: — The members of the Concord church are filled with profound joy and deep gratitude that your generous gift of one hundred thousand dollars is to be used at once to build a beautiful church edifice for your followers in the capital city of your native State. We rejoice that the prosperity of the Cause in your home city, where, without regard to class or creed, you are so highly esteemed, makes necessary the commodious and beautiful church home you have so freely bestowed. We thank you for this renewed evidence of your unselfish love."

The church will be built of the same beautiful Concord granite of which the National Library Building in Washington is constructed. This is in accord with the expressed wish of Mrs. Eddy, made known in her original deed of trust, first announced in the *Concord Monitor* of March 19, 1898. In response to an inquiry from the editor of that paper, Mrs. Eddy made the following statement: —

On January 31, 1898, I gave a deed of trust to three individuals which conveyed to them the sum of one hundred thousand dollars to be appropriated in building a granite church edifice for First Church of Christ, Scientist, in this city.

Very truly,
MARY BAKER EDDY.

CORNER-STONE LAID AT CONCORD

Beloved Brethren: — This day drops down upon the glories of summer; it is a glad day, in attune with faith's fond trust. We live in an age of Love's divine adventure to be All-in-all. This day is the natal hour of my lone earth life; and for all mankind to-day hath its gloom and glory: it endureth all things; it points to the new birth, heaven here, the struggle over; it profits by the past and joys in the present — to-day lends a new-born beauty to holiness, patience, charity, love.

Having all faith in Christian Science, we must have faith in whatever manifests love for God and man. The burden of proof that Christian Science is Science rests on Christian Scientists. The letter without the spirit is dead: it is the Spirit that heals the sick and the sinner — that makes the heart tender, faithful, true. Most men and women talk well, and some practise what they say.

God has blessed and will bless this dear band of brethren. He has laid the chief corner-stone of the temple which to-day you commemorate, to-morrow complete, and thereafter dedicate to Truth and Love. O may your temple and all who worship therein stand through all time for God and humanity!

MARY BAKER EDDY.

Message on the Occasion of the Dedication of Mrs. Eddy's Gift, July 17, 1904

Beloved Brethren: — Never more sweet than to-day, seem to me, and must seem to thee, those words of our loved Lord, "Lo, I am with you alway, even unto the end." Thus may it ever be that Christ rejoiceth and comforteth us. Sitting at his feet, I send to you the throbbing of every pulse of my desire for the ripening and rich fruit of this branch of his vine, and I thank God who hath sent forth His word to heal and to save.

At this period, the greatest man or woman on earth stands at the vestibule of Christian Science, struggling to enter into the perfect love of God and man. The infinite will not be buried in the finite; the true thought escapes from the inward to the outward, and this is the only right activity, that whereby we reach our higher nature. Material theories tend to check spiritual attraction — the tendency towards God, the infinite and eternal — by an opposite attraction towards the temporary and finite. Truth, life, and love are the only legitimate and eternal demands upon man; they are spiritual laws enforcing obedience and punishing disobedience.

Even Epictetus, a heathen philosopher who held that Zeus, the master of the gods, could not control human will, writes, "What is the essence of God? Mind." The general thought chiefly regards material things, and keeps

Copyright, 1904, by Mary Baker G. Eddy. All rights reserved.

Mind much out of sight. The Christian, however, strives for the spiritual; he abides in a right purpose, as in laws which it were impious to transgress, and follows Truth fearlessly. The heart that beats mostly for self is seldom alight with love. To live so as to keep human consciousness in constant relation with the divine, the spiritual, and the eternal, is to individualize infinite power; and this is Christian Science.

It is of less importance that we receive from mankind justice, than that we deserve it. Most of us willingly accept dead truisms which can be buried at will; but a live truth, even though it be a sapling within rich soil and with blossoms on its branches, frightens people. The trenchant truth that cuts its way through iron and sod, most men avoid until compelled to glance at it. Then they open their hearts to it for actual being, health, holiness, and immortality.

I am asked, "Is there a hell?" Yes, there is a hell for all who persist in breaking the Golden Rule or in disobeying the commandments of God. Physical science has sometimes argued that the internal fires of our earth will eventually consume this planet. Christian Science shows that hidden unpunished sin is this internal fire, — even the fire of a guilty conscience, waking to a true sense of itself, and burning in torture until the sinner is consumed, — his sins destroyed. This may take millions of cycles, but of the time no man knoweth. The advanced psychist knows that this hell is mental, not material, and that the Christian has no part in it. Only the makers of hell burn in their fire.

Concealed crimes, the wrongs done to others, are millstones hung around the necks of the wicked. Christ Jesus paid our debt and set us free by enabling us to pay it; for which we are still his debtors, washing the Way-shower's feet with tears of joy.

The intentional destroyer of others would destroy himself eternally, were it not that his suffering reforms him, thus balancing his account with divine Love, which never remits the sentence necessary to reclaim the sinner. Hence these words of Christ Jesus: "Depart from me, all ye workers of iniquity. There shall be weeping and gnashing of teeth, when ye shall see Abraham, and Isaac, and Jacob, and all the prophets, in the kingdom of God, and you yourselves thrust out." (Luke 13: 27, 28.) He who gains self-knowledge, self-control, and the kingdom of heaven within himself, within his own consciousness, is saved through Christ, Truth. Mortals must drink sufficiently of the cup of their Lord and Master to unself mortality and to destroy its erroneous claims. Therefore, said Jesus, "Ye shall drink indeed of my cup, and be baptized with the baptism that I am baptized with."

We cannot boast ourselves of to-morrow; sufficient unto each day is the duty thereof. Lest human reason becloud spiritual understanding, say not in thy heart: Sickness is possible because one's thought and conduct do not afford a sufficient defence against it. Trust in God, and "He shall direct thy paths." When evil was avenging itself on its destroyer, his preeminent goodness, the Godlike man said, "My burden is light." Only he who learns through meekness and love the falsity of supposititious life and intelligence in matter, can triumph over their ultimatum, sin, suffering, and death.

God's mercy for mortal ignorance and need is assured; then who shall question our want of more faith in His "very present help in trouble"? Jesus said: "Suffer it to be so now: for thus it becometh us to fulfil all righteousness."

Strength is in man, not in muscles; unity and power are not in atom or in dust. A small group of wise thinkers is better than a wilderness of dullards and stronger than the might of empires. Unity is spiritual cooperation, heart to heart, the bond of blessedness such as my beloved Christian Scientists all over the field, and the dear Sunday School children, have demonstrated in gifts to me of about eighty thousand dollars, to be applied to building, embellishing, and furnishing our church edifice in Concord, N. H.

We read in Holy Writ: "This man began to build, and was not able to finish." This was spoken derisively. But the love that rebukes praises also, and methinks the same wisdom which spake thus in olden time would say to the builder of the Christian Scientists' church edifice in Concord: "Well done, good and faithful." Our proper reason for church edifices is, that in them Christians may worship God, — not that Christians may worship church edifices!

May the loving Shepherd of this feeble flock lead it gently into "green pastures . . . beside the still waters." May He increase its members, and may their faith never falter — their faith in and their understanding of divine Love. This church, born in my nativity, may it build upon the rock of ages against which the waves and winds beat in vain. May the towering top of its goodly temple — burdened with beauty, pointing to the heavens, bursting into the rapture of song — long call the worshipper to seek the haven of hope, the heaven of Soul, the sweet sense of angelic song chiming chaste challenge to praise him who won the way and taught mankind to win through meekness to might, goodness to grandeur, — from cross to crown, from sense to Soul, from gleam to glory, from matter to Spirit.

Announcement

Not having the time to receive all the beloved ones who have so kindly come to the dedication of this church, I must not allow myself the pleasure of receiving any of them. I always try to be just, if not generous; and I cannot show my love for them in social ways without neglecting the sacred demands on my time and attention for labors which I think do them more good.

A Kindly Greeting

Dear Editor: — When I removed from Boston in 1889 and came to Concord, N. H., it was that I might find retirement from many years of incessant labor for the Cause of Christian Science, and the opportunity in Concord's quiet to revise our textbook, "Science and Health with Key to the Scriptures." Here let me add that, together with the retirement I so much coveted, I have also received from the leading people of this pleasant city all and more than I anticipated. I love its people — love their scholarship, friendship, and granite character. I respect their religious beliefs, and thank their ancestors for helping to form mine. The movement of establishing in this city a church of our faith was far from my purpose, when I came here, knowing that such an effort would involve a lessening of the retirement I so much desired. But the demand increased, and I consented, hoping thereby to give to many in this city a church home.

Acknowledgment of Gifts

TO THE CHICAGO CHURCHES

My Beloved Brethren: — I have yearned to express my thanks for your munificent gift to First Church of Christ, Scientist, in Concord, of ten thousand dollars. What is gratitude but a powerful *camera obscura*, a thing focusing light where love, memory, and all within the human heart is present to manifest light.

Is it not a joy to compare the beginning of Christian Science in Chicago with its present prosperity? Now [1904] six dear churches are there, the members of which not only possess a sound faith, but that faith also possesses them. A great sanity, a mighty something buried in the depths of the unseen, has wrought a resurrection among you, and has leaped into living love. What is this something, this phœnix fire, this pillar by day, kindling, guiding, and guarding your way? It is *unity*, the bond of perfectness, the thousandfold expansion that will engirdle the world, — unity, which unfolds the thought most within us into the greater and better, the sum of all reality and good.

This unity is reserved wisdom and strength. It builds upon the rock, against which envy, enmity, or malice beat in vain. Man lives, moves, and has his being in God, Love. Then man must live, he cannot die; and Love must necessarily promote and pervade all his success. Of two things fate cannot rob us; namely, of choosing the best, and of helping others thus to choose. But in doing this the Master became the servant. The grand must stoop to the menial. There is scarcely an indignity which I have not endured for the cause of Christ, Truth, and I returned blessing for cursing. The best help the worst; the righteous suffer for the unrighteous; and by this spirit man lives and thrives, and by it God governs.

TO FIRST CHURCH OF CHRIST, SCIENTIST, NEW YORK

Beloved Brethren: — I beg to thank the dear brethren of this church for the sum of ten thousand dollars presented to me for First Church of Christ, Scientist, in Concord, N. H. Goodness never fails to receive its reward, for goodness makes life a blessing. As an active portion of one stupendous whole, goodness identifies man with universal good. Thus may each member of this church rise above the oft-repeated inquiry, What am I? to the scientific response: I am able to impart truth, health, and happiness, and this is my rock of salvation and my reason for existing.

Human reason becomes tired and calls for rest. It has a relapse into the common hope. Goodness and benevolence never tire. They maintain themselves and others and never stop from exhaustion. He who is afraid of being too generous has lost the power of being magnanimous. The best man or woman is the most unselfed. God grant that this church is rapidly nearing the maximum of might, — the means that build to the heavens, — that it has indeed found and felt the infinite source where is *all*, and from which it can help its neighbor. Then efforts to be great will never end in anarchy but will continue with divine approbation. It is insincerity and a half-persuaded faith that fail to succeed and fall to the earth.

Religions may waste away, but the fittest survives; and so long as we have the right ideal, life is worth living and God takes care of our life.

TO THE MOTHER CHURCH

My Beloved Brethren: — Your munificent gift of ten thousand dollars, with which to furnish First Church of Christ, Scientist, of Concord, N. H., with an organ, is positive proof of your remembrance and love. Days of shade and shine may come and go, but we will live on and never drift apart. Life's ills are its chief recompense; they develop hidden strength. Had I never suffered for The Mother Church, neither she nor I would be practising the virtues that lie concealed in the smooth seasons and calms of human existence. When we are willing to help and to be helped, divine aid is near. If all our years were holidays, sport would be more irksome than work. So, my dear ones, let us together sing the old-new song of salvation, and let our measure of time and joy be spiritual, not material.

TO FIRST CHURCH OF CHRIST, SCIENTIST, NEW LONDON, CONN.

Beloved Brethren: — I am for the first time informed of your gift to me of a beautiful cabinet, costing one hundred and seventy-five dollars, for my books, placed in my room at First Church of Christ, Scientist, Concord, N. H.

Accept my deep thanks therefor, and especially for the self-sacrifice it may have cost the dear donors.

The mysticism of good is unknown to the flesh, for goodness is "the fruit of the Spirit." The suppositional world within us separates us from the spiritual world, which is apart from matter, and unites us to one another. Spirit teaches us to resign what we are not and to understand what we are in the unity of Spirit — in that Love which is faithful, an ever-present help in trouble, which never deserts us.

I pray that heaven's messages of "on earth peace, good will toward men," may fill your hearts and leave their loving benedictions upon your lives.

Thanksgiving Day, 1904

Beloved Students: — May this, your first Thanksgiving Day, according to time-tables, in our new church edifice, be one acceptable in His sight, and full of love, peace, and good will for yourselves, your flock, and the race. Give to all the dear ones my love, and my prayer for their health, happiness, and holiness this and every day.

Religious Freedom

Beloved Brethren: — Allow me to send forth a pæan of praise for the noble disposal of the legislative question as to the infringement of rights and privileges guaranteed to you by the laws of my native State. The constituted religious rights in New Hampshire will, I trust, never be marred by the illegitimate claims of envy, jealousy, or persecution.

In our country the day of heathenism, illiberal views,

or of an uncultivated understanding has passed. Freedom to worship God according to the dictates of enlightened conscience, and practical religion in agreement with the demand of our common Christ, the Holy One of Israel, are forever the privileges of the people of my dear old New Hampshire.

Lovingly yours,
MARY BAKER EDDY.

Box G, Brookline, Mass.,
    April 12, 1909.

CHAPTER VII

PLEASANT VIEW AND CONCORD, N. H.

INVITATION TO CONCORD, JULY 4, 1897

MY BELOVED CHURCH: — I invite you, one and all, to Pleasant View, Concord, N. H., on July 5, at 12.30 P.M., if you would enjoy so long a trip for so small a purpose as simply seeing Mother.

My precious Busy Bees, under twelve years of age, are requested to visit me at a later date, which I hope soon to name to them.

With love, Mother,
MARY BAKER EDDY.

PLEASANT VIEW, CONCORD, N. H.,
June 30, 1897.

[New York Journal]

VISIT TO CONCORD, 1901

Please say through the *New York Journal*, to the Christian Scientists of New York City and of the world at large, that I was happy to receive at Concord, N. H., the call of about three thousand believers of my faith, and that I was rejoiced at the appropriate beauty of time and place which greeted them.

I am especially desirous that it should be understood that this was no festal occasion, no formal church ceremonial, but simply my acquiescence in the request of my church members that they might see the Leader of Christian Science.

The brevity of my remarks was due to a desire on my part that the important sentiments uttered in my annual Message to the church last Sunday should not be confused with other issues, but should be emphasized in the minds of all present here in Concord.

Address at Pleasant View, June, 1903

Beloved Brethren: — Welcome home! To your home in my heart! Welcome to Pleasant View, but not to varying views. I would present a gift to you to-day, only that this gift is already yours. God hath given it to all mankind. It is His coin, His currency; it has His image and superscription. This gift is a passage of Scripture; it is my sacred motto, and it reads thus: —

"Trust in the Lord, and do good; so shalt thou dwell in the land, and verily thou shalt be fed. Delight thyself also in the Lord; and He shall give thee the desires of thine heart. Commit thy way unto the Lord; trust also in Him; and He shall bring it to pass. And He shall bring forth thy righteousness as the light, and thy judgment as the noonday."

Beloved, some of you have come long distances to kneel with us in sacred silence in blest communion — unity of faith, understanding, prayer, and praise — and to return in joy, bearing your sheaves with you. In parting I repeat to these dear members of my church: *Trust in Truth, and have no other trusts.*

To-day is fulfilled the prophecy of Isaiah: "And the ransomed of the Lord shall return, and come to Zion with songs and everlasting joy upon their heads: they shall obtain joy and gladness, and sorrow and sighing shall flee away."

Visit to Concord, 1904

Beloved Students: — The new Concord church is so nearly completed that I think you would enjoy seeing it. Therefore I hereby invite all my church communicants who attend this communion, to come to Concord, and view this beautiful structure, at two o'clock in the afternoon, Monday, June 13, 1904.

Lovingly yours,
MARY BAKER EDDY.

PLEASANT VIEW, CONCORD, N. H.,
June 11, 1904.

THE DAY IN CONCORD

While on her regular afternoon drive Mrs. Eddy responded graciously to the silent greetings of the people who were assembled on the lawn of the Unitarian church and of the high school. Her carriage came to a standstill on North State Street, and she was greeted in behalf of the church by the President, Mr. E. P. Bates, to whom she presented as a love-token for the church a handsome rosewood casket beautifully bound with burnished brass.

The casket contained a gavel for the use of the

President of The Mother Church. The wood of the head of the gavel was taken from the old Yale College Athenæum, the first chapel of the college. It was built in 1761, and razed in 1893 to make room for Vanderbilt Hall. The wood in the handle was grown on the farm of Mark Baker, father of the Rev. Mary Baker Eddy, at Bow, N. H.

In presenting this gavel to President Bates, Mrs. Eddy spoke as follows to the members of her church, The First Church of Christ, Scientist, Boston, Mass.: —

"My Beloved Brethren: — Permit me to present to you a little gift that has no intrinsic value save that which it represents — namely, a material symbol of my spiritual call to this my beloved church of over thirty thousand members; and this is that call: In the words of our great Master, 'Go ye into all the world,' 'heal the sick,' cast out evil, disease, and death; 'Freely ye have received, freely give.' You will please accept my thanks for your kind, expert call on me."

In reply Mr. Bates said, —

"I accept this gift in behalf of the church, and for myself and my successors in office."

The box containing the gavel was opened the following day in Boston at the annual meeting of The Mother Church of Christ, Scientist, and the enclosed note from Mrs. Eddy was read: —

"My Beloved Brethren: — You will please accept from me the accompanying gift as a simple token of love."

I would love to be with you at this deeply interesting anniversary, but my little church in Boston, Mass., of thirty-six thousand communicants, together with the organizations connected therewith, requires my constant attention and time, with the exception of a daily drive.

Please accept the enclosed check for five hundred dollars, to aid in repairing your church building.

Pleasant View, Concord, N. H.,
November 14, 1905.

Greetings

Allow me to say to the good folk of Concord that the growth and prosperity of our city cheer me. Its dear churches, reliable editors, intelligent medical faculty, up-to-date academies, humane institutions, provisions for the army, and well-conducted jail and state prison, — if, indeed, such must remain with us a little longer, — speak for themselves. Our picturesque city, however, greatly needs improved streets. May I ask in behalf of the public this favor of our city government; namely, to macadamize a portion of Warren Street and to macadamize North State Street throughout?

Sweeter than the balm of Gilead, richer than the diamonds of Golconda, dear as the friendship of those we love, are justice, fraternity, and Christian charity. The song of my soul must remain so long as I remain. Let brotherly love continue.

I am sure that the counterfeit letters in circulation, purporting to have my signature, must fail to influence the minds of this dear people to conclusions the very opposite of my real sentiments.

To First Church of Christ, Scientist, Wilmington, N. C.

In Appreciation of a Gift of Fifty Dollars in Gold towards the Concord (N. H.) Street Fund

My Beloved Brethren: — Long ago you of the dear South paved the way to my forever gratitude, and now illustrate the past by your present love. God grant that such great goodness, pointing the path to heaven within you, hallow your Palmetto home with palms of victory and songs of glory.

CHAPTER VIII

DEDICATORY MESSAGES TO BRANCH CHURCHES

First Church of Christ, Scientist, Chicago, Ill.

BELOVED BRETHREN: — Most happily would I comply with your cordial invitation and be with you on so interesting an occasion as the dedication of First Church of Christ, Scientist, in Chicago. But daily duties require attention elsewhere, and I am glad to say that there seems to be no special need of my personal presence at your religious jubilee. I am quite able to take the trip to your city, and if wisdom lengthens my sum of years to fourscore (already imputed to me), I shall then be even younger and nearer the eternal meridian than now, for the true knowledge and proof of life is in putting off the limitations and putting on the possibilities and permanence of Life.

In your renowned city, the genesis of Christian Science was allied to that olden axiom: "The blood of the martyrs is the seed of the Church;" but succeeding years show in livid lines that the great Shepherd has nurtured and nourished this church as a fatling of the flock. To-day the glory of His presence rests upon it, the joy of many generations awaits it, and this prophecy of Isaiah is fulfilled among you: "I will direct their work in truth, and I will make an everlasting covenant with them."

Your Bible and your textbook, pastor and ethical tenets, do not mislead the seeker after Truth. These unpretentious preachers cloud not the spiritual meaning of Holy Writ by material interpretations, nor lose the invincible process and purity of Christianity whereby the sick are healed and sinners saved. The Science of Christianity is not generally understood, but it hastens hourly to this end. This Science is the essence of religion, distilled in the laboratory of infinite Love and prepared for all peoples. And because Science is naturally divine, is this natural Science less profitable or scientific than "counting the legs of insects"? The Scripture declares that God is All. Then all is Spirit and spiritual. The true sense of life is lost to those who regard being as material. The Scripture pronounces all that God made "good;" therefore if evil exists, it exists without God. But this is impossible in reality, for He made all "that was made." Hence the inevitable revelation of Christian Science — that evil is unreal; and this is the best of it.

On April 15, 1891, the Christian Science textbook lay on a table in a burning building. A Christian Scientist entered the house through a window and snatched this book from the flames. Instantly the table sank a charred mass. The covers of the book were burned up, but not one word in the book was effaced. If the world were in ashes, the contents of "Science and Health with Key to the Scriptures" would remain immortal.

It is said that the nearest approach to the sayings of the great Master is the *Logia* of Papias, written in A.D. 145, and that all else reported as his sayings are translations. The ancient *Logia*, or imputed sayings of Jesus by Papias, are undoubtedly the beginning of the gospel writings. The synoptic Scriptures, as set forth in the first and second chapters of Genesis, were in two distinct manuscripts. The first gave an account of the spiritual creation, and the second was an opposite story, or allegory, of a material universe and man made of dust. In this allegorical document the power and prerogative of Spirit are submerged in matter. In other words, soul enters non-intelligent dust and man becomes both good and evil, both mind and matter, mortal and immortal, — all of which divine Science shows to be an impossibility.

The Old and the New Testaments contain self-evident truths that cannot be lost, but being translations, the Scriptures are criticized. Some dangerous skepticism exists as to the verification of our Master's sayings. But Christians and Christian Scientists know that if the Old Testament and gospel narratives had never been written, the nature of Christianity, as depicted in the life of our Lord, and the truth in the Scriptures, are sufficient to authenticate Christ's Christianity as the perfect ideal. The character of the Nazarene Prophet illustrates the Principle and practice of a true divinity and humanity. The different renderings or translations of Scripture in no wise affect Christian Science. Christianity and Science, being contingent on nothing written and based on the divine Principle of being, must be, are, irrefutable and eternal.

We are indeed privileged in having the untranslated revelations of Christian Science. They afford such expositions of the therapeutics, ethics, and Christianity of Christ as make even God demonstrable, the divine Love practical, and so furnish rules whereby man can prove God's love, healing the sick and the sinner.

Whosoever understands Christian Science knows beyond a doubt that its life-giving truths were preached and practised in the first century by him who proved their practicality, who uttered Christ's Sermon on the Mount, who taught his disciples the healing Christianity which applies to all ages, and who dated time. A spiritual understanding of the Scriptures restores their original tongue in the language of Spirit, that primordial standard of Truth.

Christian Science contains no element whatever of hypnotism or animal magnetism. It appeals alone to God, to the divine Principle, or Life, Truth, and Love, to whom all things are possible; and this Principle heals sin, sickness, disease, and death. Christian Science meets error with Truth, death with Life, hate with Love, and thus, and only thus, does it overcome evil and heal disease. The obstinate sinner, however, refuses to see this grand verity or to acknowledge it, for he knows not that in justice, as well as in mercy, God is Love.

In our struggles with sin and sinners, when we drop compliance with their desires, insist on what we know is right, and act accordingly, the disguised or the self-satisfied mind, not ready to be uplifted, rebels, misconstrues our best motives, and calls them unkind. But this is the cross. Take it up, — it wins the crown; and in the spirit of our great Exemplar pray: "Father, forgive them; for they know not what they do."

No warfare exists between divine theology and Christian Science, for the latter solves the whence and why of the cosmos and defines noumenon and phenomena spiritually,

MESSAGES TO BRANCH CHURCHES

not materially. The specific quest of Christian Science is to settle all points beyond cavil, on the Biblical basis that God is All-in-all; whereas philosophy and so-called natural science, dealing with human hypotheses, or material cause and effect, are aided only at long intervals with elementary truths, and ultimate in unsolved problems and outgrown, proofless positions.

Progress is spiritual. Progress is the maturing conception of divine Love; it demonstrates the scientific, sinless life of man and mortal's painless departure from matter to Spirit, not through death, but through the true idea of Life, — and Life not in matter but in Mind.

The Puritans possessed the motive of true religion, which, demonstrated on the Golden Rule, would have solved ere this the problem of religious liberty and human rights. It is "a consummation devoutly to be wished" that all nations shall speedily learn and practise the intermediate line of justice between the classes and masses of mankind, and thus exemplify in all things the universal equity of Christianity.

Thirty years ago (1866) Christian Science was discovered in America. Within those years it is estimated that Chicago has gained from a population of 238,000 to the number of 1,650,000 inhabitants.

The statistics of mortality show that thirty years ago the death-rate was at its maximum. Since that time it has steadily decreased. It is authentically said that one expositor of Daniel's dates fixed the year 1866 or 1867 for the return of Christ — the return of the spiritual idea to the material earth or antipode of heaven. It is a marked coincidence that those dates were the first two years of my discovery of Christian Science.

Thirty years ago Chicago had few Congregational churches. To-day it is said to have a majority of these churches over any other city in the United States. Thirty years ago at my request I received from the Congregational Church a letter of dismissal and recommendation to evangelical churches — thenceforth to exemplify my early love for this church and a membership of thirty years by establishing a new-old church, the foundations of which are the same, even Christ, Truth, as the chief corner-stone.

In 1884, I taught a class in Christian Science and formed a Christian Scientist Association in Chicago. From this small sowing of the seed of Truth, which, when sown, seemed the least among seeds, sprang immortal fruits through God's blessing and the faithful labor of loyal students, — the healing of the sick, the reforming of the sinner, and First Church of Christ, Scientist, with its large membership and majestic cathedral.

Humbly, gratefully, trustingly, I dedicate this beautiful house of worship to the God of Israel, the divine Love that reigns above the shadow, that launched the earth in its orbit, that created and governs the universe — guarding, guiding, giving grace, health, and immortality to man.

May the wanderer in the wilderness of mortal beliefs and fears turn hither with satisfied hope. May the birds of passage rest their weary wings amid the fair foliage of this vine of His husbanding, find shelter from the storm and a covert from the tempest. May this beloved church adhere to its tenets, abound in the righteousness of Love, honor the name of Christian Science, prove the practicality of perfection, and press on to the infinite uses of Christ's creed, namely, — "Thou shalt love the Lord thy God with all thy heart, and with all thy soul, and with all thy strength, and with all thy mind; and thy neighbor as thyself." Thus may First Church of Christ, Scientist, in this great city of Chicago, verify what John Robinson wrote in 1620 to our Pilgrim Fathers: "When Christ reigns, and not till then, will the world have rest."

First Church of Christ, Scientist,
London, England

Beloved Brethren across the Sea: — To-day a nation is born. Spiritual apprehension unfolds, transfigures, heals. With you be there no more sea, no ebbing faith, no night. Love be thy light upon the mountain of Israel. God will multiply thee.

First Church of Christ, Scientist,
Brooklyn, N. Y.

Beloved Brethren: — I rejoice with you; the day has come when the forest becomes a fruitful field, and the deaf hear the words of the Book, and the eyes of the blind see out of obscurity.

First Church of Christ, Scientist,
Detroit, Mich.

Beloved Students and Church: — Thanks for invitation to your dedication. Not afar off I am blending with thine my prayer and rejoicing. God is with thee. "Arise, shine; for thy light is come, and the glory of the Lord is risen upon thee."

First Church of Christ, Scientist, Toronto, Canada

My Beloved Brethren: — Have just received your despatch. Since the world was, men have not heard with the ear, neither hath the eye seen, what God hath prepared for them that wait upon Him and work righteousness.

White Mountain Church

My Beloved Brethren: — To-day I am privileged to congratulate the Christian Scientists of my native State upon having built First Church of Christ, Scientist, at the White Mountains. Your kind card, inviting me to be present at its dedication, came when I was so occupied that I omitted to wire an acknowledgment thereof and to return my cordial thanks at an earlier date. The beautiful birch bark on which it was written pleased me; it was so characteristic of our Granite State, and I treasure it next to your compliments. That rustic scroll brought back to me the odor of my childhood, a love which stays the shadows of years. God grant that this little church shall prove a historic gem on the glowing records of Christianity, and lay upon its altars a sacrifice and service acceptable in God's sight.

Your rural chapel is a social success quite sacred in its results. The prosperity of Zion is very precious in the sight of divine Love, holding unwearied watch over a world. Isaiah said: "How beautiful upon the mountains are the feet of him that bringeth good tidings, . . . that saith unto Zion, Thy God reigneth!" Surely, the Word that is God must at some time find utterance and acceptance throughout the earth, for he that soweth shall reap. To such as have waited patiently for the appearing of Truth, the day dawns and the harvest bells are ringing.

> "Let us, then, be up and doing,
>   With a heart for any fate;
> Still achieving, still pursuing,
>   Learn to labor and to wait."

The peace of Love is published, and the sword of the Spirit is drawn; nor will it be sheathed till Truth shall reign triumphant over all the earth. Truth, Life, and Love are formidable, wherever thought, felt, spoken, or written, — in the pulpit, in the court-room, by the wayside, or in our homes. They are the victors never to be vanquished. Love is the generic term for God. Love formed this trinity, Truth, Life, Love, the trinity no man can sunder. Life is the spontaneity of Love, inseparable from Love, and Life is the "Lamb slain from the foundation of the world," — even that which "was dead, and is alive again; and was lost, and is found;" for Life is Christ, and Christ, as aforetime, heals the sick, saves sinners, and destroys the last enemy, death.

In 1888 I visited these mountains and spoke to an attentive audience collected in the hall at the Fabyan House. Then and there I foresaw this hour, and spoke of the little church to be in the midst of the mountains, closing my remarks with the words of Mrs. Hemans: —

> For the strength of the hills, we bless Thee,
>   Our God, our fathers' God!

The sons and daughters of the Granite State are rich in signs and symbols, sermons in stones, refuge in mountains, and good universal. The rocks, rills, mountains, meadows, fountains, and forests of our native State should be prophetic of the finger divine that writes in living characters their lessons on our lives. May God's little ones cluster around this rock-ribbed church like tender nestlings in the crannies of the rocks, and preen their thoughts for upward flight.

Though neither dome nor turret tells the tale of your little church, its song and sermon will touch the heart, point the path above the valley, up the mountain, and on to the celestial hills, echoing the Word welling up from the infinite and swelling the loud anthem of one Father-Mother God, o'er all victorious! Rest assured that He in whom dwelleth all life, health, and holiness, will supply all your needs according to His riches in glory.

First Church of Christ, Scientist, Duluth, Minn.

First Church of Christ, Scientist, Duluth, Minn.: — May our God make this church the fold of flocks, and may those that plant the vineyard eat the fruit thereof. Here let His promise be verified: "Before they call, I will answer; and while they are yet speaking, I will hear."

First Church of Christ, Scientist, Salt Lake City, Utah

Beloved Brethren: — Accept my thanks for your cordial card inviting me to be with you on the day of your church dedication. It gives me great pleasure to know that you have erected a Church of Christ, Scientist, in your city. Surely, your fidelity, faith, and Christian zeal fairly indicate that, spiritually as well as literally, the church in Salt Lake City hath not lost its saltness. I may at some near future visit your city, but am too busy to think of doing so at present.

May the divine light of Christian Science that lighteth every enlightened thought illumine your faith and understanding, exclude all darkness or doubt, and signal the perfect path wherein to walk, the perfect Principle whereby to demonstrate the perfect man and the perfect law of God. In the words of St. Paul: "Now the end of the commandment is charity out of a pure heart, and of a good conscience, and of faith unfeigned;" and St. John says: "For this is the message that ye heard from the beginning, that we should love one another."

May the grace and love of God be and abide with you all.

PLEASANT VIEW, CONCORD, N. H.,
    November 16, 1898.

FIRST CHURCH OF CHRIST, SCIENTIST,
ATLANTA, GEORGIA

My Beloved Brethren: — You have met to consecrate your beautiful temple to the worship of the only true God. Since the day in which you were brought into the light and liberty of His children, it has been in the hearts of this people to build a house unto Him whose name they would glorify in a new commandment — "that ye love one another." In this new recognition of the riches of His love and the majesty of His might you have built this house — laid its foundations on the rock of Christ, and the stone which the builders rejected you have made the head of the corner. This house is hallowed by His promise: "I have hallowed this house, which thou hast built, to put my name there forever; and mine eyes and mine heart shall be there perpetually." "Now mine eyes shall be open, and mine ears attent unto the prayer that is made in this place." Your feast days will not be in commemoration, but in recognition of His presence; your ark of the covenant will not be brought out of the city of David, but out of "the secret place of the most High," whereof the Psalmist sang, even the omniscience of omnipotence; your tabernacle of the congregation will not be temporary, but a "house not made with hands, eternal in the heavens;" your oracle, under the wings of the cherubim, is Truth's evangel, enunciating, "God is Love."

In spirit I enter your inner sanctuary, your heart's heart, breathing a benediction for God's largess. He surely will not shut me out from your presence, and the ponderous walls of your grand cathedral cannot prevent me from entering where the heart of a Southron has welcomed me.

Christian Science has a place in its court, in which, like beds in hospitals, one man's head lies at another's feet. As you work, the ages win; for the majesty of Christian Science teaches the majesty of man. When it is learned that spiritual sense and not the material senses convey all impressions to man, man will naturally seek the Science of his spiritual nature, and finding it, be God-endowed for discipleship.

When divine Love gains admittance to a humble heart, that individual ascends the scale of miracles and meets the warmest wish of men and angels. Clad in invincible armor, grasping the sword of Spirit, you have started in this sublime ascent, and should reach the mount of revelation; for if ye would run, who shall hinder you? So dear, so due, to God is *obedience*, that it reaches high heaven in the common walks of life, and it affords even me a perquisite of joy.

You worship no distant deity, nor talk of unknown love. The silent prayers of our churches, resounding through the dim corridors of time, go forth in waves of sound, a diapason of heart-beats, vibrating from one pulpit to another and from one heart to another, till truth and love, commingling in one righteous prayer, shall encircle and cement the human race.

The government of divine Love derives its omnipotence from the love it creates in the heart of man; for love is allegiant, and there is no loyalty apart from love. When the human senses wake from their long slumber to see how soon earth's fables flee and faith grows wearisome, then that which defies decay and satisfies the immortal cravings is sought and found. In the twilight of the world's pageantry, in the last-drawn sigh of a glory gone, we are drawn towards God.

Beloved brethren, I cannot forget that yours is the first church edifice of our denomination erected in the sunny South — once my home. There my husband died, and the song and the dirge, surging my being, gave expression to a poem written in 1844, from which I copy this verse: —

> Friends, why throng in pity round me?
>   Wherefore, pray, the bell did toll?
> Dead is he who loved me dearly:
>   Am I not alone in soul?

Did that midnight shadow, falling upon the bridal wreath, bring the recompense of human woe, which is the merciful design of divine Love, and so help to evolve that larger sympathy for suffering humanity which is emancipating it with the morning beams and noonday glory of Christian Science?

The age is fast answering this question: Does Christian Science equal *materia medica* in healing the worst forms of contagious and organic diseases? My experience in both practices — *materia medica* and the scientific metaphysical practice of medicine — shows the latter not only equalling but vastly excelling the former.

Christians who accept our Master as authority, regard his sayings as infallible. Jesus' students, failing to cure a severe case of lunacy, asked their great Teacher, "Why could not we cast him out?" He answered, "This kind goeth not out but by prayer and fasting." This declaration of our Master, as to the relative value, skill, and certainty of the divine laws of Mind over the human mind and *above matter* in healing disease, remains beyond questioning a divine decision in behalf of Mind.

Jesus gave his disciples (students) power over all manner of diseases; and the Bible was written in order that all peoples, in all ages, should have the same opportunity to become students of the Christ, Truth, and thus become God-endued with power (knowledge of divine law) and with "signs following." Jesus declared that his teaching and practice would remain, even as it did, "for them also which shall believe on me through their word." Then, in the name of God, wherefore vilify His prophets to-day who are fulfilling Jesus' prophecy and verifying his last promise, "Lo, I am with you alway"? It were well for the world if there survived more of the wisdom of Nicodemus of old, who said, "No man can do these miracles that thou doest, except God be with him."

Be patient towards persecution. Injustice has not a tithe of the power of justice. Your enemies will advertise for you. Christian Science is spreading steadily throughout the world. Persecution is the weakness of tyrants engendered by their fear, and love will cast it out. Continue steadfast in love and good works. Children of light, you are not children of darkness. Let your light shine. Keep in mind the foundations of Christian Science — one God and one Christ. Keep personality out of sight, and Christ's "Blessed are ye" will seal your apostleship.

This glad Easter morning witnesseth a risen Saviour, a higher human sense of Life and Love, which wipes away all tears. With grave-clothes laid aside, Christ, Truth, has come forth from the tomb of the past, clad in immortality. The sepulchres give up their dead. Spirit is saying unto matter: I am not there, am not within you. Behold the place where they laid me; but human thought has risen!

Mortality's thick gloom is pierced. The stone is rolled away. Death has lost its sting, and the grave its victory. Immortal courage fills the human breast and lights the living way of Life.

Second Church of Christ, Scientist, Chicago, Ill.

My Beloved Brethren: — Your card of invitation to this feast of soul — the dedication of your church — was duly received. Accept my thanks.

Ye sit not in the idol's temple. Ye build not to an unknown God. Ye worship Him whom ye serve. Boast not thyself, thou ransomed of divine Love, but press on unto the possession of unburdened bliss. Heal the sick, make spotless the blemished, raise the living dead, cast out fashionable lunacy.

The ideal robe of Christ is seamless. Thou hast touched its hem, and thou art being healed. The risen Christ is thine. The haunting mystery and gloom of his glory rule not this century. Thine is the upspringing hope, the conquest over sin and mortality, that lights the living way to Life, not to death.

May the God of our fathers, the infinite Person whom we worship, be and abide with you. May the blessing of divine Love rest with you. My heart hovers around your churches in Chicago, for the dove of peace sits smilingly on these branches and sings of our Redeemer.

First Church of Christ, Scientist,
Los Angeles, Cal.

Beloved Students: — Your kind letter, inviting me to be present at the dedication of your church, was duly received. It would indeed give me pleasure to visit you, to witness your prosperity, and "rejoice with them that do rejoice," but the constant recurring demands upon my time and attention pin me to my post. Of this, however, I can sing: My love can fly on wings of joy to you and leave a leaf of olive; it can whisper to you of the divine ever-presence, answering your prayers, crowning your endeavors, and building for you a house "eternal in the heavens."

You will dedicate your temple in faith unfeigned, not to
the unknown God, but unto Him whom to know aright
is life everlasting. His presence with you will bring to
your hearts so much of heaven that you will not feel my
absence. The privilege remains mine to watch and work
for all, from East to West, from the greensward and
gorgeous skies of the Orient to your dazzling glory
in the Occident, and to thank God forever "for His
goodness, and for His wonderful works to the children
of men."

PLEASANT VIEW, CONCORD, N. H.,
    November 20, 1902.

SECOND CHURCH OF CHRIST, SCIENTIST,
MINNEAPOLIS, MINN.

Beloved: — The spiritual dominates the temporal. Love
gives nothing to take away. Nothing dethrones His
house. You are dedicating yours to Him. Protesting
against error, you unite with all who believe in Truth.
God guard and guide you.

FIRST CHURCH OF CHRIST, SCIENTIST,
NEW YORK, N. Y.

Beloved Brethren: — Carlyle writes, "Give a thing time;
if it succeeds, it is a right thing." Here I aver that you
have grasped time and labor, taking the first by the fore-
lock and the last by love. In this lofty temple, dedicated
to God and humanity, may the prophecy of Isaiah be
fulfilled: "Fear not: . . . I have called thee by thy
name; thou art mine." Within its sacred walls may

song and sermon generate only that which Christianity writes in broad facts over great continents — sermons that fell forests and remove mountains, songs of joy and gladness.

The letter of your work dies, as do all things material, but the spirit of it is immortal. Remember that a temple but foreshadows the idea of God, the "house not made with hands, eternal in the heavens," while a silent, grand man or woman, healing sickness and destroying sin, builds that which reaches heaven. Only those men and women gain greatness who gain themselves in a complete subordination of self.

The tender memorial engraven on your grand edifice stands for human self lost in divine light, melted into the radiance of His likeness. It stands for meekness and might, for Truth as attested by the Founder of your denomination and emblazoned on the fair escutcheon of your church.

Beloved Students:—Your telegram, in which you present to me the princely gift of your magnificent church edifice in New York City, is an unexpected token of your gratitude and love. I deeply appreciate it, profoundly thank you for it, and gratefully accept the spirit of it; but I must decline to receive that for which you have sacrificed so much and labored so long. May divine Love abundantly bless you, reward you according to your works, guide and guard you and your church through the depths; and may you

"Who stood the storm when seas were rough,
    Ne'er in a sunny hour fall off."

First Church of Christ, Scientist, Cleveland, Ohio

Beloved Brethren: — You will pardon my delay in acknowledging your card of invitation to the dedicatory services of your church. Adverse circumstances, loss of help, new problems to be worked out for the field, *etc.*, have hitherto prevented my reply. However, it is never too late to repent, to love more, to work more, to watch and pray; but those privileges I have not had time to express, and so have submitted to necessity, letting the deep love which I cherished for you be hidden under an appearance of indifference.

We must resign with good grace what we are denied, and press on with what we are, for we cannot do more than we are nor understand what is not ripening in us. To do good to all because we love all, and to use in God's service the one talent that we all have, is our only means of adding to that talent and the best way to silence a deep discontent with our shortcomings.

Christian Science is at length learned to be no miserable piece of ideal legerdemain, by which we poor mortals expect to live and die, but a deep-drawn breath fresh from God, by whom and in whom man lives, moves, and has deathless being. The praiseworthy success of this church, and its united efforts to build an edifice in which to worship the infinite, sprang from the temples erected first in the hearts of its members — the unselfed love that builds without hands, eternal in the heaven of Spirit. God grant that this unity remain, and that you continue to build, rebuild, adorn, and fill these spiritual temples with grace, Truth, Life, and Love.

First Church of Christ, Scientist, Pittsburgh, Pa.

My Beloved Brethren: — I congratulate you upon erecting the first edifice of our denomination in the Keystone State, a State whose metropolis is called the "city of brotherly love." May this dear church militant accept my tender counsel in these words of the Scripture, to be engrafted in church and State: —

"Let every man be swift to hear, slow to speak, slow to wrath." "He that is slow to anger is better than the mighty; and he that ruleth his spirit than he that taketh a city." "If any man offend not in word, the same is a perfect man, and able also to bridle the whole body." "By thy words thou shalt be condemned." "Love thy neighbor as thyself."

"Christ also suffered for us, leaving us an example, that [we] should follow his steps: . . . who, when he was reviled, reviled not again; when he suffered, he threatened not; but committed himself to Him that judgeth righteously." "Consider him that endured such contradiction of sinners against himself, lest ye be wearied and faint in your minds."

First Church of Christ, Scientist, St. Louis, Mo.

My Beloved Brethren: — The good in being, even the spiritually indispensable, is your daily bread. Work and pray for it. The poor toil for our bread, and we should work for their health and holiness. Over the glaciers of winter the summer glows. The beauty of holiness comes with the departure of sin. Enjoying good things is not evil, but becoming slaves to pleasure is. That error is most forcible which is least distinct to conscience. Attempt nothing without God's help.

May the beauty of holiness be upon this dear people, and may this beloved church be glorious, without spot or blemish.

First Church of Christ, Scientist, San José, Cal.

Beloved Students: — Words are inadequate to express my deep appreciation of your labor and success in completing and dedicating your church edifice, and of the great hearts and ready hands of our far Western students, the Christian Scientists.

Comparing such students with those whose words are but the substitutes for works, we learn that the translucent atmosphere of the former must illumine the midnight of the latter, else Christian Science will disappear from among mortals.

I thank divine Love for the hope set before us in the Word and in the doers thereof, "for of such is the kingdom of heaven."

First Church of Christ, Scientist, Wilmington, N. C.

My Beloved Brethren: — At this dedicatory season of your church edifice in the home of my heart, I send loving congratulations, join with you in song and sermon. God will bless the work of your hearts and hands.

Pleasant View, Concord, N. H.,
July 27, 1907.

First Church of Christ, Scientist, London, England

Beloved Students and Brethren: — Your letters of May 1 and June 19, informing me of the dedication of your magnificent church edifice, have been received with many thanks to you and great gratitude to our one Father.

May God grant not only the continuance of His favors, but their abundant and ripened fruit.

Chestnut Hill, Mass.,
June 26, 1909.

CHAPTER IX

LETTERS TO BRANCH CHURCHES

First Church of Christ, Scientist, Philadelphia, Pa.

My Beloved Students and Brethren: — I rejoice with thee. Blessed art thou. In place of darkness, light hath sprung up. The reward of thy hands is given thee to-day. May God say this of the church in Philadelphia: I have naught against thee.

First Church of Christ, Scientist, Washington, D. C.

Beloved Brethren: — The Board of Directors and Trustees of this church will please accept my grateful acknowledgment of the receipt of their Christian canon pertaining to the hour. The joint resolutions contained therein show explicitly the attitude of this church in our capital towards me and towards the Cause of Christian Science, so dear to our hearts and to all loyal lovers of God and man.

This year, standing on the verge of the twentieth century, has sounded the tocsin of a higher hope, of strengthened hands, of unveiled hearts, of fourfold unity between the churches of our denomination in this and in other lands. Religious liberty and individual rights under the Constitution of our nation are rapidly advancing, avowing and consolidating the genius of Christian Science.

Heaven be praised for the signs of the times. Let "the heathen rage, and the people imagine a vain thing;" our trust is in the Almighty God, who ruleth in heaven and upon earth, and none can stay His hand or say, "What doest thou?"

First Church of Christ, Scientist, London, England

My Beloved Brethren: — The chain of Christian unity, unbroken, stretches across the sea and rises upward to the realms of incorporeal Life — even to the glorious beatitudes of divine Love. Striving to be good, to do good, and to love our neighbor as ourself, man's soul is safe; man emerges from mortality and receives his rights inalienable — the love of God and man. What holds us to the Christian life is the seven-fold shield of honesty, purity, and unselfed love. I need not say this to you, for you know the way in Christian Science.

Pale, sinful sense, at work to lift itself on crumbling thrones of justice by pulling down its benefactors, will tumble from this scheme into the bottomless abyss of self-damnation, there to relinquish its league with evil. Wide yawns the gap between this course and Christian Science.

God spare this plunge, lessen its depths, save sinners and fit their being to recover its connection with its divine Principle, Love. For this I shall continue to pray.

God is blessing you, my beloved students and brethren. Press on towards the high calling whereunto divine Love has called us and is fast fulfilling the promises.

Satan is unchained only for a season, as the Revelator foresaw, and love and good will to man, sweeter than a sceptre, are enthroned now and forever.

First Church of Christ, Scientist,
New York, N. Y.

My Beloved Brethren: — Your Soul-full words and song repeat my legacies in blossom. Such elements of friendship, faith, and hope repossess us of heaven. I thank you out of a full heart. Even the crown of thorns, which mocked the bleeding brow of our blessed Lord, was overcrowned with a diadem of duties done. So let us meekly meet, mercifully forgive, wisely ponder, and lovingly scan the convulsions of mortal mind, that its sudden sallies may help us, not to a start, but to a tenure of unprecarious joy. Rich hope have I in him who says in his heart: —

> I will listen for Thy voice,
>   Lest my footsteps stray;
> I will follow and rejoice
>   All the rugged way.

Second Church of Christ, Scientist,
New York, N. Y.

Beloved Brethren: — Please accept a line from me in lieu of my presence on the auspicious occasion of the opening of your new church edifice. Hope springs exultant on this blest morn. May its white wings overshadow this white temple and soar above it, pointing the path from earth to heaven — from human ambition, fear, or distrust to the faith, meekness, and might of him who hallowed this Easter morn.

Now may his salvation draw near, for the night is far spent and the day is at hand. In the words of St. Paul: "Render therefore to all their dues: tribute to whom tribute is due; custom to whom custom; ... honor to whom honor. Owe no man any thing, but to love one another: for he that loveth another hath fulfilled the law."

May the benediction of "Well done, good and faithful," rest worthily on the builders of this beautiful temple, and the glory of the resurrection morn burst upon the spiritual sense of this people with renewed vision, infinite meanings, endless hopes, and glad victories in the onward and upward chain of being.

First Church of Christ, Scientist,
Oakland, Cal.

Beloved Brethren: — I thank you for the words of cheer and love in your letter. The taper unseen in sunlight cheers the darkness. My work is reflected light, — a drop from His ocean of love, from the underived glory, the divine *Esse*. From the dear tone of your letter, you must be bringing your sheaves into the storehouse. Press on. The way is narrow at first, but it expands as we walk in it. "Herein is my Father glorified, that ye bear much fruit." God bless this vine of His planting.

FIRST CHURCH OF CHRIST, SCIENTIST,
WASHINGTON, D. C.

Beloved Brethren: — I have nothing new to communicate; all is in your textbooks. Pray aright and demonstrate your prayer; sing in faith. Know that religion should be distinct in our consciousness and life, but not clamorous for worldly distinction. Church laws which are obeyed without mutiny are God's laws. Goodness and philanthropy begin with work and never stop working. All that is worth reckoning is what we do, and the best of everything is not too good, but is economy and riches. Be great not as a grand obelisk, nor by setting up to be great, — only as good. A spiritual hero is a mark for gamesters, but he is unutterably valiant, the summary of suffering here and of heaven hereafter. Our thoughts beget our actions; they make us what we are. Dishonesty is a mental malady which kills its possessor; it is a sure precursor that its possessor is mortal. A deep sincerity is sure of success, for God takes care of it. God bless this dear church, and I am sure that He will if it is ready for the blessing.

FIRST CHURCH OF CHRIST, SCIENTIST,
LONDON, ENGLAND

Beloved Students: — You have laid the corner-stone of your church edifice impressively, and buried immortal truths in the bosom of earth safe from all chance of being challenged.

You whose labors are doing so much to benefit mankind will not be impatient if you have not accomplished all you desire, nor will you be long in doing more. My faith in God and in His followers rests in the fact that He is infinite good, and that He gives His followers opportunity to use their hidden virtues, to put into practice the power which lies concealed in the calm and which storms awaken to vigor and to victory.

It is only by looking heavenward that mutual friendships such as ours can begin and never end. Over sea and over land, Christian Science unites its true followers in one Principle, divine Love, that sacred *ave* and essence of Soul which makes them one in Christ.

First Church of Christ, Scientist, Columbus, Ohio

In Reply to a Letter Announcing the Purpose of the Christian Scientists to Practise without Fees in Compliance with the State Laws

Beloved Brethren: — I congratulate you tenderly on the decision you have made as to the present practice of Christian Science in your State, and thoroughly recommend it under the circumstances. I practised gratuitously when starting this great Cause, which was then the scoff of the age.

The too long treatment of a disease, the charging of the sick whom you have not healed a full fee for treatment, the suing for payment, hypnotism, and the resenting of injuries, are not the fruits of Christian Science, while returning good for evil, loving one's enemies, and overcoming evil with good, — these are its fruits; and its therapeutics, based as aforetime on this divine Principle, heals all disease.

We read in the Scriptures: "There is therefore now no condemnation to them which are in Christ Jesus, who walk not after the flesh, but after the Spirit." "Stand fast therefore in the liberty wherewith Christ hath made us free." "Be ye therefore wise as serpents, and harmless as doves."

Wisdom is won through faith, prayer, experience; and God is the giver.

> "God moves in a mysterious way
> His wonders to perform;
> He plants His footsteps in the sea
> And rides upon the storm."

Third Church of Christ, Scientist, London, England

Beloved Brethren: — Love and unity are hieroglyphs of goodness, and their philosophical impetus, spiritual Æsculapius and Hygeia, saith, "As the thought is, so is the deed; as the thing made is good or bad, so is its maker." This idealism connects itself with spiritual understanding, and so makes God more supreme in consciousness, man more His likeness, friends more faithful, and enemies harmless. Scholastic theology at its best touches but the hem of Christian Science, shorn of all personality, wholly apart from human hypotheses, matter, creed and dogma, the lust of the flesh and the pride of power. Christian Science is the full idea of its divine Principle, God; it is forever based on Love, and it is demonstrated by perfect rules; it is unerring. Hence health, holiness, immortality, are its natural effects. The practitioner may fail, but the Science never.

Philosophical links, which would unite dead matter with animate, Spirit with matter and material means, prayer with power and pride of position, hinder the divine influx and lose Science, — lose the Principle of divine metaphysics and the tender grace of spiritual understanding, that love-linked holiness which heals and saves.

Schisms, imagination, and human beliefs are not parts of Christian Science; they darken the discernment of Science; they divide Truth's garment and cast lots for it.

Seeing a man in the moon, or seeing a person in the picture of Jesus, or believing that you see an individual who has passed through the shadow called death, is not seeing the spiritual idea of God; but it is seeing a human belief, which is far from the fact that portrays Life, Truth, Love.

May these words of the Scriptures comfort you: "The Lord shall be unto thee an everlasting light, and thy God thy glory." "The city had no need of the sun, neither of the moon, to shine in it: for the glory of God did lighten it, and the Lamb is the light thereof." "Ye are a chosen generation, a royal priesthood, an holy nation, a peculiar people; that ye should show forth the praises of Him who hath called you out of darkness into His marvellous light." "Giving thanks unto the Father, which hath made us meet to be partakers of the inheritance of the saints in light: who hath delivered us from the power of darkness, and hath translated us into the kingdom of His dear Son." "Ye were sometimes darkness, but now are ye light in the Lord: walk as children of light."

First Church of Christ, Scientist,
Milwaukee, Wis.

Beloved Brethren: — Your communication is gratefully received. Press on! The wrath of men shall praise God, and the remainder thereof He will restrain.

A Telegram and Mrs. Eddy's Reply

Beloved Leader: — The representatives of churches and societies of Christian Science in Missouri, in annual conference assembled, unite in loving greetings to you, and pledge themselves to strive more earnestly, day by day, for the clearer understanding and more perfect manifestation of the truth which you have unfolded to the world, and by which sin and sickness are destroyed and life and immortality brought to light.

Yours in loving obedience,

Churches and Societies of Christian
Science in Missouri.

St. Joseph, Missouri,
January 5, 1909.

MRS. EDDY'S REPLY

"Well done, thou good and faithful servant: . . . enter thou into the joy of thy lord" — the satisfaction of meeting and mastering evil and defending good, thus predicating man upon divine Science. (See Science and Health, p. 227.)

Chestnut Hill, Mass.,
January 6, 1909.

First Church of Christ, Scientist, Sydney, Australia

Beloved Brethren:— Accept my deep thanks for your highly interesting letter. It would seem as if the whole import of Christian Science had been mirrored forth by your loving hearts, to reflect its heavenly rays over all the earth.

Box G, Brookline, Mass.,
July 15, 1909.

First Church of Christ, Scientist, Edinburgh, Scotland

Beloved Christian Scientists:— Like the gentle dews of heaven and the refreshing breeze of morn, comes your dear letter to my waiting heart, — waiting in due expectation of just such blessedness, crowning the hope and hour of divine Science, than which nothing can exceed its ministrations of God to man.

I congratulate you on the prospect of erecting a church building, wherein to gather in praise and prayer for the whole human family.

Box G, Brookline, Mass.,
November 2, 1909.

The Committees in Conference, Chicago, Ill.

The Committees:— God bless the courageous, far-seeing committees in conference for their confidence in His ways and means of reaching the very acme of Christian Science.

Comment on Letter from First Church of Christ, Scientist, Ottawa, Ontario

God will abundantly bless this willing and obedient church with the rich reward of those that seek and serve Him. No greater hope have we than in right thinking and right acting, and faith in the blessing of fidelity, courage, patience, and grace.

CHAPTER X

ADMONITION AND COUNSEL

What Our Leader Says

BELOVED Christian Scientists, keep your minds so filled with Truth and Love, that sin, disease, and death cannot enter them. It is plain that nothing can be added to the mind already full. There is no door through which evil can enter, and no space for evil to fill in a mind filled with goodness. Good thoughts are an impervious armor; clad therewith you are completely shielded from the attacks of error of every sort. And not only yourselves are safe, but all whom your thoughts rest upon are thereby benefited.

The self-seeking pride of the evil thinker injures him when he would harm others. Goodness involuntarily resists evil. The evil thinker is the proud talker and doer. The right thinker abides under the shadow of the Almighty. His thoughts can only reflect peace, good will towards men, health, and holiness.[1]

Ways that are Vain

Certain individuals entertain the notion that Christian Science Mind-healing should be two-sided, and only denounce error in general, — saying nothing, in particu-

[1] Copyright, 1909, by Mary Baker Eddy.

WAYS THAT ARE VAIN

lar, of error that is damning men. They are sticklers for a false, convenient peace, straining at gnats and swallowing camels. The unseen wrong to individuals and society they are too cowardly, too ignorant, or too wicked to uncover, and excuse themselves by denying that this evil exists. This mistaken way, of hiding sin in order to maintain harmony, has licensed evil, allowing it first to smoulder, and then break out in devouring flames. All that error asks is to be let alone; even as in Jesus' time the unclean spirits cried out, "Let us alone; what have we to do with thee?"

Animal magnetism, in its ascending steps of evil, entices its victim by unseen, silent arguments. Reversing the modes of good, in their silent allurements to health and holiness, it impels mortal mind into error of thought, and tempts into the committal of acts foreign to the natural inclinations. The victims lose their individuality, and lend themselves as willing tools to carry out the designs of their worst enemies, even those who would induce their self-destruction. Animal magnetism fosters suspicious distrust where honor is due, fear where courage should be strongest, reliance where there should be avoidance, a belief in safety where there is most danger; and these miserable lies, poured constantly into his mind, fret and confuse it, spoiling that individual's disposition, undermining his health, and sealing his doom, unless the cause of the mischief is found out and destroyed.

Other minds are made dormant by it, and the victim is in a state of semi-individuality, with a mental haziness which admits of no intellectual culture or spiritual growth. The state induced by this secret evil influence is a species of intoxication, in which the victim is led to believe and do what he would never, otherwise, think or do voluntarily.

This intricate method of animal magnetism is the essence, or spirit, of evil, which makes mankind drunken. In this era it is taking the place of older and more open sins, and other forms of intoxication. A harder fight will be necessary to expose the cause and effects of this evil influence, than has been required to put down the evil effects of alcohol. The alcoholic habit is the use of higher forms of matter, wherewith to do evil; whereas animal magnetism is the highest form of mental evil, wherewith to complete the sum total of sin.

The question is often asked, Why is there so much dissension among mental practitioners? We answer, Because they do not practise in strict accordance with the teaching of Christian Science Mind-healing. If they did, there would be unity of action. Being like the disciples of old, "with one accord in one place," they would receive a spiritual influx impossible under other conditions, and so would recognize and resist the animal magnetism by which they are being deceived and misled.

The mental malpractitioner, interfering with the rights of Mind, destroys the true sense of Science, and loses his own power to heal. He tries to compensate himself for his own loss by hindering in every way conceivable the success of others. You will find this practitioner saying that animal magnetism never troubles him, but that Mrs. Eddy teaches animal magnetism; and he says this to cover his crime of mental malpractice, in furtherance of unscrupulous designs.

The natural fruits of Christian Science Mind-healing are harmony, brotherly love, spiritual growth and activity. The malicious aim of perverted mind-power, or animal magnetism, is to paralyze good and give activity to evil. It starts factions and engenders envy and hatred, but as activity is by no means a right of evil and its emissaries, they ought not to be encouraged in it. Because this age is cursed with one rancorous and lurking foe to human weal, those who are the truest friends of mankind, and conscientious in their desire to do right and to live pure and Christian lives, should be more zealous to do good, more watchful and vigilant. Then they will be proportionately successful and bring out glorious results.

Unless one's eyes are opened to the modes of mental malpractice, working so subtly that we mistake its suggestions for the impulses of our own thought, the victim will allow himself to drift in the wrong direction without knowing it. Be ever on guard against this enemy. Watch your thoughts, and see whether they lead you to God and into harmony with His true followers. Guard and strengthen your own citadel more strongly. Thus you will grow wiser and better through every attack of your foe, and the Golden Rule will not rust for lack of use or be misinterpreted by the adverse influence of animal magnetism.

Only One Quotation

The following three quotations from "Science and Health with Key to the Scriptures" are submitted to the dear Churches of Christ, Scientist. From these they may select one only to place on the walls of their church. Otherwise, as our churches multiply, promiscuous selections would write your textbook on the walls of your churches.

Divine Love always has met and always will meet every human need.

MARY BAKER EDDY.

Christianity is again demonstrating the Life that is Truth, and the Truth that is Life.

MARY BAKER EDDY.

Jesus' three days' work in the sepulchre set the seal of eternity on time. He proved Life to be deathless and Love to be the master of hate.

MARY BAKER EDDY.

THE LABORER AND HIS HIRE

In reply to letters questioning the consistency of Christian Scientists taking pay for their labors, and with the hope of relieving the questioners' perplexity, I will say: Four years after my discovery of Christian Science, while taking no remuneration for my labors, and for healing all manner of diseases, I was confronted with the fact that I had no monetary means left wherewith to hire a hall in which to speak, or to establish a Christian Science home for indigent students, which I yearned to do, or even to meet my own current expenses. I therefore halted from necessity.

I had cast my all into the treasury of Truth, but where were the means with which to carry on a Cause? To desert the Cause never occurred to me, but nobody

THE LABORER AND HIS HIRE

then wanted Christian Science, or gave it a halfpenny. Though sorely oppressed, I was above begging and knew well the priceless worth of what had been bestowed without money or price. Just then God stretched forth His hand. He it was that bade me do what I did, and it prospered at every step. I wrote "Science and Health with Key to the Scriptures," taught students for a tuition of three hundred dollars each, though I seldom taught without having charity scholars, sometimes a dozen or upward in one class. Afterwards, with touching tenderness, those very students sent me the full tuition money. However, I returned this money with love; but it was again mailed to me in letters begging me to accept it, saying, "Your teachings are worth much more to me than money can be."

It was thus that I earned the means with which to start a Christian Science home for the poor worthy student, to establish a Metaphysical College, to plant our first magazine, to purchase the site for a church edifice, to give my church *The Christian Science Journal*, and to keep "the wolves in sheep's clothing," preying upon my pearls, from clogging the wheels of Christian Science.

When the great Master first sent forth his students, he bade them take no scrip for their journey, saying, "The laborer is worthy of his hire." Next, on the contrary, he bade them take scrip. Can we find a better example for our lives than that of our Master? Why did he send forth his students first without, and then with, provision for their expenses? Doubtless to test the effect of both methods on mankind. That he preferred the latter is evident, since we have no hint of his changing this direction; and that his divine wisdom should temper human affairs, is plainly set forth in the Scriptures. Till Christian Scientists give all their time to spiritual things, live without eating, and obtain their money from a fish's mouth, they must earn it in order to help mankind with it. All systems of religion stand on this basis.

The law and the gospel, — Christian, civil, and educational means, — manufacture, agriculture, tariff, and revenue subsist on demand and supply, regulated by a government currency, by which each is provided for and maintained. What, then, can a man do with truth and without a cent to sustain it? Either his life must be a miracle that frightens people, or his truth not worth a cent.

THE CHILDREN CONTRIBUTORS

My Beloved Children: — Tenderly thanking you for your sweet industry and love on behalf of the room of the Pastor Emeritus in The First Church of Christ, Scientist, Boston, I say: The purpose of God to youward indicates another field of work which I present to your thought, work by which you can do much good and which is adapted to your present unfolding capacity. I request that from this date you disband as a society, drop the insignia of "Busy Bees," work in your own several localities, and no longer contribute to The Mother Church flower fund.

As you grow older, advance in the knowledge of self-support, and see the need of self-culture, it is to be expected you will feel more than at present that charity begins at home, and that you will want money for your own uses. Contemplating these important wants, I see that you should begin now to earn for a purpose even higher, the money that you expend for flowers. You will want it for academics, for your own school education, or, if need be, to help your parents, brothers, or sisters.

Further to encourage your early, generous incentive for action, and to reward your hitherto unselfish toil, I have deeded in trust to The Mother Church of Christ, Scientist, in Boston, the sum of four thousand dollars to be invested in safe municipal bonds for my dear children contributors to the room of the Pastor Emeritus. This sum is to remain on interest till it is disbursed in equal shares to each contributor. This disbursal will take place when the contributors shall have arrived at legal age, and each contributor will receive his dividend with interest thereon up to date, provided he has complied with my request as above named.

A Correction

In the last *Sentinel* [Oct. 12, 1899] was the following question: "If all matter is unreal, why do we deny the existence of disease in the material body and not the body itself?"

We deny *first* the existence of disease, because we can meet this negation more readily than we can negative all that the material senses affirm. It is written in "Science and Health with Key to the Scriptures": "An improved belief is one step out of error, and aids in taking the next step and in understanding the situation in Christian Science" (p. 296).

Thus it is that our great Exemplar, Jesus of Nazareth, first takes up the subject. He does not require the last step to be taken first. He came to the world not to destroy the law of being, but to fulfil it in righteousness.

He restored the diseased body to its normal action, functions, and organization, and in explanation of his deeds he said, "Suffer it to be so now: for thus it becometh us to fulfil all righteousness." Job said, "In my flesh shall I see God." Neither the Old nor the New Testament furnishes reasons or examples for the destruction of the human body, but for its restoration to life and health as the scientific proof of "God with us." The power and prerogative of Truth are to destroy all disease and to raise the dead — even the self-same Lazarus. The *spiritual* body, the incorporeal idea, came with the *ascension*.

Jesus demonstrated the divine Principle of Christian Science when he presented his *material* body absolved from death and the grave. The introduction of pure abstractions into Christian Science, without their correlatives, leaves the divine Principle of Christian Science unexplained, tends to confuse the mind of the reader, and ultimates in what Jesus denounced, namely, straining at gnats and swallowing camels.

QUESTION ANSWERED

A fad of belief is the fool of mesmerism. The belief that an individual can either teach or heal by proxy is a false faith that will end bitterly. My published works are teachers and healers. My private life is given to a servitude the fruit of which all mankind may share. Such labor is impartial, meted out to one no more than to another. Therefore an individual should not enter the Massachusetts Metaphysical College with the expectation of receiving instruction from me, other than that which my books afford, unless I am personally present. Nor should patients anticipate being helped by me through some favored student. Such practice would be erroneous, and such an anticipation on the part of the sick a hindrance rather than help.

My good students have all the honor of their success in teaching or in healing. I by no means would pluck their plumes. Human power is most properly used in preventing the occasion for its use; otherwise its use is abuse.

Christian Science Healing

To say that it is sin to ride to church on an electric car, would not be more preposterous than to believe that man's Maker is not equal to the destruction of disease germs. Christ, Truth, the ever-present spiritual idea, who raises the dead, is equal to the giving of life and health to man and to the healing, as aforetime, of all manner of diseases. I would not charge Christians with doubting the Bible record of our great Master's life of healing, since Christianity must be predicated of what Christ Jesus taught and did; but I do say that Christian Science cannot annul nor make void the laws of the land, since Christ, the great demonstrator of Christian Science, said, "Think not that I am come to destroy the law, or the prophets: I am not come to destroy, but to fulfil."

I have expressed my opinion publicly as to the precautions against the spread of so-called infectious and contagious diseases in the following words: —

"Rather than quarrel over vaccination, I recommend, if the law demand, that an individual submit to this process, that he obey the law, and then appeal to the gospel to save him from bad physical results. Whatever changes come to this century or to any epoch, we may safely submit to the providence of God, to common justice, to the maintenance of individual rights, and to governmental usages. This statement should be so interpreted as to apply, on the basis of Christian Science, to the reporting of a contagious case to the proper authorities when the law so requires. When Jesus was questioned concerning obedience to human law, he replied: 'Render to Cæsar the things that are Cæsar's,' even while you render 'to God the things that are God's.'"

I believe in obeying the laws of the land. I practise and teach this obedience, since justice is the moral signification of law. Injustice denotes the absence of law. Each day I pray for the pacification of all national difficulties, for the brotherhood of man, for the end of idolatry and infidelity, and for the growth and establishment of Christian religion — Christ's Christianity. I also have faith that my prayer availeth, and that He who is overturning will overturn until He whose right it is shall reign. Each day I pray: "God bless my enemies; make them Thy friends; give them to know the joy and the peace of love."

Past, present, or future philosophy or religion, which departs from the instructions and example of the great Galilean Prophet, cannot be Christlike. Jesus obeyed human laws and fell a victim to those laws. But nineteen centuries have greatly improved human nature and human statutes. That the innocent should suffer for the guilty, seems less divine, and that humanity should share alike liberty of conscience, seems more divine to-day than it did yesterday.

CHRISTIAN SCIENCE HEALING

The earthly price of spirituality in religion and medicine in a material age is persecution, and the moral distance between Christianity and materialism precludes Jesus' doctrine, now as then, from finding favor with certain purely human views. The prophets of old looked for something higher than the systems and practices of their times. They foresaw the new dispensation of Truth and the demonstration of God in His more infinite meanings,—the demonstration which was to destroy sin, disease, and death, establish the definition of omnipotence, and illustrate the Science of Mind. Earth has not known another so great and good as Christ Jesus. Then can we find a better moral philosophy, a more complete, natural, and divine Science of medicine, or a better religion than his?

God is Spirit. Then modes of healing, other than the spiritual and divine, break the First Commandment of the Decalogue, "Thou shalt have no other gods before me." There are no other heaven-appointed means than the spiritual with which to heal sin and disease. Our Master conformed to this law, and instructed his followers, saying, "He that believeth on me, the works that I do shall he do also." This is enough.

All issues of morality, of Christianity, of pleasure, or of pain must come through a correct or incorrect state of thought, since matter is not conscious; then, like a watchman forsaking his post, shall we have no faith in God, in the divine Mind, thus throwing the door wide open to the intruding disease, forgetting that the divine Mind, Truth and Life, can guard the entrance?

We earnestly ask: Shall we not believe the Scripture, "The prayer of faith shall save the sick"? In the seventeenth chapter of the Gospel according to St. Matthew, we read that even the disciples of Jesus once failed mentally to cure by their faith and understanding a violent case of lunacy. And because of this Jesus rebuked them, saying: "O faithless and perverse generation, how long shall I be with you? how long shall I suffer you? bring him hither to me." When his disciples asked him why they could not heal that case, Jesus, the master Metaphysician, answered, "Because of your unbelief" (lack of *faith*); and then continued: "If ye have faith as a grain of mustard seed, ye shall say unto this mountain, Remove hence to yonder place; and it shall remove." Also he added: "This kind goeth not out but by prayer and fasting" (refraining from admitting the claims of the senses). Even in those dark days Jesus was not arrested and executed (for "insanity") because of his faith and his great demands on the faith of his followers, but he was arrested because, as was said, "he stirreth up the people." Be patient, O Christian Scientist! It is well that thou canst unloose the sandals of thy Master's feet.

The Constitution of the United States does not provide that *materia medica* shall make laws to regulate man's religion; rather does it imply that religion shall permeate our laws. Mankind will be God-governed in proportion as God's government becomes apparent, the Golden Rule utilized, and the rights of man and the liberty of conscience held sacred. Meanwhile, they who name the name of Christian Science will assist in the holding of crime in check, will aid the ejection of error, will maintain law and order, and will cheerfully await the end — justice and judgment.

Rules of Conduct

I hereby notify the public that no comers are received at Pleasant View without previous appointment by letter. Also that I neither listen to complaints, read letters, nor dictate replies to letters which pertain to church difficulties outside of The Mother Church of Christ, Scientist, or to any class of individual discords. Letters from the sick are not read by me or by my secretaries. They should be sent to the Christian Science practitioners whose cards are in *The Christian Science Journal*.

Letters and despatches from individuals with whom I have no acquaintance and of whom I have no knowledge, containing questions about secular affairs, I do not answer. First, because I have not sufficient time to waste on them; second, because I do not consider myself capable of instructing persons in regard to that of which I know nothing. All such questions are superinduced by wrong motives or by "evil suggestions," either of which I do not entertain.

All inquiries, coming directly or indirectly from a member of The Mother Church of Christ, Scientist, which relate in any manner to the keeping or the breaking of one of the Church By-laws, should be addressed to the Christian Science Board of Directors and not to the Pastor Emeritus.

A Word to the Wise

The hour is imminent. Upon it lie burdens that time will remove. Just now divine Love and wisdom saith, "Be *still*, and know that I am God." Do all Christian Scientists see or understand the importance of that demand at the moment, when human wisdom is inadequate to meet the exigencies of the hour and when they should wait on the logic of events?

I respectfully call your attention to this demand, knowing a little, as I ought, the human need, the divine command, the blessing which follows obedience and the bane which follows disobedience. Hurried conclusions as to the public thought are not apt to be correctly drawn. The public sentiment is helpful or dangerous only in proportion to its right or its wrong concept, and the forward footsteps it impels or the prejudice it instils. This prejudice the future must disclose and dispel. Avoid for the immediate present public debating clubs. Also be sure that you are not caught in some author's net, or made blind to his loss of the Golden Rule, of which Christian Science is the predicate and postulate, when he borrows the thoughts, words, and classification of one author without quotation-marks, at the same time giving full credit to another more fashionable but less correct.

My books state Christian Science correctly. They may not be as taking to those ignorant of this Science as books less correct and therefore less profound. But it is not safe to accept the latter as standards. We would not deny their authors a hearing, since the Scripture declares, "He that is not against us is on our part." And we should also speak in loving terms of their efforts, but we cannot afford to recommend any literature as wholly Christian Science which is not absolutely genuine.

Beloved students, just now let us adopt the classic saying, "They also serve who only stand and wait." Our Cause is growing apace under the present persecution

thereof. This is a crucial hour, in which the coward and
the hypocrite come to the surface to pass off, while the
loyal at heart and the worker in the spirit of Truth are
rising to the zenith of success, — the "Well done, good
and faithful," spoken by our Master.

Capitalization

A correct use of capital letters in composition caps the
climax of the old "new tongue." Christian Science is not
understood by the writer or the reader who does not comprehend where capital letters should be used in writing
about Christian Science.

In divine Science all belongs to God, for God is All;
hence the propriety of giving unto His holy name
due deference, — the capitalization which distinguishes
it from all other names, thus obeying the leading of our
Lord's Prayer.

The coming of Christ's kingdom on earth begins in the
minds of men by honoring God and sacredly holding His
name apart from the names of that which He creates.
Mankind almost universally gives to the divine Spirit
the name God. Christian Science names God as divine
Principle, Love, the infinite Person. In this, as in all
that is right, Christian Scientists are expected to stick
to their text, and by no illogical conclusion, either in
speaking or in writing, to forget their prayer, "Hallowed
be Thy name."

In their textbook it is clearly stated that God is divine
Principle and that His synonyms are Love, Truth, Life,
Spirit, Mind, Soul, which combine as *one*. The divine
Principle includes them all. The word Principle, when
referring to God, should not be written or used as a

common noun or in the plural number. To avoid using this word incorrectly, use it only where you can substitute the word God and make sense. This rule strictly observed will preserve an intelligent usage of the word and convey its meaning in Christian Science.

What are termed in common speech the principle of harmonious vibration, the principle of conservation of number in geometry, the principle of the inclined plane in mechanics, *etc.*, are but an effect of one universal cause, — an emanation of the one divine intelligent Principle that holds the earth in its orbit by evolved spiritual power, that commands the waves and the winds, that marks the sparrow's fall, and that governs all from the infinitesimal to the infinite, — namely, God. Withdraw God, divine Principle, from man and the universe, and man and the universe would no longer exist. But annihilate matter, and man and the universe would remain the forever fact, the spiritual "substance of things hoped for;" and the evidence of the immortality of man and the cosmos is sustained by the intelligent divine Principle, Love.

Beloved students, in this you learn to hallow His name, even as you value His all-power, all-presence, all-Science, and depend on Him for your existence.

Wherefore?

Our faithful laborers in the field of Science have been told by the alert editor-in-chief of the *Christian Science Sentinel* and *Journal* that "Mrs. Eddy advises, until the public thought becomes better acquainted with Christian Science, that Christian Scientists decline to doctor infectious or contagious diseases."

The great Master said, "For which of those works do ye stone me?" He said this to satisfy himself regarding that which he spake as God's representative — as one who never weakened in his own personal sense of righteousness because of another's wickedness or because of the minifying of his own goodness by another. Charity is quite as rare as wisdom, but when charity does appear, it is known by its patience and endurance.

When, under the protection of State or United States laws, good citizens are arrested for manslaughter because one out of three of their patients, having the same disease and in the same family, dies while the others recover, we naturally turn to divine justice for support and wait on God. Christian Scientists should be influenced by their own judgment in taking a case of malignant disease. They should consider well their ability to cope with the claim, and they should not overlook the fact that there are those lying in wait to catch them in their sayings; neither should they forget that in their practice, whether successful or not, *they are not specially protected by law.* The above quotation by the editor-in-chief stands for this: Inherent justice, constitutional individual rights, self-preservation, and the gospel injunction, "Neither cast ye your pearls before swine, lest they trample them under their feet, and turn again and rend you."

And it stands side by side with Christ's command, "Whosoever shall smite thee on thy right cheek, turn to him the other also." I abide by this rule and triumph by it. The sinner may sneer at this beatitude, for "the fool hath said in his heart, There is no God." Statistics show that Christian Science cures a larger per cent of malignant diseases than does *materia medica*.

I call disease by its name and have cured it thus; so there is nothing new on this score. My book Science and Health names disease, and thousands are healed by learning that so-called disease is a sensation of mind, not of matter. Evil minds signally blunder in divine metaphysics; hence I am always saying the unexpected to them. The evil mind calls it "skulking," when to me it is wisdom to "overcome evil with good." I fail to know how one can be a Christian and yet depart from Christ's teachings.

Significant Questions

Who shall be greatest? Referring to John the Baptist, of whom he said none greater had been born of women, our Master declared: "He that is least in the kingdom of heaven is greater than he." That is, he that hath the kingdom of heaven, the reign of holiness, in the least in his heart, shall be greatest.

Who shall inherit the earth? The meek, who sit at the feet of Truth, bathing the human understanding with tears of repentance and washing it clean from the taints of self-righteousness, hypocrisy, envy, — they shall inherit the earth, for "wisdom is justified of her children."

"Who shall dwell in Thy holy hill? He that walketh uprightly, and worketh righteousness, and speaketh the truth in his heart."

Who shall be called to Pleasant View? He who strives, and attains; who has the divine presumption to say: "For I know whom I have believed, and am persuaded that he is able to keep that which I have committed unto him against that day" (St. Paul). It goes without saying that such a one was never called to Pleasant View for penance or for reformation; and I call none but genuine Christian Scientists, unless I mistake their calling. No mesmerist nor disloyal Christian Scientist is fit to come hither. I have no use for such, and there cannot be found at Pleasant View one of *this sort*. "For all that do these things are an abomination unto the Lord: and because of these abominations the Lord thy God doth drive them out from before thee." (Deuteronomy 18: 12.)

It is true that loyal Christian Scientists, called to the home of the Discoverer and Founder of Christian Science, can acquire in one year the Science that otherwise might cost them a half century. But this should not be the incentive for going thither. Better far that Christian Scientists go to help their helper, and thus lose all selfishness, as she has lost it, and thereby help themselves and the whole world, as she has done, according to this saying of Christ Jesus: "And whosoever doth not bear his cross, and come after me, cannot be my disciple."

Mental Digestion

Will those beloved students, whose growth is taking in the Ten Commandments and scaling the steep ascent of Christ's Sermon on the Mount, accept profound thanks for their swift messages of rejoicing over the twentieth century Church Manual? Heaps upon heaps of praise confront me, and for what? That which I said in my heart would never be needed, — namely, laws of limitation for a Christian Scientist. Thy ways are not as ours. Thou knowest best what we need most, — hence my disappointed hope and grateful joy. The redeemed should be happier than the elect. Truth is strong with destiny; it takes life profoundly; it measures the infinite against the finite. Notwithstanding the sacrilegious moth of time, eternity awaits our Church Manual, which will maintain its rank as in the past, amid ministries aggressive and active, and will stand when those have passed to rest.

Scientific pathology illustrates the digestion of spiritual nutriment as both sweet and bitter, — sweet in expectancy and bitter in experience or during the senses' assimilation thereof, and digested only when Soul silences the dyspepsia of sense. This church is impartial. Its rules apply not to one member only, but to one and all equally. Of this I am sure, that each Rule and By-law in this Manual will increase the spirituality of him who obeys it, invigorate his capacity to heal the sick, to comfort such as mourn, and to awaken the sinner.

Teaching in the Sunday School

To the Superintendent and Teachers of The Mother Church Sunday School

Beloved Students: — I read with pleasure your approval of the amendments to Article XIX., Sections 5 and 6,[1] in our Church Manual. Be assured that fitness and fidelity such as thine in the officials of my church give my solitude sweet surcease. It is a joy to know that they who are faithful over foundational trusts, such as the Christian education of the dear children, will reap the reward of rightness, rise in the scale of being, and realize at last their Master's promise, "And they shall be all taught of God."

Pleasant View, Concord, N. H.,
November 14, 1904.

[1] Article XX., Sections 2 and 3 in 89th edition.

Charity and Invalids

Mrs. Eddy endeavors to bestow her charities for such purposes only as God indicates. Giving merely in compliance with solicitations or petitions from strangers, incurs the liability of working in wrong directions. As a rule, she has suffered most from those whom she has labored much to benefit — also from the undeserving poor to whom she has given large sums of money, worse than wasted. She has, therefore, finally resolved to spend no more time or money in such uncertain, unfortunate investments. She has qualified students for healing the sick, and has ceased practice herself in order to help God's work in other of its highest and infinite meanings, as God, not man, directs. Hence, letters from invalids demanding her help do not reach her. They are committed to the waste-basket by her secretaries.

"Charity suffereth long and is kind," but wisdom must govern charity, else love's labor is lost and giving is unkind. As it is, Mrs. Eddy is constantly receiving more important demands on her time and attention than one woman is sufficient to supply. It would therefore be as unwise for her to undertake new tasks, as for a landlord who has not an empty apartment in his house, to receive more tenants.

Lessons in the Sunday School

To the Officers of the Sunday School of Second Church of Christ, Scientist, New York

Beloved Brethren: — You will accept my thanks for your interesting report regarding the By-law, "Subject for Lessons" (Article XX., Section 3 of Church Manual).

It rejoices me that you are recognizing the proper course, unfurling your banner to the breeze of God, and sailing over rough seas with the helm in His hands. Steering thus, the waiting waves will weave for you their winning webs of life in looms of love that line the sacred shores. The right way wins the right of way, even the way of Truth and Love whereby all our debts are paid, mankind blessed, and God glorified.

Watching *versus* Watching Out

Comment on an Editorial which Appeared in the Christian Science Sentinel, September 23, 1905

Our Lord and Master left to us the following sayings as living lights in our darkness: "What I say unto you I say unto all, Watch" (Mark 13:37); and, "If the goodman of the house had known what hour the thief would come, he would have watched, and not have suffered his house to be broken through." (Luke 12:39.)

Here we ask: Are Christ's teachings the true authority for Christian Science? They are. Does the textbook of Christian Science, "Science and Health with Key to the Scriptures," read on page 252, "A knowledge of error and of its operations must precede that understanding of Truth which destroys error, until the entire mortal, material error finally disappears, and the eternal verity, man created by and of Spirit, is understood and recognized as the true likeness of his Maker"? It does. If so-called watching produces fear or exhaustion and no good results, does that watch accord with Jesus' saying? It does not. Can watching as Christ demands harm you? It cannot. Then should not "watching out" mean, watching against a negative watch, *alias*, no watch, and gaining the spirit of true watching, even the spirit of our Master's command? It must mean that.

Is there not something to watch in yourself, in your daily life, since "by their fruits ye shall know them," which prevents an effective watch? Otherwise, wherefore the Lord's Prayer, "Deliver us from evil"? And if this something, when challenged by Truth, frightens you, should you not put that out instead of *putting out your watch?* I surely should. Then are you not made better by watching? I am. Which should we prefer, ease or dis-ease in sin? Is not discomfort from sin better adapted to deliver mortals from the effects of belief in sin than ease in sin? and can you demonstrate over the effects of other people's sins by indifference thereto? I cannot.

The Scriptures say, "They have healed also the hurt of the daughter of my people slightly, saying, Peace, peace; when there is no peace" (Jeremiah 6 : 14), thus taking the name of God in vain. Ignorance of self is the most stubborn belief to overcome, for apathy, dishonesty, sin, follow in its train. One should watch to know what his errors are; and if this watching destroys his peace in error, should one watch against such a result? He should not. Our Master said, "He that taketh not his cross, and followeth after me, is not worthy of me . . . and he that loseth his life [his false sense of life] for my sake shall find it." (Matthew 10: 38, 39.)

Principle or Person?

Do Christian Scientists love God as much as they love mankind? Aye, that's the question. Let us examine it for ourselves. Thinking of person implies that one is not thinking of Principle, and fifty telegrams per holiday signalize the thinking of person. Are the holidays blest by absorbing one's time writing or reading congratulations? I cannot watch and pray while reading telegrams; they only cloud the clear sky, and they give the appearance of personal worship which Christian Science annuls. Did the dear students know how much I love them, and how I need every hour wherein to express this love in labor for them, they would gladly give me the holidays for this work and not task themselves with mistaken means. But God will reward their kind motives, and guide them every step of the way from human affection to spiritual understanding, from faith to achievement, from light to Love, from sense to Soul.

Christian Science and China

Beloved Student: — The report of the success of Christian Science in benighted China, when regarded on one side only, is cheering, but to look at both sides of the great question of introducing Christian Science into a heathen nation gives the subject quite another aspect. I believe that all our great Master's sayings are practical and scientific. If the Dowager Empress could hold her nation, there would be no danger in teaching Christian Science in her country. But a war on religion in China would be more fatal than the Boxers' rebellion. Silent prayer in and for a heathen nation is just what is needed. But to teach and to demonstrate Christian Science before the minds of the people are prepared for it, and when the laws are against it, is fraught with danger.

Inconsistency

To teach the truth of life without using the word death, the suppositional opposite of life, were as impossible as to define truth and not name its opposite, error. Straining at gnats, one may swallow camels.

The tender mother, guided by love, faithful to her instincts, and adhering to the imperative rules of Science, asks herself: Can I teach my child the correct numeration of numbers and never name a cipher? Knowing that she cannot do this in mathematics, she should know that it cannot be done in metaphysics, and so she should definitely name the error, uncover it, and teach truth scientifically.

Signs of the Times

Is God infinite? Yes. Did God make man? Yes. Did God make all that was made? He did. Is God Spirit? He is. Did infinite Spirit make that which is not spiritual? No. Who or what made matter? Matter as substance or intelligence never was made. Is mortal man a creator, is he matter or spirit? Neither one. Why? Because Spirit is God and *infinite;* hence there can be no other creator and no other creation. Man is but His image and likeness.

Are you a Christian Scientist? I am. Do you adopt as truth the above statements? I do. Then why this meaningless commemoration of birthdays, since there are none?

Had I known what was being done in time to have prevented it, that which commemorated in deed or in word what is not true, would never have entered into the history of our church buildings. Let us have no more of echoing dreams. Will the beloved students accept my full heart's love for them and their kind thoughts.

Nota Bene

My Beloved Christian Scientists: —Because I suggested the name for one central Reading Room, and this name continues to be multiplied, you will permit me to make the *amende honorable* — notwithstanding "incompetence" — and to say, please adopt generally for your name, Christian Science Reading Room. An old axiom says: Too much of one thing spoils the whole. Too many centres may become equivalent to no centre.

Here I have the joy of knowing that Christian Scientists will exchange the present name for the one which I suggest, with the sweet alacrity and uniformity with which they accepted the first name.

Merely this appellative seals the question of unity, and opens wide on the amplitude of liberty and love a far-reaching motive and success, of which we can say, the more the better.

Pleasant View, Concord, N. H.,
July 8, 1907.

Take Notice

I request the Christian Scientists universally to read the paragraph beginning at line 30 of page 442 in the edition of Science and Health which will be issued February 29 [1908]. I consider the information there given to be of great importance at this stage of the workings of animal magnetism, and it will greatly aid the students in their individual experiences.

TAKE NOTICE

The contemplated reference in Science and Health to the "higher criticism" announced in the *Sentinel* a few weeks ago, I have since decided not to publish.

Take Notice

What I wrote on Christian Science some twenty-five years ago I do not consider a precedent for a present student of this Science. The best mathematician has not attained the full understanding of the principle thereof, in his earliest studies or discoveries. Hence, it were wise to accept only my teachings that I know to be correct and adapted to the present demand.

Take Notice

To Christian Scientists: — See Science and Health, page 442, line 30, and give daily attention thereto.

Practitioners' Charges

Christian Science practitioners should make their charges for treatment equal to those of reputable physicians in their respective localities.

BROOKLINE, MASS., December 24, 1909.

Take Notice

The article on the Church Manual by Blanche Hersey Hogue, in the *Sentinel* of September 10 [1910] is practical and scientific, and I recommend its careful study to all Christian Scientists.

CHAPTER XI

QUESTIONS ANSWERED

Questions and Answers

Will the Bible, if read and practised, heal as effectually as your book, "Science and Health with Key to the Scriptures"?

THE exact degree of comparison between the effects produced by reading the above-named books can only be determined by personal proof. Rightly to read and to practise the Scriptures, their spiritual sense must be discerned, understood, and demonstrated. God being Spirit, His language and meaning are wholly spiritual. Uninspired knowledge of the translations of the Scriptures has imparted little power to practise the Word. Hence the revelation, discovery, and presentation of Christian Science — the Christ Science, or "new tongue" of which St. Mark prophesied — became requisite in the divine order. On the swift pinions of spiritual thought man rises above the letter, law, or *morale* of the inspired Word to the spirit of Truth, whereby the Science is reached that demonstrates God. When the Bible is thus read and practised, there is no possibility of misinterpretation. God is understandable, knowable, and applicable to every human need. In this is the proof that Christian Science is Science, for it demonstrates Life, not death; health, not disease; Truth, not error; Love, not hate. The Science of the Scriptures coexists with God; and "Science and Health with Key to the Scriptures" relegates Christianity to its primitive proof, wherein reason, revelation, the divine Principle, rules, and practice of Christianity acquaint the student with God. In the ratio that Christian Science is studied and understood, mankind will, as aforetime, imbibe the spirit and prove the practicality, validity, and redemptive power of Christianity by healing all manner of disease, by overcoming sin and death.

Must mankind wait for the ultimate of the millennium — until every man and woman comes into the knowledge of Christ and all are taught of God and see their apparent identity as one man and one woman — for God to be represented by His idea or image and likeness?

God is one, and His idea, image, or likeness, man, is one. But God is *infinite* and so includes *all* in one. Man is the generic term for men and women. Man, as the idea or image and likeness of the infinite God, is a compound, complex idea or likeness of the infinite *one*, or one infinite, whose image is the reflection of all that is real and eternal in infinite identity. Gender means a kind. Hence mankind — in other words, a kind of man who is identified by sex — is the material, so-called man born of the flesh, and is not the spiritual man, created by God, Spirit, who made all that was made. The millennium is a state and stage of mental advancement, going on since ever time was. Its impetus, accelerated by the advent of Christian Science, is marked, and will increase till all men shall know Him (divine Love) from the least to the greatest, and one God and the brotherhood of man shall be known and acknowledged throughout the earth.

The Higher Criticism

An earnest student writes to me: "Would it be asking too much of you to explain more fully why you call Christian Science the higher criticism?"

I called Christian Science the higher criticism in my dedicatory Message to The Mother Church, June 10, 1906, when I said, "This Science is a law of divine Mind, . . . an ever-present help. Its presence is felt, for it acts and acts wisely, always unfolding the highway of hope, faith, understanding."

I now repeat another proof, namely, that Christian Science is the higher criticism because it criticizes evil, disease, and death — all that is unlike God, good — on a Scriptural basis, and approves or disapproves according to the word of God. In the next edition of Science and Health I shall refer to this.

MARY BAKER EDDY.

Class Teaching

Mrs. Eddy thus replies, through her student, Mr. Adam Dickey, to the question, Does Mrs. Eddy approve of class teaching: —

Yes! She most assuredly does, when the teaching is done by those who are duly qualified, who have received certificates from the Massachusetts Metaphysical College or the Board of Education, and who have the necessary moral and spiritual qualifications to perform this important work. Class teaching will not be abolished until it has accomplished that for which it was established; viz., the elucidation of the Principle and rule of Christian Science through the higher meaning of the Scriptures. Students who are ready for this step should beware the net that is craftily laid and cunningly concealed to prevent their advancement in this direction.

Instruction by Mrs. Eddy

We are glad to have the privilege of publishing an extract from a letter to Mrs. Eddy, from a Christian Scientist in the West, and Mrs. Eddy's reply thereto. The issue raised is an important one and one upon which there should be absolute and correct teaching. Christian Scientists are fortunate to receive instruction from their Leader on this point. The question and Mrs. Eddy's reply follow.

"Last evening I was catechized by a Christian Science practitioner because I referred to myself as an immortal idea of the one divine Mind. The practitioner said that my statement was wrong, because I still lived in my flesh. I replied that I did not live in my flesh, that my flesh lived or died according to the beliefs I entertained about it; but that, after coming to the light of Truth, I had found that I lived and moved and had my being in God, and to obey Christ was not to know as real the beliefs of an earthly mortal. Please give the truth in the *Sentinel*, so that all may know it."

MRS. EDDY'S REPLY

You are scientifically correct in your statement about yourself. You can never demonstrate spirituality until you declare yourself to be immortal and understand that you are so. Christian Science is absolute; it is neither behind the point of perfection nor advancing towards it; it is at this point and must be practised therefrom. Unless you fully perceive that you are the child of God, hence perfect, you have no Principle to demonstrate and no rule for its demonstration. By this I do not mean that mortals are the children of God,— far from it. In practising Christian Science you must state its Principle correctly, or you forfeit your ability to demonstrate it.

TAKE NOTICE

I hereby announce to the Christian Science field that all inquiries or information relating to Christian Science practice, to publication committee work, reading-room work, or to Mother Church membership, should be sent to the Christian Science Board of Directors of The Mother Church; and I have requested my secretary not to make inquiries on these subjects, nor to reply to any received, but to leave these duties to the Clerk of The Mother Church, to whom they belong.

MARY BAKER EDDY.

September 28, 1910.

CHAPTER XII

READERS, TEACHERS, LECTURERS

The New York Churches

My Beloved Students: — According to reports, the belief is springing up among you that the several churches in New York City should come together and form one church. This is a suggestion of error, which should be silenced at its inception. You cannot have lost sight of the rules for branch churches as published in our Church Manual. The Empire City is large, and there should be more than one church in it.

The Readers of The Church of Christ, Scientist, hold important, responsible offices, and two individuals would meet meagrely the duties of half a dozen or more of the present incumbents. I have not yet had the privilege of knowing two students who are adequate to take charge of three or more churches. The students in New York and elsewhere will see that it is wise to remain in their own fields of labor and give all possible time and attention to caring for their own flocks.

The November Class, 1898

Beloved Christian Scientists: — Your prompt presence in Concord at my unexplained call witnesses your fidelity to Christian Science and your spiritual unity with your

Leader. I have awaited your arrival before informing you of my purpose in sending for you, in order to avoid the stir that might be occasioned among those who wish to share this opportunity and to whom I would gladly give it at this time if a larger class were advantageous to the students.

You have been invited hither to receive from me one or more lessons on Christian Science, prior to conferring on any or all of you who are ready for it, the degree of C.S.D., of the Massachusetts Metaphysical College. This opportunity is designed to impart a fresh impulse to our spiritual attainments, the great need of which I daily discern. I have awaited the right hour, and to be called of God to contribute my part towards this result.

The "secret place," whereof David sang, is unquestionably man's spiritual state in God's own image and likeness, even the inner sanctuary of divine Science, in which mortals do not enter without a struggle or sharp experience, and in which they put off the human for the divine. Knowing this, our Master said: "Many are called, but few are chosen." In the highest sense of a disciple, all loyal students of my books are indeed my students, and your wise, faithful teachers have come so to regard them.

What I have to say may not require more than one lesson. This, however, must depend on results. But the lessons will certainly not exceed three in number. No charge will be made for my services.

Massachusetts Metaphysical College

The Massachusetts Metaphysical College of Boston, Massachusetts, was chartered A.D. 1881. As the people observed the success of this Christian system of heal-

METAPHYSICAL COLLEGE

ing all manner of disease, over and above the approved schools of medicine, they became deeply interested in it. Now the wide demand for this universal benefice is imperative, and it should be met as heretofore, cautiously, systematically, scientifically. This Christian educational system is established on a broad and liberal basis. Law and order characterize its work and secure a thorough preparation of the student for practice.

The growth of human inquiry and the increasing popularity of Christian Science, I regret to say, have called out of their hiding-places those poisonous reptiles and devouring beasts, superstition and jealousy. Towards the animal elements manifested in ignorance, persecution, and lean glory, and to their Babel of confusion worse confounded, let Christian Scientists be charitable. Let the voice of Truth and Love be heard above the dire din of mortal nothingness, and the majestic march of Christian Science go on *ad infinitum,* praising God, doing the works of primitive Christianity, and enlightening the world.

To protect the public, students of the Massachusetts Metaphysical College have received certificates, and these credentials are still required of all who claim to teach Christian Science.

Inquiries have been made as to the precise signification of the letters of degrees that follow the names of Christian Scientists. They indicate, respectively, the degrees of Bachelor and Doctor of Christian Science, conferred by the President or Vice-President of the Massachusetts Metaphysical College. The first degree (C.S.B.) is given to students of the Primary class; the second degree (C.S.D.) is given to those who, after receiving the first degree, continue for three years as practitioners of Christian Science in good and regular standing.

Students who enter the Massachusetts Metaphysical College, or are examined under its auspices by the Board of Education, must be well educated and have practised Christian Science three years with good success.

The Board of Education

In the year 1889, to gain a higher hope for the race, I closed my College in the midst of unprecedented prosperity, left Boston, and sought in solitude and silence a higher understanding of the absolute scientific unity which must exist between the teaching and letter of Christianity and the spirit of Christianity, dwelling forever in the divine Mind or Principle of man's being and revealed through the human character.

While revising "Science and Health with Key to the Scriptures," the light and might of the divine concurrence of the spirit and the Word appeared, and the result is an auxiliary to the College called the Board of Education of The Mother Church of Christ, Scientist, in Boston, Mass.

Our Master said: "What I do thou knowest not now; but thou shalt know hereafter;" and the spirit of his mission, the wisdom of his words, and the immortality of his works are the same to-day as yesterday and forever.

The Magna Charta of Christian Science means much,

multum in parvo, — all-in-one and one-in-all. It stands for the inalienable, universal rights of men. Essentially democratic, its government is administered by the common consent of the governed, wherein and whereby man governed by his creator is self-governed. The church is the mouthpiece of Christian Science, — its law and gospel are according to Christ Jesus; its rules are health, holiness, and immortality, — equal rights and privileges, equality of the sexes, rotation in office.

To a First Reader

Beloved Student: — Christ is meekness and Truth enthroned. Put on the robes of Christ, and you will be lifted up and will draw all men unto you. The little fishes in my fountain must have felt me when I stood silently beside it, for they came out in orderly line to the rim where I stood. Then I fed these sweet little thoughts that, not fearing me, sought their food of me.

God has called you to be a fisher of men. It is not a stern but a loving look which brings forth mankind to receive your bestowal, — not so much eloquence as *tender persuasion* that takes away their fear, for it is Love alone that feeds them.

Do you come to your little flock so filled with divine food that you cast your bread upon the waters? Then be sure that after many or a few days it will return to you.

The little that I have accomplished has all been done through love, — self-forgetful, patient, unfaltering tenderness.

The Christian Science Board of Lectureship

Beloved Students: — I am more than satisfied with your work: its grandeur almost surprises me. Let your watchword always be:

> "Great, not like Caesar, stained with blood,
> But only great as I am good."

You are not setting up to be great; you are here for the purpose of grasping and defining the demonstrable, the eternal. Spiritual heroes and prophets are they whose new-old birthright is to put an end to falsities in a wise way and to proclaim Truth so winningly that an honest, fervid affection for the race is found adequate for the emancipation of the race.

You are the needed and the inevitable sponsors for the twentieth century, reaching deep down into the universal and rising above theorems into the transcendental, the infinite — yea, to the reality of God, man, nature, the universe. No fatal circumstance of idolatry can fold or falter your wings. No fetishism with a symbol can fetter your flight. You soar only as uplifted by God's power, or you fall for lack of the divine impetus. You know that to conceive God aright you must be good.

The Christ mode of understanding Life — of exterminating sin and suffering and their penalty, death — I have largely committed to you, my faithful witnesses. You go forth to face the foe with loving look and with the religion and philosophy of labor, duty, liberty, and love, to challenge universal indifference, chance, and creeds. Your highest inspiration is found nearest the divine Principle and nearest the scientific expression of Truth.

You may condemn evil in the abstract without harming any one or your own moral sense, but condemn persons seldom, if ever. Improve every opportunity to correct sin through your own perfectness. When error strives to be heard above Truth, let the "still small voice" produce God's phenomena. Meet dispassionately the raging element of individual hate and counteract its most gigantic falsities.

The moral abandon of hating even one's enemies excludes goodness. Hate is a moral idiocy let loose for one's own destruction. Unless withstood, the heat of hate burns the wheat, spares the tares, and sends forth a mental miasma fatal to health, happiness, and the morals of mankind, — and all this only to satiate its loathing of love and its revenge on the patience, silence, and lives of saints. The marvel is, that at this enlightened period a respectable newspaper should countenance such evil tendencies.

Millions may know that I am the Founder of Christian Science. I alone know what that means.

READERS IN CHURCH

The report that I prefer to have a man, rather than a woman, for First Reader in The Church of Christ, Scientist, I desire to correct. My preference lies with the individual best fitted to perform this important function. If both the First and Second Readers are my students, then without reference to sex I should prefer that student who is most spiritually-minded. What our churches need is that devout, unselfed quality of thought which spiritualizes the congregation.

Words for the Wise

The By-law of The Mother Church of Christ, Scientist, relative to a three years' term for church Readers, was entitled to and has received profound attention. Rotation in office promotes wisdom, quiets mad ambition, satisfies justice, and crowns honest endeavors.

The best Christian Scientists will be the first to adopt this By-law in their churches, and their Readers will retire *ex officio*, after three years of acceptable service as church Readers, to higher usefulness in this vast vineyard of our Lord.

The churches who adopt this By-law will please send to the Editor of our periodicals notice of their action.

Afterglow

Beloved Students: — The By-law of The Mother Church of Christ, Scientist, stipulating three years as the term for its Readers, neither binds nor compels the branch churches to follow suit; and the By-law applies only to Christian Science churches in the United States and Canada. Doubtless the churches adopting this By-law will discriminate as regards its adaptability to their conditions. But if now is not the time, the branch churches can wait for the favored moment to act on this subject.

I rest peacefully in knowing that the impulsion of this action in The Mother Church was from above. So I have faith that whatever is done in this direction by the branch churches will be blest. The Readers who have filled this sacred office many years, have beyond it duties and attainments beckoning them. What these are I cannot yet say. The great Master saith: "What I do thou knowest not now; but thou shalt know hereafter."

Teachers of Christian Science

I reply to the following question from unknown questioners:

"Are the students, whom I have taught, obliged to take both Primary and Normal class instruction in the Board of Education in order to become teachers of Primary classes?"

No, not if you and they are loyal Christian Scientists, and not if, after examination in the Board of Education, your pupils are found eligible to enter the Normal class, which at present is taught in the Board of Education only.

There is evidently some misapprehension of my meaning as to the mode of instruction in the Board of Education. A Primary student of mine can teach pupils the practice of Christian Science, and after three years of good practice, my Primary student can himself be examined in the Board of Education, and if found eligible, receive a certificate of the degree C.S.D.

The General Association of Teachers, 1903

My Beloved Students: — I call you mine, for all is thine and mine. What God gives, elucidates, armors, and tests in His service, is ours; and we are His. You have convened only to convince yourselves of this grand verity: namely, the unity in Christian Science. Cherish steadfastly this fact. Adhere to the teachings of the Bible,

Science and Health, and our Manual, and you will obey the law and gospel. Have one God and you will have no devil. Keep yourselves busy with divine Love. Then you will be toilers like the bee, always distributing sweet things which, if bitter to sense, will be salutary as Soul; but you will not be like the spider, which weaves webs that ensnare.

Rest assured that the good you do unto others you do to yourselves as well, and the wrong you may commit must, will, rebound upon you. The entire purpose of true education is to make one not only know the truth but live it — to make one enjoy doing right, make one not work in the sunshine and run away in the storm, but work midst clouds of wrong, injustice, envy, hate; and wait on God, the strong deliverer, who will reward righteousness and punish iniquity. "As thy days, so shall thy strength be."

THE LONDON TEACHERS' ASSOCIATION, 1903

Beloved Students: — Your letter and dottings are an oasis in my wilderness. They point to verdant pastures, and are already rich rays from the eternal sunshine of Love, lighting and leading humanity into paths of peace and holiness.

Your "Thanksgiving Day," instituted in England on New Year's Day, was a step in advance. It expressed your thanks, and gave to the "happy New Year" a higher hint. You are not aroused to this action by the allurements of wealth, pride, or power; the impetus comes from above — it is moral, spiritual, divine. All hail to this higher hope that neither slumbers nor is stilled by the cold impulse of a lesser gain!

It rejoices me to know that you know that healing the sick, soothing sorrow, brightening this lower sphere with the ways and means of the higher and everlasting harmony, brings to light the perfect original man and universe. What nobler achievement, what greater glory can nerve your endeavor? Press on! My heart and hope are with you.

> "Thou art not here for ease or pain,
> But manhood's glorious crown to gain."

The General Association of Teachers, 1904

Beloved Brethren: — I thank you. Jesus said: "The world hath not known Thee: but I have known Thee, and these have known that Thou hast sent me."

The Canadian Teachers, 1904

Beloved Brethren: — Accept my love and these words of Jesus: "Holy Father, keep through Thine own name those whom Thou hast given me, that they may be one, as we are."

Students in the Board of Education, December, 1904

Beloved Students: — You will accept my profound thanks for your letter and telegram. If wishing is wise, I send with this a store of wisdom in three words: God bless you. If faith is fruition, you have His rich blessing already and my joy therewith.

We understand best that which begins in ourselves and by education brightens into birth. Dare to be faithful to God and man. Let the creature become one with his creator, and mysticism departs, heaven opens, right reigns, and you have begun to be a Christian Scientist.

The May Class, 1905

Beloved: — I am glad you enjoy the dawn of Christian Science; you must reach its meridian. Watch, pray, demonstrate. Released from materialism, you shall run and not be weary, walk and not faint.

The December Class, 1905

Beloved Students: — Responding to your kind letter, let me say: You will reap the sure reward of right thinking and acting, of watching and praying, and you will find the ever-present God an ever-present help. I thank the faithful teacher of this class and its dear members.

"Rotation in Office"

Dear Leader: — May we have permission to print, as a part of the preamble to our By-laws, the following extract from your article "Christian Science Board of Education" in the June *Journal* of 1904, page 184: —

"The Magna Charta of Christian Science means much, *multum in parvo*, — all-in-one and one-in-all. It stands for the inalienable, universal rights of men. Essentially democratic, its government is administered by the common consent of the governed, wherein and whereby man governed by his creator is self-governed. The church is the mouthpiece of Christian Science, — its law and gospel are according to Christ Jesus;

its rules are health, holiness, and immortality, — equal rights and privileges, equality of the sexes, rotation in office."

MRS. EDDY'S REPLY

Christian Science churches have my consent to publish the foregoing in their By-laws. By "rotation in office" I do not mean that minor officers who are filling their positions satisfactorily should be removed every three years, or be elevated to offices for which they are not qualified.

CHESTNUT HILL, MASS.,
March 6, 1909.

CHAPTER XIII

CHRISTMAS

Early Chimes, December, 1898

BEFORE the Christmas bells shall ring, allow me to improvise some new notes, not specially musical to be sure, but admirably adapted to the key of my feeling and emphatically phrasing strict observance or note well.

This year, my beloved Christian Scientists, you must grant me my request that I be permitted total exemption from Christmas gifts. Also I beg to send to you all a deep-drawn, heartfelt breath of thanks for those things of beauty and use forming themselves in your thoughts to send to your Leader. Thus may I close the door of mind on this subject, and open the volume of Life on the pure pages of impersonal presents, pleasures, achievements, and *aid*.

Christmas, 1900

Again loved Christmas is here, full of divine benedictions and crowned with the dearest memories in human history — the earthly advent and nativity of our Lord and Master. At this happy season the veil of time springs aside at the touch of Love. We count our blessings and see whence they came and whither they tend. Parents call home their loved ones, the Yule-fires burn, the festive boards are spread, the gifts glow in the dark green branches of the Christmas-tree. But alas for the broken household band! God give to them more of His dear love that heals the wounded heart.

To-day the watchful shepherd shouts his welcome over the new cradle of an old truth. This truth has traversed night, through gloom to glory, from cradle to crown. To the awakened consciousness, the Bethlehem babe has left his swaddling-clothes (material environments) for the form and comeliness of the divine ideal, which has passed from a corporeal to the spiritual sense of Christ and is winning the heart of humanity with ineffable tenderness. The Christ is speaking for himself and for his mother, Christ's heavenly origin and aim. To-day the Christ is, more than ever before, "the way, the truth, and the life," — "which lighteth every man that cometh into the world," healing all sorrow, sickness, and sin. To this auspicious Christmastide, which hallows the close of the nineteenth century, our hearts are kneeling humbly. We own his grace, reviving and healing. At this immortal hour, all human hate, pride, greed, lust should bow and declare Christ's power, and the reign of Truth and Life divine should make man's being pure and blest.

Christmas Gifts

Beloved Students: — For your manifold Christmas memorials, too numerous to name, I group you in one benison and send you my Christmas gift, two words enwrapped, — *love* and *thanks*.

To-day Christian Scientists have their record in the monarch's palace, the Alpine hamlet, the Christian traveller's resting-place. Wherever the child looks up in prayer, or the Book of Life is loved, there the sinner is reformed and the sick are healed. Those are the "signs following." What is it that lifts a system of religion to deserved fame? Nothing is worthy the name of religion save one lowly offering — love.

This period, so fraught with opposites, seems illuminated for woman's hope with divine light. It bids her bind the tenderest tendril of the heart to all of holiest worth. To the woman at the sepulchre, bowed in strong affection's anguish, one word, "Mary," broke the gloom with Christ's all-conquering love. Then came her resurrection and task of glory, to know and to do God's will, — in the words of St. Paul: "Looking unto Jesus the author and finisher of our faith; who for the joy that was set before him endured the cross, despising the shame, and is set down at the right hand of the throne of God."

The memory of the Bethlehem babe bears to mortals gifts greater than those of Magian kings, — hopes that cannot deceive, that waken prophecy, gleams of glory, coronals of meekness, diadems of love. Nor should they who drink their Master's cup repine over blossoms that mock their hope and friends that forsake. Divinely beautiful are the Christmas memories of him who sounded all depths of love, grief, death, and humanity.

To the dear children let me say: Your Christmas gifts are hallowed by our Lord's blessing. A transmitted charm rests on them. May this consciousness of God's dear love for you give you the might of love, and may you move onward and upward, lowly in its majesty.

To the children who sent me that beautiful statuette in alabaster — a child with finger on her lip reading a book — I write: Fancy yourselves with me; take a peep into my studio; look again at your gift, and you will see the sweetest sculptured face and form conceivable, mounted on its pedestal between my bow windows, and on either side lace and flowers. I have named it my *white student*.

From First Church of Christ, Scientist, in London, Great Britain, I received the following cabled message: —

Rev. Mrs. Eddy, Pleasant View,
    Concord, N. H.

Loving, grateful Christmas greetings from members London, England, church.

December 24, 1901.

To this church across the sea I return my heart's wireless love. All our dear churches' Christmas telegrams to me are refreshing and most pleasing Christmas presents, for they require less attention than packages and give me more time to think and work for others. I hope that in 1902 the churches will remember me only thus. Do not forget that an honest, wise zeal, a lowly, triumphant trust, a true heart, and a helping hand constitute man, and nothing less is man or woman.

[*New York World*]

The Significance of Christmas

Certain occasions, considered either collectively or individually and observed properly, tend to give the activity of man infinite scope; but mere merry-making or needless gift-giving is not that in which human capacities find the most appropriate and proper exercise. Christmas respects the Christ too much to submerge itself in merely temporary means and ends. It represents the eternal informing Soul recognized only in harmony, in the beauty and bounty of Life everlasting, — in the truth that is Life, the Life that heals and saves mankind. An eternal Christmas would make matter an alien save as phenomenon, and matter would reverentially withdraw itself before Mind. The despotism of material sense or the flesh would flee before such reality, to make room for substance, and the shadow of frivolity and the inaccuracy of material sense would disappear.

In Christian Science, Christmas stands for the real, the absolute and eternal, — for the things of Spirit, not of matter. Science is divine; it hath no partnership with human means and ends, no half-way stations. Nothing conditional or material belongs to it. Human reason and philosophy may pursue paths devious, the line of liquids, the lure of gold, the doubtful sense that falls short of substance, the things hoped for and the evidence unseen.

The basis of Christmas is the rock, Christ Jesus; its fruits are inspiration and spiritual understanding of joy and rejoicing, — not because of tradition, usage, or corporeal pleasures, but because of fundamental and demonstrable truth, because of the heaven within us. The basis of Christmas is love loving its enemies, returning good for evil, love that "suffereth long, and is kind." The true spirit of Christmas elevates medicine to Mind; it casts out evils, heals the sick, raises the dormant faculties, appeals to all conditions, and supplies every need of man. It leaves hygiene, medicine, ethics, and religion to God and His Christ, to that which is the Way, in word and in deed, — the Way, the Truth, and the Life.

There is but one Jesus Christ on record. Christ is incorporeal. Neither the you nor the I in the flesh can be or is Christ.

Christmas for the Children

Methinks the loving parents and guardians of youth ofttimes query: How shall we cheer the children's Christmas and profit them withal? The wisdom of their elders, who seek wisdom of God, seems to have amply provided for this, according to the custom of the age and to the full supply of juvenile joy. Let it continue thus with one exception: the children should not be taught to believe that Santa Claus has aught to do with this pastime. A deceit or falsehood is never wise. Too much cannot be done towards guarding and guiding well the germinating and inclining thought of childhood. To mould aright the first impressions of innocence, aids in perpetuating purity and in unfolding the immortal model, man in His image and likeness. St. Paul wrote, "When I was a child, I spake as a child, I understood as a child, . . . but when I became a man, I put away childish things."

PLEASANT VIEW, CONCORD, N.H.,
December 28, 1905.

[*The Ladies' Home Journal*]

What Christmas Means to Me

To me Christmas involves an open secret, understood by few — or by none — and unutterable except in Christian Science. Christ was not born of the flesh. Christ is the Truth and Life born of God — born of Spirit and not of matter. Jesus, the Galilean Prophet, was born of the Virgin Mary's spiritual thoughts of Life and its manifestation.

God creates man perfect and eternal in His own image. Hence man is the image, idea, or likeness of perfection — an ideal which cannot fall from its inherent unity with divine Love, from its spotless purity and original perfection.

Observed by material sense, Christmas commemorates the birth of a human, material, mortal babe — a babe born in a manger amidst the flocks and herds of a Jewish village.

This homely origin of the babe Jesus falls far short of my sense of the eternal Christ, Truth, never born and never dying. I celebrate Christmas with my soul, my spiritual sense, and so commemorate the entrance into human understanding of the Christ conceived of Spirit, of God and not of a woman — as the birth of Truth, the dawn of divine Love breaking upon the gloom of matter and evil with the glory of infinite being.

Human doctrines or hypotheses or vague human philosophy afford little divine effulgence, deific presence or power. Christmas to me is the reminder of God's great gift, — His spiritual idea, man and the universe, — a gift which so transcends mortal, material, sensual giving that the merriment, mad ambition, rivalry, and ritual of our common Christmas seem a human mockery in mimicry of the real worship in commemoration of Christ's coming.

I love to observe Christmas in quietude, humility, benevolence, charity, letting good will towards man, eloquent silence, prayer, and praise express my conception of Truth's appearing.

The splendor of this nativity of Christ reveals infinite meanings and gives manifold blessings. Material gifts and pastimes tend to obliterate the spiritual idea in consciousness, leaving one alone and without His glory.

Mrs. Eddy's Christmas Message

My Household.

Beloved: — A word to the wise is sufficient. Mother wishes you all a *happy Christmas,* a feast of Soul and a famine of sense.

Lovingly thine,
MARY BAKER EDDY.

Box G, Brookline, Mass.,
   December 25, 1909.

CHAPTER XIV

CONTRIBUTIONS TO NEWSPAPERS AND MAGAZINES

[*Boston Herald*, May 5, 1900]

A Word in Defence

I EVEN hope that those who are kind enough to speak well of me may do so honestly and not too earnestly, and this seldom, until mankind learn more of my meaning and can speak justly of my living.

[*Boston Globe*, November 29, 1900]

Christian Science Thanks

On the threshold of the twentieth century, will you please send through the *Globe* to the people of New England, which is the birthplace of Thanksgiving Day, a sentiment on what the last Thanksgiving Day of the nineteenth century should signify to all mankind?

MRS. EDDY'S RESPONSE

New England's last Thanksgiving Day of this century signifies to the minds of men the Bible better understood and Truth and Love made more practical; the First Commandment of the Decalogue more imperative, and

"Love thy neighbor as thyself" more possible and pleasurable.

It signifies that love, unselfed, knocks more loudly than ever before at the heart of humanity and that it finds admittance; that revelation, spiritual voice and vision, are less subordinate to material sight and sound and more apparent to reason; that evil flourishes less, invests less in trusts, loses capital, and is bought at par value; that the Christ-spirit will cleanse the earth of human gore; that civilization, peace between nations, and the brotherhood of man should be established, and justice plead not vainly in behalf of the sacred rights of individuals, peoples, and nations.

It signifies that the Science of Christianity has dawned upon human thought to appear full-orbed in millennial glory; that scientific religion and scientific therapeutics are improving the morals and increasing the longevity of mankind, are mitigating and destroying sin, disease, and death; that religion and *materia medica* should be no longer tyrannical and proscriptive; that divine Love, impartial and universal, as understood in divine Science, forms the coincidence of the human and divine, which fulfils the saying of our great Master, "The kingdom of God is within you;" that the atmosphere of the human mind, when cleansed of self and permeated with divine Love, will reflect this purified subjective state in clearer skies, less thunderbolts, tornadoes, and extremes of heat and cold; that agriculture, manufacture, commerce, and wealth should be governed by honesty, industry, and justice, reaching out to all classes and peoples. For these signs of the times we thank our Father-Mother God.

[*New York World*, December, 1900]

INSUFFICIENT FREEDOM

To my sense, the most imminent dangers confronting the coming century are: the robbing of people of life and liberty under the warrant of the Scriptures; the claims of politics and of human power, industrial slavery, and insufficient freedom of honest competition; and ritual, creed, and trusts in place of the Golden Rule, "Whatsoever ye would that men should do to you, do ye even so to them."

[*Concord* (N. H.) *Monitor*, July, 1902]

CHRISTIAN SCIENCE AND THE TIMES

Your article on the decrease of students in the seminaries and the consequent vacancies occurring in the pulpits, points unmistakably to the "signs of the times" of which Jesus spoke. This flux and flow in one direction, so generally apparent, tends in one ultimate — the final spiritualization of all things, of all codes, modes, hypotheses, of man and the universe. How can it be otherwise, since God is Spirit and the origin of all that really is, and since this great fact is to be verified by the spiritualization of all?

Since 1877, these special "signs of the times" have increased year by year. My book, "Science and Health with Key to the Scriptures," was published in 1875. Note, if you please, that many points in theology and *materia medica*, at that date undisturbed, are now agitated, modified, and disappearing, and the more spiritual modes and significations are adopted.

It is undoubtedly true that Christian Science is destined

to become the one and the only religion and therapeutics on this planet. And why not, since Christianity is fully demonstrated to be divine Science? Nothing can be correct and continue forever which is not divinely scientific, for Science is the law of the Mind that is God, who is the originator of all that really is. The Scripture reads: "All things were made by Him; and without Him was not any thing made that was made." Here let us remember that God is not the Alpha and Omega of man and the universe; He is supreme, infinite, the great forever, the eternal Mind that hath no beginning and no end, no Alpha and no Omega.

[*New York American*, February, 1905]

HEAVEN

Is heaven spiritual?

Heaven is spiritual. Heaven is harmony, — infinite, boundless bliss. The dying or the departed enter heaven in proportion to their progress, in proportion to their fitness to partake of the quality and the quantity of heaven. One individual may first awaken from his dream of life in matter with a sense of music; another with that of relief from fear or suffering, and still another with a bitter sense of lost opportunities and remorse. Heaven is the reign of divine Science. Material thought tends to obscure spiritual understanding, to darken the true conception of man's divine Principle, Love, wherein and whereby soul is emancipate and environed with everlasting Life. Our great Teacher hath said: "Behold, the kingdom of God is within you" — within man's spiritual understanding of all the divine modes, means, forms, expression, and manifestation of goodness and happiness.

[*Boston Herald*, March 5, 1905]

Prevention and Cure of Divorce

The nuptial vow should never be annulled so long as the *morale* of marriage is preserved. The frequency of divorce shows that the imperative nature of the marriage relation is losing ground, — hence that some fundamental error is engrafted on it. What is this error? If the motives of human affection are right, the affections are enduring and achieving. What God hath joined together, man cannot sunder.

Divorce and war should be exterminated according to the Principle of law and gospel, — the maintenance of individual rights, the justice of civil codes, and the power of Truth uplifting the motives of men. Two commandments of the Hebrew Decalogue, "Thou shalt not commit adultery" and "Thou shalt not kill," obeyed, will eliminate divorce and war. On what hath not a "Thus saith the Lord," I am as silent as the dumb centuries without a living Divina.

This time-world flutters in my thought as an unreal shadow, and I can only solace the sore ills of mankind by a lively battle with "the world, the flesh and the devil," in which Love is the liberator and gives man the victory over himself. Truth, canonized by life and love, lays the axe at the root of all evil, lifts the curtain on the Science of being, the Science of wedlock, of living and of loving, and harmoniously ascends the scale of life. Look high enough, and you see the heart of humanity warming and winning. Look long enough, and you see male and female one — sex or gender eliminated; you see the designation *man* meaning woman as well, and you see the whole universe included in one infinite Mind and reflected in the intelligent compound idea, image or likeness, called man, showing forth the infinite divine Principle, Love, called God, — man wedded to the Lamb, pledged to innocence, purity, perfection. Then shall humanity have learned that "they which shall be accounted worthy to obtain that world, and the resurrection from the dead, neither marry, nor are given in marriage: neither can they die any more: for they are equal unto the angels; and are the children of God." (Luke 20: 35, 36.) This, therefore, is Christ's plan of salvation from divorce.

> All are but parts of one stupendous whole,
> Whose body nature is, and God the Soul.
> — POPE.

[*The Independent*, November, 1906]

HARVEST

God hath thrust in the sickle, and He is separating the tares from the wheat. This hour is molten in the furnace of Soul. Its harvest song is world-wide, world-known, world-great. The vine is bringing forth its fruit; the beams of right have healing in their light. The windows of heaven are sending forth their rays of reality — even Christian Science, pouring out blessing for cursing, and rehearsing: "I will rebuke the devourer for your sakes, and he shall not destroy the fruits of your ground." "Prove me now herewith, saith the Lord of hosts, if I will not open you the windows of heaven, and pour you out a blessing, that there shall not be room enough to receive it."

The lie and the liar are self-destroyed. Truth is immortal. "Rejoice, and be exceeding glad: . . . for so persecuted they the prophets which were before you." The cycle of good obliterates the epicycle of evil.

Because of the magnitude of their spiritual import, we repeat the signs of these times. In 1905, the First Congregational Church, my first religious home in this capital city of Concord, N. H., kindly invited me to its one hundred and seventy-fifth anniversary; the leading editors and newspapers of my native State congratulate me; the records of my ancestry attest honesty and valor. Divine Love, nearer my consciousness than before, saith: I am rewarding your waiting, and "thy people shall be my people."

Let error rage and imagine a vain thing. Mary Baker Eddy is not dead, and the words of those who say that she is are the father of their *wish*. Her life is proven under trial, and evidences "as thy days, so shall thy strength be."

Those words of our dear, departing Saviour, breathing love for his enemies, fill my heart: "Father, forgive them; for they know not what they do." My writings heal the sick, and I thank God that for the past forty years I have returned good for evil, and that I can appeal to Him as my witness to the truth of this statement.

What we love determines what we are. I love the prosperity of Zion, be it promoted by Catholic, by Protestant, or by Christian Science, which anoints with Truth, opening the eyes of the blind and healing the sick. I would no more quarrel with a man because of his religion than I would because of his art. The divine Principle of Christian Science will ultimately be seen to control both religion and art in unity and harmony. God is Spirit, and "they that worship Him must worship Him in spirit

MRS. EDDY'S HUMAN IDEAL

and in truth." If, as the Scriptures declare, God, Spirit, is infinite, matter and material sense are null, and there are no vertebrata, mollusca, or radiata.

When I wrote "Science and Health with Key to the Scriptures," I little understood all that I indited; but when I practised its precepts, healing the sick and reforming the sinner, then I learned the truth of what I had written. It is of comparatively little importance what a man thinks or believes he knows; the good that a man does is the one thing needful and the sole proof of rightness.

[*The Evening Press*, Grand Rapids, Mich., August, 1907]

Mrs. Eddy Describes her Human Ideal

In a modest, pleasantly situated home in the city of Concord, N. H., lives at eighty-six years of age the most discussed woman in all the world. This lady with sweet smile and snowy hair is Mrs. Mary Baker Eddy, Founder and Leader of Christian Science, beloved of thousands of believers and followers of the thought that has made her famous. It was to this aged woman of world-wide renown that the editor of *The Evening Press* addressed this question, requesting the courtesy of a reply: —

"What is nearest and dearest to your heart to-day?"

Mrs. Eddy's reply will be read with deep interest by all Americans, who, whatever their religious beliefs, cannot fail to be impressed by the personality of this remarkable woman.

MRS. EDDY'S ANSWER

Editor of The Evening Press: — To your courtesy and to your question permit me to say that, insomuch as I know myself, what is "nearest and dearest" to my heart is an honest man or woman — one who steadfastly and actively strives for perfection, one who leavens the loaf of life with justice, mercy, truth, and love.

Goodness is greatness, and the logic of events pushes onward the centuries; hence the Scripture, "The law of the Spirit of life in Christ Jesus hath made me [man] free from the law of sin and death."

This predicate and ultimate of scientific being presents, however, no claim that man is equal to God, for the finite is not the altitude of the infinite.

The real man was, is, and ever shall be the divine ideal, that is, God's image and likeness; and Christian Science reveals the divine Principle, the example, the rule, and the demonstration of this idealism.

Sincerely yours,
MARY BAKER EDDY.

PLEASANT VIEW, CONCORD, N. H.

[*Cosmopolitan*, November, 1907]

YOUTH AND YOUNG MANHOOD

EDITOR'S NOTE. — The *Cosmopolitan* presents this month to its readers a facsimile of an article sent to us by Mrs. Eddy, with the corrections on the manuscript reproduced in her own handwriting. Not only Mrs. Eddy's own devoted followers, but the public generally, will be interested in this communication from the extraordinary woman who, nearly eighty-seven years of age, plays so great a part in the world and leads with such conspicuous success her very great following.

Mrs. Eddy writes very rarely for any publications outside of the Christian Science periodicals, and our readers will be interested in this presentation of the thought of a mind that has had so much influence on this generation.

The *Cosmopolitan* gives no editorial indorsement to the teachings of Christian Science, it has no religious opinions or predilections to put before its readers. This manuscript is presented simply as an interesting and remarkable proof of Mrs. Eddy's ability in old age to vindicate in her own person the value of her teachings.

Certainly, Christian Scientists, enthusiastic in their belief, are fortunate in being able to point to a Leader far beyond the allotted years of man, emerging triumphantly from all attacks upon her, and guiding with remarkable skill, determination, and energy a very great organization that covers practically the civilized world.

King David, the Hebrew bard, sang, "I have been young, and now am old; yet have I not seen the righteous forsaken, nor his seed begging bread."

I for one accept his wise deduction, his ultimate or spiritual sense of thinking, feeling, and acting, and its reward. This sense of rightness acquired by experience and wisdom, should be early presented to youth and to manhood in order to forewarn and forearm humanity.

The ultimatum of life here and hereafter is utterly apart from a material or personal sense of pleasure, pain, joy, sorrow, life, and death. The truth of life, or life in truth, is a scientific knowledge that is portentous; and is won only by the spiritual understanding of Life as God, good, ever-present good, and therefore life eternal.

You will agree with me that the material body is mortal, but Soul is immortal; also that the five personal senses are perishable: they lapse and relapse, come and go, until at length they are consigned to dust. But say you, "Man awakes from the dream of death in possession of the five personal senses, does he not?" Yes, because death alone does not awaken man in God's image and likeness. The divine Science of Life alone gives

Copyright, 1907, by Mary Baker G. Eddy.

the true sense of life and of righteousness, and demonstrates the Principle of life eternal; even the Life that is Soul apart from the so-called life of matter or the material senses.

Death alone does not absolve man from a false material sense of life, but goodness, holiness, and love do this, and so consummate man's being with the harmony of heaven; the omnipotence, omnipresence, and omniscience of Life, even its all-power, all-presence, all-Science.

Dear reader, right thinking, right feeling, and right acting — honesty, purity, unselfishness — in youth tend to success, intellectuality, and happiness in manhood. To begin rightly enables one to end rightly, and thus it is that one achieves the Science of Life, demonstrates health, holiness, and immortality.

[*Boston Herald*, April, 1908]

Mrs. Eddy Sends Thanks

Mrs. Mary Baker Eddy has sent the following to the *Herald:* —

Will the dear Christian Scientists accept my thanks for their magnificent gifts, and allow me to say that I am not fond of an abundance of material presents; but I am cheered and blessed when beholding Christian healing, unity among brethren, and love to God and man; this is my crown of rejoicing, for it demonstrates Christian Science.

The Psalmist sang, "That thy way may be known upon earth, thy saving health among all nations."

[*Minneapolis* (Minn.) *News*]

Universal Fellowship

Christian Science can and does produce universal fellowship. As the sequence of divine Love it explains love, it lives love, it demonstrates love. The human, material, so-called senses do not perceive this fact until they are controlled by divine Love; hence the Scripture, "Be still, and know that I am God."

BROOKLINE, MASS.,
May 1, 1908.

[*New York Herald*]

Mrs. Eddy's Own Denial that She is Ill

Permit me to say, the report that I am sick (and I trust the desire thereof) is dead, and should be buried. Whereas the fact that I am well and keenly alive to the truth of being — the Love that is Life — is sure and steadfast. I go out in my carriage daily, and have omitted my drive but twice since I came to Massachusetts. Either my work, the demands upon my time at home, or the weather, is all that prevents my daily drive.

Working and praying for my dear friends' and my dear enemies' health, happiness, and holiness, the true sense of being goes on.

Doing unto others as we would that they do by us, is immortality's self. Intrepid, self-oblivious love fulfils the law and is self-sustaining and eternal. With white-winged charity brooding over all, spiritually understood and demonstrated, let us unite in one *Te Deum* of praise.

BOX G, BROOKLINE, MASS.,
May 15, 1908.

[*Christian Science Sentinel*, May 16, 1908]

To Whom It May Concern

Since Mrs. Eddy is watched, as one watches a criminal or a sick person, she begs to say, in her own behalf, that she is neither; therefore to be criticized or judged by either a daily drive or a dignified stay at home, is superfluous. When accumulating work requires it, or because of a preference to remain within doors she omits her drive, do not strain at gnats or swallow camels over it, but try to be composed and resigned to the shocking fact that she is minding her own business, and recommends this surprising privilege to all her dear friends and enemies.

MARY BAKER EDDY.

[*Boston Post*, November, 1908]

Politics

Mrs. Mary Baker Eddy has always believed that those who are entitled to vote should do so, and she has also believed that in such matters no one should seek to dictate the actions of others.

In reply to a number of requests for an expression of her political views, she has given out this statement: —

I am asked, "What are your politics?" I have none, in reality, other than to help support a righteous government; to love God supremely, and my neighbor as myself.

CHAPTER XV

PEACE AND WAR

[*Boston Herald*, March, 1898]

OTHER WAYS THAN BY WAR

IN reply to your question, "Should difficulties between the United States and Spain be settled peacefully by statesmanship and diplomacy, in a way honorable and satisfactory to both nations?" I will say I can see no other way of settling difficulties between individuals and nations than by means of their wholesome tribunals, equitable laws, and sound, well-kept treaties.

A bullet in a man's heart never settles the question of his life. The mental animus goes on, and urges that the answer to the sublime question as to man's life shall come from God and that its adjustment shall be according to His laws. The characters and lives of men determine the peace, prosperity, and life of nations. Killing men is not consonant with the higher law whereby wrong and injustice are righted and exterminated.

Whatever weighs in the eternal scale of equity and mercy tips the beam on the right side, where the immortal words and deeds of men alone can settle all questions amicably and satisfactorily. But if our nation's rights or honor were seized, every citizen would be a soldier and woman would be armed with power girt for the hour.

To coincide with God's government is the proper incentive to the action of all nations. If His purpose for peace is to be subserved by the battle's plan or by the intervention of the United States, so that the Cubans may learn to make war no more, this means and end will be accomplished.

The government of divine Love is supreme. Love rules the universe, and its edict hath gone forth: "Thou shalt have no other gods before me," and "Love thy neighbor as thyself." Let us have the molecule of faith that removes mountains, — faith armed with the understanding of Love, as in divine Science, where right reigneth. The revered President and Congress of our favored land are in God's hands.

[*Boston Globe*, December, 1904]

How Strife may be Stilled

Follow that which is good.

A Japanese may believe in a heaven for him who dies in defence of his country, but the steadying, elevating power of civilization destroys such illusions and should overcome evil with good.

Nothing is gained by fighting, but much is lost.

Peace is the promise and reward of rightness. Governments have no right to engraft into civilization the burlesque of uncivil economics. War is in itself an evil, barbarous, devilish. Victory in error is defeat in Truth. War is not in the domain of good; war weakens power and must finally fall, pierced by its own sword.

The Principle of all power is God, and God is Love. Whatever brings into human thought or action an element opposed to Love, is never requisite, never a necessity, and is not sanctioned by the law of God, the law of Love. The Founder of Christianity said: "My peace I give unto you: not as the world giveth, give I unto you."

Christian Science reinforces Christ's sayings and doings. The Principle of Christian Science demonstrates peace. Christianity is the chain of scientific being reappearing in all ages, maintaining its obvious correspondence with the Scriptures and uniting all periods in the design of God. The First Commandment in the Hebrew Decalogue — "Thou shalt have no other gods before me" — obeyed, is sufficient to still all strife. God is the divine Mind. Hence the sequence: Had all peoples one Mind, peace would reign.

God is Father, infinite, and this great truth, when understood in its divine metaphysics, will establish the brotherhood of man, end wars, and demonstrate "on earth peace, good will toward men."

[*Christian Science Sentinel*, June 17, 1905]

THE PRAYER FOR PEACE

Dearly Beloved: — I request that every member of The Mother Church of Christ, Scientist, in Boston, pray each day for the amicable settlement of the war between Russia and Japan; and pray that God bless that great nation and those islands of the sea with peace and prosperity.

MARY BAKER EDDY.

PLEASANT VIEW, CONCORD, N. H.,
June 13, 1905.

280 MISCELLANY

Rev. Mary Baker Eddy,
Pleasant View, Concord, N. H.

Beloved Leader: — We acknowledge with rejoicing the receipt of your message, which again gives assurance of your watchful care and guidance in our behalf and of your loving solicitude for the welfare of the nations and the peaceful tranquillity of the race. We rejoice also in this new reminder from you that all the things which make for the establishment of a universal, loving brotherhood on earth may be accomplished through the righteous prayer which availeth much.

William B. Johnson, *Clerk.*
Boston, Mass., June 13, 1905.

[*Christian Science Sentinel*, July 1, 1905]

"Hear, O Israel: The Lord our God is one Lord"

I now request that the members of my church cease special prayer for the peace of nations, and cease in full faith that God does not hear our prayers only because of oft speaking, but that He will bless all the inhabitants of the earth, and none can stay His hand nor say unto Him, What doest Thou? Out of His allness He must bless all with His own truth and love.

Mary Baker Eddy.
Pleasant View, Concord, N. H.,
June 27, 1905.

[*Christian Science Sentinel*, July 22, 1905]

An Explanation

In no way nor manner did I request my church to cease praying for the peace of nations, but simply to pause in special prayer for peace. And why this asking? Because a spiritual foresight of the nations' drama presented itself and awakened a wiser want, even to know how to pray other than the daily prayer of my church, — "Thy kingdom come. Thy will be done in earth, as it is in heaven."

I cited, as our present need, faith in God's disposal of events. Faith full-fledged, soaring to the Horeb height, brings blessings infinite, and the spirit of this orison is the fruit of rightness, — "on earth peace, good will toward men." On this basis the brotherhood of all peoples is established; namely, one God, one Mind, and "Love thy neighbor as thyself," the basis on which and by which the infinite God, good, the Father-Mother Love, is ours and we are His in divine Science.

[*Boston Globe*, August, 1905]

Practise the Golden Rule

[Telegram]

"Official announcement of peace between Russia and Japan seems to offer an appropriate occasion for the expression of congratulations and views by representative persons. Will you do us the kindness to wire a sentiment on some phase of the subject, on the ending of the war, the effect on the two parties to the treaty of Portsmouth, the influence which President Roosevelt has exerted for peace, or the advancement of the cause of arbitration."

MRS. EDDY'S REPLY

To the Editor of the *Globe:*

War will end when nations are ripe for progress. The treaty of Portsmouth is not an executive power, although its purpose is good will towards men. The government of a nation is its peace maker or breaker.

I believe strictly in the Monroe doctrine, in our Constitution, and in the laws of God. While I admire the faith and friendship of our chief executive in and for all nations, my hope must still rest in God, and the Scriptural injunction, — "Look unto me, and be ye saved, all the ends of the earth."

The Douma recently adopted in Russia is no uncertain ray of dawn. Through the wholesome chastisements of Love, nations are helped onward towards justice, righteousness, and peace, which are the landmarks of prosperity. In order to apprehend more, we must practise what we already know of the Golden Rule, which is to all mankind a light emitting light.

MARY BAKER EDDY.

MRS. EDDY AND THE PEACE MOVEMENT

MR. HAYNE DAVIS, American Secretary,
   International Conciliation Committee,
      542 Fifth Avenue, New York City.

Dear Mr. Davis: — Deeply do I thank you for the interest you manifest in the success of the Association for International Conciliation. It is of paramount importance to every son and daughter of all nations under the sunlight of the law and gospel.

May God guide and prosper ever this good endeavor.

                Most truly yours,
                     MARY BAKER EDDY.

PLEASANT VIEW, CONCORD, N. H.,
     April 3, 1907.

Mrs. Eddy's Acknowledgment of Appointment as Fondateur of the Association for International Conciliation

First Church of Christ, Scientist, New York City,
  Mr. John D. Higgins, *Clerk.*

My Beloved Brethren: — Your appointment of me as *Fondateur* of the Association for International Conciliation is most gracious.

To aid in this holy purpose is the leading impetus of my life. Many years have I prayed and labored for the consummation of "on earth peace, good will toward men." May the fruits of said grand Association, pregnant with peace, find their birthright in divine Science.

Right thoughts and deeds are the sovereign remedies for all earth's woe. Sin is its own enemy. Right has its recompense, even though it be betrayed. Wrong may be a man's highest idea of right until his grasp of goodness grows stronger. It is always safe to be just.

When pride, self, and human reason reign, injustice is rampant.

Individuals, as nations, unite harmoniously on the basis of justice, and this is accomplished when self is lost in Love — or God's own plan of salvation. "To do justly, and to love mercy, and to walk humbly" is the standard of Christian Science.

Human law is right only as it patterns the divine. Consolation and peace are based on the enlightened sense of God's government.

Lured by fame, pride, or gold, success is dangerous, but the choice of folly never fastens on the good or the great. Because of my rediscovery of Christian Science, and honest efforts (however meagre) to help human purpose and peoples, you may have accorded me more than is deserved, — but 'tis sweet to be remembered.

Lovingly yours,
MARY BAKER EDDY.

PLEASANT VIEW, CONCORD, N. H.,
April 22, 1907.

[Concord (N. H.) Daily Patriot]

A CORRECTION

Dear Editor: — In the issue of your good paper, the *Patriot*, May 21, when referring to the Memorial service of the E. E. Sturtevant Post held in my church building, it read, "It is said to be the first time in the history of the church in this country that such an event has occurred." In your next issue please correct this mistake. Since my residence in Concord, 1889, the aforesaid Memorial service has been held annually in some church in Concord, N. H.

When the Veterans indicated their desire to assemble in my church building, I consented thereto only as other churches had done. But here let me say that I am absolutely and religiously opposed to war, whereas I do believe implicitly in the full efficacy of divine Love to conciliate by arbitration all quarrels between nations and peoples.

MARY BAKER EDDY.

PLEASANT VIEW, CONCORD, N. H.,
May 28, 1907.

To a Student

Dear Student: — Please accept my thanks for your kind invitation, on behalf of the Civic League of San Francisco, to attend the Industrial Peace Conference, and accept my hearty congratulations.

I cannot spare the time requisite to meet with you; but I rejoice with you in all your wise endeavors for industrial, civic, and national peace. Whatever adorns Christianity crowns the great purposes of life and demonstrates the Science of being. Bloodshed, war, and oppression belong to the darker ages, and shall be relegated to oblivion.

It is a matter for rejoicing that the best, bravest, most cultured men and women of this period unite with us in the grand object embodied in the Association for International Conciliation.

In Revelation 2:26, St. John says: "And he that overcometh, and keepeth my works unto the end, to him will I give power over the nations." In the words of St. Paul, I repeat: —

"And they neither found me in the temple disputing with any man, neither raising up the people, neither in the synagogues, nor in the city: neither can they prove the things whereof they now accuse me. But this I confess unto thee, that after the way which they call heresy, so worship I the God of my fathers, believing all things which are written in the law and in the prophets."

Most sincerely yours,
MARY BAKER EDDY.

PLEASANT VIEW, CONCORD, N. H.

[*The Christian Science Journal*, May, 1908]

WAR

For many years I have prayed daily that there be no more war, no more barbarous slaughtering of our fellow-beings; prayed that all the peoples on earth and the islands of the sea have one God, one Mind; love God supremely, and love their neighbor as themselves.

National disagreements can be, and should be, arbitrated wisely, fairly; and fully settled.

It is unquestionable, however, that at this hour the armament of navies is necessary, for the purpose of preventing war and preserving peace among nations.

CHAPTER XVI

TRIBUTES

[*New York Mail and Express*]

Monument to Baron and Baroness de Hirsch

THE movement to erect a monument to the late Baron and Baroness de Hirsch enlists my hearty sympathy. They were unquestionably used in a remarkable degree as instruments of divine Love.

Divine Love reforms, regenerates, giving to human weakness strength, serving as admonition, instruction, and governing all that really is. Divine Love is the noumenon and phenomenon, the Principle and practice of divine metaphysics. Love talked and not lived is a poor shift for the weak and worldly. Love lived in a court or cot is God exemplified, governing governments, industries, human rights, liberty, life.

In love for man we gain the only and true sense of love for God, practical good, and so rise and still rise to His image and likeness, and are made partakers of that Mind whence springs the universe.

Philanthropy is loving, ameliorative, revolutionary; it wakens lofty desires, new possibilities, achievements, and energies; it lays the axe at the root of the tree that bringeth not forth good fruit; it touches thought to spiritual issues, systematizes action, and insures success;

it starts the wheels of right reason, revelation, justice, and mercy; it unselfs men and pushes on the ages. Love unfolds marvellous good and uncovers hidden evil. The philanthropist or reformer gives little thought to self-defence; his life's incentive and sacrifice need no apology. The good done and the good to do are his ever-present reward.

Love for mankind is the elevator of the human race; it demonstrates Truth and reflects divine Love. Good is divinely natural. Evil is unnatural; it has no origin in the nature of God, and He is the Father of all.

The great Galilean Prophet was, is, the reformer of reformers. His piety partook not of the travesties of human opinions, pagan mysticisms, tribal religion, Greek philosophy, creed, dogma, or *materia medica*. The divine Mind was his only instrumentality in religion or medicine. The so-called laws of matter he eschewed; with him matter was not the auxiliary of Spirit. He never appealed to matter to perform the functions of Spirit, divine Love.

Jesus cast out evil, disease, death, showing that all suffering is commensurate with sin; therefore, he cast out devils and healed the sick. He showed that every effect or amplification of wrong will revert to the wrongdoer; that sin punishes itself; hence his saying, "Sin no more, lest a worse thing come unto thee." Love atones for sin through love that destroys sin. His rod is love.

We cannot remake ourselves, but we can make the best of what God has made. We can know that all is good because God made all, and that evil is not a fatherly grace.

All education is work. The thing most important is
what we do, not what we say. God's open secret is seen
through grace, truth, and love.

I enclose a check for five hundred dollars for the
De Hirsch monument fund.

TRIBUTES TO QUEEN VICTORIA

Mr. William B. Johnson, C.S.B., *Clerk*.

Beloved Student: — I deem it proper that The Mother
Church of Christ, Scientist, in Boston, Massachusetts, the
first church of Christian Science known on earth, should
upon this solemn occasion congregate; that a special meeting of its First Members convene for the sacred purpose of
expressing our deep sympathy with the bereaved nation,
its loss and the world's loss, in the sudden departure of
the late lamented Victoria, Queen of Great Britain and
Empress of India, — long honored, revered, beloved.
"God save the Queen" is heard no more in England, but
this shout of love lives on in the heart of millions.

With love,

MARY BAKER EDDY.

Pleasant View, Concord, N. H.,
January 27, 1901.

It being inconvenient for me to attend the memorial
meeting in the South Congregational church on Sunday
evening, February 3, I herewith send a few words of condolence, which may be read on that tender occasion.

I am interested in a meeting to be held in the capital of my native State *in memoriam* of the late lamented
Victoria, Queen of Great Britain and Empress of India.

It betokens a love and a loss felt by the strong hearts of New England and the United States. When contemplating this sudden international bereavement, the near seems afar, the distant nigh, and the tried and true seem few. The departed Queen's royal and imperial honors lose their lustre in the tomb, but her personal virtues can never be lost. Those live on in the affection of nations.

Few sovereigns have been as venerable, revered, and beloved as this noble woman, born in 1819, married in 1840, and deceased the first month of the new century.

Letter to Mrs. McKinley

My Dear Mrs. McKinley: — My soul reaches out to God for your support, consolation, and victory. Trust in Him whose love enfolds thee. "Thou wilt keep him in perfect peace, whose mind is stayed on Thee: because he trusteth in Thee." "Out of the depths have I cried unto Thee." Divine Love is never so near as when all earthly joys seem most afar.

Thy tender husband, our nation's chief magistrate, has passed earth's shadow into Life's substance. Through a momentary mist he beheld the dawn. He awaits to welcome you where no arrow wounds the eagle soaring, where no partings are for love, where the high and holy call you again to meet.

"I knew that Thou hearest me always," are the words of him who suffered and subdued sorrow. Hold this attitude of mind, and it will remove the sackcloth from thy home.

With love,

MARY BAKER EDDY.

PLEASANT VIEW, CONCORD, N. H.,
September 14, 1901.

Tribute to President McKinley

Imperative, accumulative, holy demands rested on the life and labors of our late beloved President, William McKinley. Presiding over the destinies of a nation meant more to him than a mere rehearsal of aphorisms, a uniting of breaches soon to widen, a quiet assent or dissent. His work began with heavy strokes, measured movements, reaching from the infinitesimal to the infinite. It began by warming the marble of politics into zeal according to wisdom, quenching the volcanoes of partizanship, and uniting the interests of all peoples; and it ended with a universal good overcoming evil.

His home relations enfolded a wealth of affection, — a tenderness not talked but felt and lived. His humanity, weighed in the scales of divinity, was not found wanting. His public intent was uniform, consistent, sympathetic, and so far as it fathomed the abyss of difficulties was wise, brave, unselfed. May his history waken a tone of truth that shall reverberate, renew euphony, emphasize humane power, and bear its banner into the vast forever.

While our nation's ensign of peace and prosperity waves over land and sea, while her reapers are strong, her sheaves garnered, her treasury filled, she is suddenly stricken, — called to mourn the loss of her renowned leader! Tears blend with her triumphs. She stops to think, to mourn, yea, to pray, that the God of harvests send her more laborers, who, while they work for their own country, shall sacredly regard the liberty of other peoples and the rights of man.

What cannot love and righteousness achieve for the race? All that can be accomplished, and more than history has yet recorded. All good that ever was written, taught, or wrought comes from God and human faith in the right. Through divine Love the right government is assimilated, the way pointed out, the process shortened, and the joy of acquiescence consummated. May God sanctify our nation's sorrow in this wise, and His rod and His staff comfort the living as it did the departing. O may His love shield, support, and comfort the chief mourner at the desolate home!

POWER OF PRAYER

My answer to the inquiry, "Why did Christians of every sect in the United States fail in their prayers to save the life of President McKinley," is briefly this: Insufficient faith or spiritual understanding, and a compound of prayers in which one earnest, tender desire works unconsciously against the *modus operandi* of another, would prevent the result desired. In the June, 1901, Message to my church in Boston, I refer to the effect of one human desire or belief unwittingly neutralizing another, though both are equally sincere.

In the practice of *materia medica*, croton oil is not mixed with morphine to remedy dysentery, for those drugs are supposed to possess opposite qualities and so to produce opposite effects. The spirit of the prayer of the righteous heals the sick, but this spirit is of God, and the divine Mind is the same yesterday, to-day, and forever; whereas the human mind is a compound of faith and doubt, of fear and hope, of faith in truth and faith in error.

POWER OF PRAYER

The knowledge that all things are possible to God excludes doubt, but differing human concepts as to the divine power and purpose of infinite Mind, and the so-called power of matter, act as the different properties of drugs are supposed to act — one against the other — and this compound of mind and matter neutralizes itself.

Our lamented President, in his loving acquiescence, believed that his martyrdom was God's way. Hundreds, thousands of others believed the same, and hundreds of thousands who prayed for him feared that the bullet would prove fatal. Even the physicians may have feared this.

These conflicting states of the human mind, of trembling faith, hope, and of fear, evinced a lack of the absolute understanding of God's omnipotence, and thus they prevented the power of absolute Truth from reassuring the mind and through the mind resuscitating the body of the patient.

The divine power and poor human sense — yea, the spirit and the flesh — struggled, and to mortal sense the flesh prevailed. Had prayer so fervently offered possessed no opposing element, and President McKinley's recovery been regarded as wholly contingent on the power of God, — on the power of divine Love to overrule the purposes of hate and the law of Spirit to control matter, — the result would have been scientific, and the patient would have recovered.

St. Paul writes: "For the law of the Spirit of life in Christ Jesus hath made me free from the law of sin and death." And the Saviour of man saith: "What things soever ye desire, when ye pray, believe that ye receive them, and ye shall have them." Human governments maintain the right of the majority to rule. Christian Scientists are yet in a large minority on the subject of divine metaphysics; but they improve the morals and the lives of men, and they heal the sick on the basis that God has all power, is omnipotent, omniscient, omnipresent, supreme over *all*.

In a certain city the Master "did not many mighty works there because of their unbelief," — because of the mental counteracting elements, the startled or the unrighteous contradicting minds of mortals. And if he were personally with us to-day, he would rebuke whatever accords not with a full faith and spiritual knowledge of God. He would mightily rebuke a single doubt of the ever-present power of divine Spirit to control all the conditions of man and the universe.

If the skilful surgeon or the faithful M.D. is not dismayed by a fruitless use of the knife or the drug, has not the Christian Scientist with his conscious understanding of omnipotence, in spite of the constant stress of the hindrances previously mentioned, reason for his faith in what is shown him by God's works?

On the Death of Pope Leo XIII., July 20, 1903

The sad, sudden announcement of the decease of Pope Leo XIII., touches the heart and will move the pen of millions. The intellectual, moral, and religious energy of this illustrious pontiff have animated the Church of Rome for one quarter of a century. The august ruler of two hundred and fifty million human beings has now passed through the shadow of death into the great forever. The court of the Vatican mourns him; his relatives shed "the unavailing tear." He is the loved and lost of many millions. I sympathize with those who mourn, but rejoice in knowing our dear God comforts such with the blessed assurance that life is not lost; its influence remains in the minds of men, and divine Love holds its substance safe in the certainty of immortality. "In Him was life; and the life was the light of men." (John 1:4.)

A Tribute to the Bible

LETTER OF THANKS FOR THE GIFT OF A COPY OF MARTIN LUTHER'S TRANSLATION INTO GERMAN OF THE BIBLE, PRINTED IN NUREMBERG IN 1733

Dear Student: — I am in grateful receipt of your time-worn Bible in German. This Book of books is also the gift of gifts; and kindness in its largest, profoundest sense is goodness. It was kind of you to give it to me. I thank you for it.

Christian Scientists are fishers of men. The Bible is our sea-beaten rock. It guides the fishermen. It stands the storm. It engages the attention and enriches the being of all men.

A Benediction

[Copy of Cablegram]

COUNTESS OF DUNMORE AND FAMILY,
 55 Lancaster Gate, West, London, England.

Divine Love is your ever-present help. You, I, and mankind have cause to lament the demise of Lord Dunmore; but as the Christian Scientist, the servant of God and man, he still lives, loves, labors.

MARY BAKER EDDY.

PLEASANT VIEW, CONCORD, N. H.,
 August 31, 1907.

Hon. Clarence A. Buskirk's Lecture

The able discourse of our "learned judge," his flash of flight and insight, lays the axe "unto the root of the trees," and shatters whatever hinders the Science of being.

MARY BAKER EDDY.

PLEASANT VIEW, CONCORD, N. H.,
October 14, 1907.

"Hear, O Israel"

The late lamented Christian Scientist brother and the publisher of my books, Joseph Armstrong, C.S.D., is not dead, neither does he sleep nor rest from his labors in divine Science; and his works do follow him. Evil has no power to harm, to hinder, or to destroy the real spiritual man. He is wiser to-day, healthier and happier, than yesterday. The mortal dream of life, substance, or mind in matter, has been lessened, and the reward of good and punishment of evil and the waking out of his Adam-dream of evil will end in harmony, — evil powerless, and God, good, omnipotent and infinite.

MARY BAKER EDDY.

PLEASANT VIEW, CONCORD, N. H.,
December 10, 1907.

Miss Clara Barton

In the *New York American*, January 6, 1908, Miss Clara Barton dipped her pen in my heart, and traced its emotions, motives, and object. Then, lifting the curtains of mortal mind, she depicted its rooms, guests, standing and seating capacity, and thereafter gave her discovery to the press. Now if Miss Barton were not a venerable soldier, patriot, philanthropist, moralist, and stateswoman, I should shrink from such salient praise. But in consideration of all that Miss Barton really is, and knowing that she can bear the blows which may follow said description of her soul-visit, I will say, Amen, so be it.

MARY BAKER EDDY.

PLEASANT VIEW, CONCORD, N. H.,
    January 10, 1908.

THERE IS NO DEATH

A suppositional gust of evil in this evil world is the dark hour that precedes the dawn. This gust blows away the baubles of belief, for there is in reality no evil, no disease, no death; and the Christian Scientist who believes that he dies, gains a rich blessing of disbelief in death, and a higher realization of heaven.

My beloved Edward A. Kimball, whose clear, correct teaching of Christian Science has been and is an inspiration to the whole field, is here now as veritably as when he visited me a year ago. If we would awaken to this recognition, we should see him here and realize that he never died; thus demonstrating the fundamental truth of Christian Science.

MARY BAKER EDDY.

MRS. EDDY'S HISTORY

I have not had sufficient interest in the matter to read or to note from others' reading what the enemies of Christian Science are said to be circulating regarding my history, but my friends have read Sibyl Wilbur's book,

"The Life of Mary Baker Eddy," and request the privilege of buying, circulating, and recommending it to the public. I briefly declare that nothing has occurred in my life's experience which, if correctly narrated and understood, could injure me; and not a little is already reported of the good accomplished therein, the self-sacrifice, *etc.*, that has distinguished all my working years.

I thank Miss Wilbur and the Concord Publishing Company for their unselfed labors in placing this book before the public, and hereby say that they have my permission to publish and circulate this work.

MARY BAKER EDDY.

CHAPTER XVII

ANSWERS TO CRITICISMS

[Letter to the *New York Commercial Advertiser*]

CHRISTIAN SCIENCE AND THE CHURCH

OVER the signature "A Priest of the Church," somebody, kindly referring to my address to First Church of Christ, Scientist, in Concord, N. H., writes: "If they [Christian Scientists] have any truth to reveal which has not been revealed by the church or the Bible, let them make it known to the world, before they claim the allegiance of mankind."

I submit that Christian Science has been widely made known to the world, and that it contains the entire truth of the Scriptures, as also whatever portions of truth may be found in creeds. In addition to this, Christian Science presents the demonstrable divine Principle and rules of the Bible, hitherto undiscovered in the translations of the Bible and lacking in the creeds.

Therefore I query: Do Christians, who believe in sin, and especially those who claim to pardon sin, believe that God is good, and that God is *All?* Christian Scientists firmly subscribe to this statement; yea, they understand it and the law governing it, namely, that God, the divine Principle of Christian Science, is "of purer eyes than to behold evil." On this basis they endeavor to cast out the belief in sin or in aught besides God, thus enabling the sinner to overcome sin according to the Scripture, "Work out your own salvation with fear and trembling. For it is God which worketh in you both to will and to do of His good pleasure."

Does he who believes in sickness know or declare that there is no sickness or disease, and thus heal disease? Christian Scientists, who do not believe in the reality of disease, heal disease, for the reason that the divine Principle of Christian Science, demonstrated, heals the most inveterate diseases. Does he who believes in death understand or aver that there is no death, and proceed to overcome "the last enemy" and raise the dying to health? Christian Scientists raise the dying to health in Christ's name, and are striving to reach the summit of Jesus' words, "If a man keep my saying, he shall never see death."

If, as this kind priest claims, these things, inseparable from Christian Science, are common to his church, we propose that he make known his doctrine to the world, that he teach the Christianity which heals, and send out students according to Christ's command, "Go ye into all the world, and preach the gospel to every creature," "Heal the sick, cleanse the lepers, raise the dead, cast out devils."

The tree is known by its fruit. If, as he implies, Christian Science is not a departure from the first century churches,—as surely it is not,—why persecute it? Are the churches opening fire on their own religious ranks, or are they attacking a peaceable party quite their antipode? Christian Science is a reflected glory; it shines with borrowed rays — from Light emitting light. Christian Science is the new-old Christianity, that which was and is the revelation of divine Love.

The present flux in religious faith may be found to be a healthy fermentation, by which the lees of religion will be lost, dogma and creed will pass off in scum, leaving a solid Christianity at the bottom — a foundation for the builders. I would that all the churches on earth could unite as brethren in one prayer: Father, teach us the life of Love.

PLEASANT VIEW, CONCORD, N. H.,
    March 22, 1899.

[Letter to the *New York World*]

FAITH IN METAPHYSICS

Is faith in divine metaphysics insanity?

All sin is insanity, but healing the sick is *not* sin. There is a universal insanity which mistakes fable for fact throughout the entire testimony of the material senses. Those unfortunate people who are committed to insane asylums are only so many well-defined instances of the baneful effects of illusion on mortal minds and bodies. The supposition that we can correct insanity by the use of drugs is in itself a species of insanity. A drug cannot of itself go to the brain or affect cerebral conditions in any manner whatever. Drugs cannot remove inflammation, restore disordered functions, or destroy disease without the aid of mind.

If mind be absent from the body, drugs can produce no curative effect upon the body. The mind must be, is, the vehicle of all modes of healing disease and of producing disease. Through the mandate of mind or according to a man's belief, can he be helped or be killed by a drug; but mind, not matter, produces the result in either case.

Neither life nor death, health nor disease, can be produced on a corpse, whence mind has departed. This self-evident fact is proof that mind is the cause of all effect made manifest through so-called matter. The general craze is that matter masters mind; the specific insanity is that brain, matter, is insane.

[Letter to the *New York Herald*]

Reply to Mark Twain

It is a fact well understood that I begged the students who first gave me the endearing appellative "Mother," not to name me thus. But without my consent, the use of the word spread like wildfire. I still must think the name is not applicable to me. I stand in relation to this century as a Christian Discoverer, Founder, and Leader. I regard self-deification as blasphemous. I may be more loved, but I am less lauded, pampered, provided for, and cheered than others before me — and wherefore? Because Christian Science is not yet popular, and I refuse adulation.

My first visit to The Mother Church after it was built and dedicated pleased me, and the situation was satisfactory. The dear members wanted to greet me with escort and the ringing of bells, but I declined and went alone in my carriage to the church, entered it, and knelt in thanks upon the steps of its altar. There the foresplendor of the beginnings of truth fell mysteriously upon my spirit. I believe in one Christ, teach one Christ, know of but one Christ. I believe in but one incarnation, one Mother Mary. I know that I am not that one, and I have never claimed to be. It suffices me to learn the Science of the Scriptures relative to this subject.

Christian Scientists have no quarrel with Protestants, Catholics, or any other sect. Christian Scientists need to be understood as following the divine Principle — God, Love — and not imagined to be unscientific worshippers of a human being.

In his article, of which I have seen only extracts, Mark Twain's wit was not wasted in certain directions. Christian Science eschews divine rights in human beings. If the individual governed human consciousness, my statement of Christian Science would be disproved; but to demonstrate Science and its pure monotheism — one God, one Christ, no idolatry, no human propaganda — it is essential to understand the spiritual idea. Jesus taught and proved that what feeds a few feeds all. His life-work subordinated the material to the spiritual, and he left his legacy of truth to mankind. His metaphysics is not the sport of philosophy, religion, or science; rather is it the pith and finale of them all.

I have not the inspiration nor the aspiration to be a first or second Virgin-mother — her duplicate, antecedent, or subsequent. What I am remains to be proved by the good I do. We need much humility, wisdom, and love to perform the functions of foreshadowing and foretasting heaven within us. This glory is molten in the furnace of affliction.

[*Boston Journal*, June 8, 1903]

A MISSTATEMENT CORRECTED

I was early a pupil of Miss Sarah J. Bodwell, the principal of Sanbornton Academy, New Hampshire, and finished my course of studies under Professor Dyer H. Sanborn, author of Sanborn's Grammar. Among my early studies were Comstock's Natural Philosophy, Chemistry, Blair's Rhetoric, Whateley's Logic, Watt's "On the Mind and Moral Science." At sixteen years of age, I began writing for the leading newspapers, and for many years I wrote for the best magazines in the South and North. I have lectured in large and crowded halls in New York City, Chicago, Boston, Portland, and at Waterville College, and have been invited to lecture in London, England, and Edinburgh, Scotland. In 1883, I started *The Christian Science Journal*, and for several years was the proprietor and sole editor of that periodical. In 1893, Judge S. J. Hanna became editor of *The Christian Science Journal*, and for ten subsequent years he knew my ability as an editor. In a lecture in Chicago, he said: "Mrs. Eddy is from every point of view a woman of sound education and liberal culture."

Agassiz, the celebrated naturalist and author, wisely said: "Every great scientific truth goes through three stages. First, people say it conflicts with the Bible. Next, they say it has been discovered before. Lastly, they say they have always believed it."

The first attack upon me was: Mrs. Eddy misinterprets the Scriptures; second, she has stolen the contents of her book, "Science and Health with Key to the Scriptures,"

A PLEA FOR JUSTICE

from one P. P. Quimby (an obscure, uneducated man), and that he is the founder of Christian Science. Failing in these attempts, the calumniator has resorted to Ralph Waldo Emerson's philosophy as the authority for Christian Science! Lastly, the defamer will declare as honestly (?), "I have always known it."

In Science and Health, page 68, third paragraph, I briefly express myself unmistakably on the subject of "vulgar metaphysics," and the manuscripts and letters in my possession, which "vulgar" defamers have circulated, stand in evidence. People do not know who is referred to as "an ignorant woman in New Hampshire." Many of the nation's best and most distinguished men and women were natives of the Granite State.

I am the author of the Christian Science textbook, "Science and Health with Key to the Scriptures;" and the demand for this book constantly increases. I am rated in the *National Magazine* (1903) as "standing eighth in a list of twenty-two of the foremost living authors."

I claim no special merit of any kind. All that I am in reality, God has made me. I still wait at the cross to learn definitely more from my great Master, but not of the Greek nor of the Roman schools — simply how to do his works.

A Plea for Justice

My recent reply to the reprint of a scandal in the *Literary Digest* was not a question of "Who shall be greatest?" but of "Who shall be just?" Who is or is not the founder of Christian Science was not the trend of thought, but my purpose was to lift the curtain on wrong, on falsehood which persistently misrepresents my character, education, and authorship, and attempts to narrow my life into a conflict for fame.

Far be it from me to tread on the ashes of the dead or to dissever any unity that may exist between Christian Science and the philosophy of a great and good man, for such was Ralph Waldo Emerson; and I deem it unwise to enter into a newspaper controversy over a question that is no longer a question. The false should be antagonized only for the purpose of making the true apparent. I have quite another purpose in life than to be thought great. Time and goodness determine greatness. The greatest reform, with almost unutterable truths to translate, must wait to be transfused into the practical and to be understood in the "new tongue." Age, with experience-acquired patience and unselfed love, waits on God. Human merit or demerit will find its proper level. Divinity alone solves the problem of humanity, and that in God's own time. "By their fruits ye shall know them."

Reminiscences

In 1862, when I first visited Dr. Quimby of Portland, Me., his scribblings were descriptions of his patients, and these comprised the manuscripts which in 1887 I advertised that I would pay for having published. Before his decease, in January, 1866, Dr. Quimby had tried to get them published and had failed.

Quotations have been published, purporting to be Dr. Quimby's own words, which were written while I was his patient in Portland and holding long conversations with him on my views of mental therapeutics. Some words in these quotations certainly read like words that I said to him, and which I, at his request, had added to his copy when I corrected it. In his conversations with me and in his scribblings, the word science was not used at all, till one day I declared to him that back of his magnetic treatment and manipulation of patients, there was a science, and it was the science of mind, which had nothing to do with matter, electricity, or physics.

After this I noticed he used that word, as well as other terms which I employed that seemed at first new to him. He even acknowledged this himself, and startled me by saying what I cannot forget — it was this: "I see now what you mean, and I see that I am John, and that you are Jesus."

At that date I was a staunch orthodox, and my theological belief was offended by his saying and I entered a demurrer which rebuked him. But afterwards I concluded that he only referred to the *coming* anew of Truth, which we both desired; for in some respects he was quite a seer and understood what I said better than some others did. For one so unlearned, he was a remarkable man. Had his remark related to my personality, I should still think that it was profane.

At first my case improved wonderfully under his treatment, but it relapsed. I was gradually emerging from *materia medica*, dogma, and creeds, and drifting whither I knew not. This mental struggle might have caused my illness. The fallacy of *materia medica*, its lack of science, and the want of divinity in scholastic theology, had already dawned on me. My idealism, however, limped, for then it lacked Science. But the divine Love will accomplish what all the powers of earth combined can never prevent being accomplished — the advent of divine healing and its divine Science.

Reply to McClure's Magazine

It is calumny on Christian Science to say that man is aroused to thought or action only by ease, pleasure, or recompense. Something higher, nobler, more imperative impels the impulse of Soul.

It becomes my duty to be just to the departed and to tread not ruthlessly on their ashes. The attack on me and my late father and his family in *McClure's Magazine*, January, 1907, compels me as a dutiful child and the Leader of Christian Science to speak.

McClure's Magazine refers to my father's "tall, gaunt frame" and pictures "the old man tramping doggedly along the highway, regularly beating the ground with a huge walking-stick." My father's person was erect and robust. He never used a walking-stick. To illustrate: One time when my father was visiting Governor Pierce, President Franklin Pierce's father, the Governor handed him a gold-headed walking-stick as they were about to start for church. My father thanked the Governor, but declined to accept the stick, saying, "I never use a cane."

Although *McClure's Magazine* attributes to my father language unseemly, his household law, constantly enforced, was no profanity and no slang phrases. *McClure's Magazine* also declares that the Bible was the only book in his house. On the contrary, my father was a great reader. The man whom *McClure's Magazine* characterizes as "ignorant, dominating, passionate, fearless," was uniformly dignified — a well-informed, intellectual man, cultivated in mind and manners. He was called upon to do much business for his town, making out deeds, settling quarrels, and even acting as counsel in a lawsuit involving a question of pauperism between the towns of Loudon and Bow, N. H. Franklin Pierce, afterwards President of the United States, was the counsel for Loudon and Mark Baker for Bow. Both entered their pleas, and my father won the suit. After it was decided, Mr. Pierce bowed to my father and congratulated him. For several years father was chaplain of the New Hampshire State Militia, and as I recollect it, he was justice of the peace at one time. My father was a strong believer in States' rights, but slavery he regarded as a great sin.

Mark Baker was the youngest of his father's family, and inherited his father's real estate, an extensive farm situated in Bow and Concord, N. H. It is on record that Mark Baker's father paid the largest tax in the colony. *McClure's Magazine* says, describing the Baker homestead at Bow: "The house itself was a small, square box building of rudimentary architecture." My father's house had a sloping roof, after the prevailing style of architecture at that date.

McClure's Magazine states: "Alone of the Bakers, he [Albert] received a liberal education. . . . Mary Baker passed her first fifteen years at the ancestral home at Bow. It was a lonely and unstimulating existence. The church supplied the only social diversions, the district school practically all the intellectual life."

Let us see what were the fruits of this "lonely and

unstimulating existence." All my father's daughters were given an academic education, sufficiently advanced so that they all taught school acceptably at various times and places. My brother Albert was a distinguished lawyer. In addition to my academic training, I was privately tutored by him. He was a member of the New Hampshire Legislature, and was nominated for Congress, but died before the election. *McClure's Magazine* calls my youngest brother, George Sullivan Baker, "a workman in a Tilton woolen mill." As a matter of fact, he was joint partner with Alexander Tilton, and together they owned a large manufacturing establishment in Tilton, N. H. His military title of Colonel came from appointment on the staff of the Governor of New Hampshire. My oldest brother, Samuel D. Baker, carried on a large business in Boston, Mass.

Regarding the allegation by *McClure's Magazine* that all the family, "excepting Albert, died of cancer," I will say that there was never a death in my father's family reported by physician or post-mortem examination as caused by cancer.

McClure's Magazine says that "the quarrels between Mary, a child ten years old, and her father, a gray-haired man of fifty, frequently set the house in an uproar," and adds that these "fits" were diagnosed by Dr. Ladd as "hysteria mingled with bad temper." My mother often presented my disposition as exemplary for her other children to imitate, saying, "When do you ever see Mary angry?" When the first edition of Science and Health was published, Dr. Ladd said to Alexander Tilton: "Read it, for it will do you good. It does not surprise me, it so resembles the author."

I will relate the following incident, which occurred later in life, as illustrative of my disposition: —

While I was living with Dr. Patterson at his country home in North Groton, N. H., a girl, totally blind, knocked at the door and was admitted. She begged to be allowed to remain with me, and my tenderness and sympathy were such that I could not refuse her. Shortly after, however, my good housekeeper said to me: "If this blind girl stays with you, I shall have to leave; she troubles me so much." It was not in my heart to turn the blind girl out, and so I lost my housekeeper.

My reply to the statement that the clerk's book shows that I joined the Tilton Congregational Church at the age of seventeen is that my religious experience seemed to culminate at twelve years of age. Hence a mistake may have occurred as to the exact date of my first church membership.

The facts regarding the McNeil coat-of-arms are as follows: —

Fanny McNeil, President Pierce's niece, afterwards Mrs. Judge Potter, presented me my coat-of-arms, saying that it was taken in connection with her own family coat-of-arms. I never doubted the veracity of her gift. I have another coat-of-arms, which is of my mother's ancestry. When I was last in Washington, D. C., Mrs. Judge Potter and myself knelt in silent prayer on the mound of her late father, General John McNeil, the hero of Lundy Lane.

Notwithstanding that *McClure's Magazine* says, "Mary Baker completed her education when she finished Smith's grammar and reached long division in arithmetic," I was called by the Rev. R. S. Rust, D.D., Principal of the

Methodist Conference Seminary at Sanbornton Bridge, to supply the place of his leading teacher during her temporary absence.

Regarding my first marriage and the tragic death of my husband, *McClure's Magazine* says: "He [George Washington Glover] took his bride to Wilmington, South Carolina, and in June, 1844, six months after his marriage, he died of yellow fever. He left his young wife in a miserable plight. She was far from home and entirely without money or friends. Glover, however, was a Free Mason, and thus received a decent burial. The Masons also paid Mrs. Glover's fare to New York City, where she was met and taken to her father's home by her brother George. . . . Her position was an embarrassing one. She was a grown woman, with a child, but entirely without means of support. . . . Mrs. Glover made only one effort at self-support. For a brief season she taught school."

My first husband, Major George W. Glover, resided in Charleston, S. C. While on a business trip to Wilmington, N. C., he was suddenly seized with yellow fever and died in about nine days. I was with him on this trip. He took with him the usual amount of money he would need on such an excursion. At his decease I was surrounded by friends, and their provisions in my behalf were most tender. The Governor of the State and his staff, with a long procession, followed the remains of my beloved one to the cemetery. The Free Masons selected my escort, who took me to my father's home in Tilton, N. H. My salary for writing gave me ample support. I did open an infant school, but it was for the purpose of starting that educational system in New Hampshire.

The rhyme attributed to me by *McClure's Magazine* is

not mine, but is, I understand, a paraphrase of a silly song of years ago. Correctly quoted, it is as follows, so I have been told: —

> Go to Jane Glover,
> Tell her I love her;
> By the light of the moon
> I will go to her.

The various stories told by *McClure's Magazine* about my father spreading the road in front of his house with tan-bark and straw, and about persons being hired to rock me, I am ignorant of. Nor do I remember any such stuff as Dr. Patterson driving into Franklin, N. H., with a couch or cradle for me in his wagon. I only know that my father and mother did everything they could think of to help me when I was ill.

I was never "given to long and lonely wanderings, especially at night," as stated by *McClure's Magazine*. I was always accompanied by some responsible individual when I took an evening walk, but I seldom took one. I have always consistently declared that I was not a medium for spirits. I never was especially interested in the Shakers, never "dabbled in mesmerism," never was "an amateur clairvoyant," nor did "the superstitious country folk frequently" seek my advice. I never went into a trance to describe scenes far away, as *McClure's Magazine* says.

My oldest sister dearly loved me, but I wounded her pride when I adopted Christian Science, and to a Baker that was a sorry offence. I was obliged to be parted from my son, because after my father's second marriage my little boy was not welcome in my father's house.

McClure's Magazine calls Dr. Daniel Patterson, my second husband, "an itinerant dentist." It says that after my marriage we "lived for a short time at Tilton, then moved to Franklin. . . . During the following nine years the Pattersons led a roving existence. The doctor practised in several towns, from Tilton to North Groton and then to Rumney." When I was married to him, Dr. Daniel Patterson was located in Franklin, N. H. He had the degree D.D.S., was a popular man, and considered a rarely skilful dentist. He bought a place in North Groton, which he fancied, for a summer home. At that time he owned a house in Franklin, N. H.

Although, as *McClure's Magazine* claims, the court record may state that my divorce from Dr. Patterson was granted on the ground of desertion, the cause nevertheless was adultery. Individuals are here to-day who were present in court when the decision was given by the judge and who know the following facts: After the evidence had been submitted that a husband was about to have Dr. Patterson arrested for eloping with his wife, the court instructed the clerk to record the divorce in my favor. What prevented Dr. Patterson's arrest was a letter from me to this self-same husband, imploring him not to do it. When this husband recovered his wife, he kept her a prisoner in her home, and I was also the means of reconciling the couple. A Christian Scientist has told me that with tears of gratitude the wife of this husband related these facts to her just as I have stated them. I lived with Dr. Patterson peaceably, and he was kind to me up to the time of the divorce.

The following affidavit by R. D. Rounsevel of Littleton, N. H., proprietor of the White Mountain House, Fabyans,

REPLY TO McCLURE'S MAGAZINE

N. H., the original of which is in my possession, is of interest in this connection: —

About the year 1874, Dr. Patterson, a dentist, boarded with me in Littleton, New Hampshire. During his stay, at different times, I had conversation with him about his wife, from whom he was separated. He spoke of her being a pure and Christian woman, and the cause of the separation being wholly on his part; that if he had done as he ought, he might have had as pleasant and happy home as one could wish for.

At that time I had no knowledge of who his wife was. Later on I learned that Mary Baker G. Eddy, the Discoverer and Founder of Christian Science, was the above-mentioned woman.

(Signed) R. D. ROUNSEVEL.

Grafton S. S. Jan'y, 1902. Then personally appeared R. D. Rounsevel and made oath that the within statement by him signed is true.

Before me, (Signed) H. M. MORSE,
Justice of the Peace.

Who or what is the *McClure* "history," so called, presenting? Is it myself, the veritable Mrs. Eddy, whom the *New York World* declared dying of cancer, or is it her alleged double or dummy heretofore described?

If indeed it be I, allow me to thank the enterprising historians for the testimony they have thereby given of the divine power of Christian Science, which they admit has snatched me from the *cradle* and the grave, and made me the beloved Leader of millions of the good men and women in our own and in other countries, — and all this because the truth I have promulgated has separated the tares from the wheat, uniting in one body those who love Truth; because Truth divides between sect and Science and renews the heavenward impulse; because I still hear the harvest song of the Redeemer awakening the nations, causing man to love his enemies; because "blessed are ye, when men shall revile you, and persecute you, and shall say all manner of evil against you falsely, for my sake."

[*Christian Science Sentinel*, January 19, 1907]

A CARD

The article in the January number of *The Arena* magazine, entitled "The Recent Reckless and Irresponsible Attacks on Christian Science and its Founder, with a Survey of the Christian Science Movement," by the scholarly editor, Mr. B. O. Flower, is a grand defence of our Cause and its Leader. Such a dignified, eloquent appeal to the press in behalf of common justice and truth demands public attention. It defends human rights and the freedom of Christian sentiments, and tends to turn back the foaming torrents of ignorance, envy, and malice. I am pleased to find this "twentieth-century review of opinion" once more under Mr. Flower's able guardianship and manifesting its unbiased judgment by such sound appreciation of the rights of Christian Scientists and of all that is right.

MARY BAKER EDDY.

CHAPTER XVIII

AUTHORSHIP OF SCIENCE AND HEALTH

THE following statement, which was published in the *Sentinel* of December 1, 1906, exactly defining her relations with the Rev. James Henry Wiggin of Boston, was made by Mrs. Eddy in refutation of allegations in the public press to the effect that Mr. Wiggin had a share in the authorship of "Science and Health with Key to the Scriptures."

MRS. EDDY'S STATEMENT

It is a great mistake to say that I employed the Rev. James Henry Wiggin to correct my diction. It was for no such purpose. I engaged Mr. Wiggin so as to avail myself of his criticisms of my statement of Christian Science, which criticisms would enable me to explain more clearly the points that might seem ambiguous to the reader.

Mr. Calvin A. Frye copied my writings, and he will tell you that Mr. Wiggin left my diction quite out of the question, sometimes saying, "I wouldn't express it that way." He often dissented from what I had written, but I quieted him by quoting corroborative texts of Scripture.

My diction, as used in explaining Christian Science, has been called original. The liberty that I have taken with capitalization, in order to express the "new tongue," has well-nigh constituted a new style of language. In almost every case where Mr. Wiggin added words, I have erased them in my revisions.

Mr. Wiggin was not my proofreader for my book "Miscellaneous Writings," and for only two of my books. I especially employed him on "Science and Health with Key to the Scriptures," because at that date some critics declared that my book was as ungrammatical as it was misleading. I availed myself of the name of the former proofreader for the University Press, Cambridge, to defend my grammatical construction, and confidently awaited the years to declare the moral and spiritual effect upon the age of "Science and Health with Key to the Scriptures."

I invited Mr. Wiggin to visit one of my classes in the Massachusetts Metaphysical College, and he consented on condition that I should not ask him any questions. I agreed not to question him just so long as he refrained from questioning me. He held himself well in check until I began my attack on agnosticism. As I proceeded, Mr. Wiggin manifested more and more agitation, until he could control himself no longer and, addressing me, burst out with:

"How do you know that there ever was such a man as Christ Jesus?"

He would have continued with a long argument, framed from his ample fund of historical knowledge, but I stopped him.

"Now, Mr. Wiggin," I said, "you have broken our agreement. I do not find my authority for Christian Science in history, but in revelation. If there had never

AUTHORSHIP OF SCIENCE AND HEALTH

existed such a person as the Galilean Prophet, it would make no difference to me. I should still know that God's spiritual ideal is the only real man in His image and likeness."

My saying touched him, and I heard nothing further from him in the class, though afterwards he wrote a kind little pamphlet, signed "Phare Pleigh."

I hold the late Mr. Wiggin in loving, grateful memory for his high-principled character and well-equipped scholarship.

LETTERS FROM STUDENTS

The following letters from students of Mrs. Eddy confirm her statement regarding the work which the Rev. Mr. Wiggin did for her, and also indicate what he himself thought of that work and of Mrs. Eddy: —

My Dear Teacher: — I am conversant with some facts which perhaps have not come under the observation of many of your students, and considering the questions which have recently appeared, it may interest you to be advised that I have this information. On the tenth day of January, 1887, I entered your Primary class at Boston. A few days later, in conversation with you about the preparation of a theme, you suggested that I call on the late J. Henry Wiggin to assist me in analyzing and arranging the topics, which I did about the twentieth of the above-named month. These dates are very well fixed in my memory, as I considered the time an important one in my experience, and do so still. I also recall very plainly the conversation with you in general as regards Mr. Wiggin. You told me that he had done some literary work for you and that he was a fine literary student and a good proofreader.

Upon calling on Mr. Wiggin, I presented my matter for a theme to him, and he readily consented to assist me, which he did. He also seemed very much pleased to converse about you and your work, and I found that his statement of what he had done for you exactly agreed with what you had told me. He also expressed himself freely as to his high regard for you as a Christian lady, as an author, and as a student of ability. Mr. Wiggin spoke of "Science and Health with Key to the Scriptures" as being a very unique book, and seemed quite proud of his having had something to do with some editions. He always spoke of you as the author of this book and the author of all your works. Mr. Wiggin did not claim to be a Christian Scientist, but was in a measure in sympathy with the movement, although he did not endorse all the statements in your textbook; but his tendency was friendly.

I called on Mr. Wiggin several times while I was in your Primary class at the time above referred to, and several times subsequent thereto, and he always referred to you as the author of your works and spoke of your ability without any hesitation or restriction. Our conversations were at times somewhat long and went into matters of detail regarding your work, and I am of the opinion that he was proud of his acquaintance with you.

I saw Mr. Wiggin several times after the class closed, and the last conversation I had with him was at the time of the dedication of the first Mother Church edifice in 1895. I met him in the vestibule of the church and he spoke in a very animated manner of your

AUTHORSHIP OF SCIENCE AND HEALTH

grand demonstration in building this church for your followers. He seemed very proud to think that he had been in a way connected with your work, but he always referred to you as the one who had accomplished this great work.

My recollections of Mr. Wiggin place him as one of your devoted and faithful friends, one who knew who and what you are, also your position as regards your published works; and he always gave you that position without any restriction. I believe that Mr. Wiggin was an honest man and that he told the same story to every one with whom he had occasion to talk, so I cannot believe that he has ever said anything whatever of you and your relations to your published works differing from what he talked so freely in my presence.

There is nothing in the circumstances which have arisen recently, and the manner in which the statements have been made, to change my opinion one iota in this respect.

It will soon be twenty years since I first saw you and entered your class. During that time, from my connection with the church, the Publishing Society, and my many conversations with you, my personal knowledge of the authorship of your works is conclusive to me in every detail, and I am very glad that I was among your early students and have had this experience and know of my own personal knowledge what has transpired during the past twenty years.

I am also pleased to have had conversations with people who knew you years before I did, and who have told me of their knowledge of your work.

It is not long since I met a lady who lived in Lynn, and she told me she knew you when you were writing Science and Health, and that she had seen the manuscript. These are facts which cannot be controverted and they must stand.

> Your affectionate student,
> EDWARD P. BATES.

BOSTON, MASS., November 21, 1906.

My Beloved Teacher: — I have just read your statement correcting mistakes widely published about the Rev. James H. Wiggin's work for and attitude towards you; also Mr. Edward P. Bates' letter to you on the same subject; which reminds me of a conversation I had with Mr. Wiggin on Thanksgiving Day twenty years ago, when a friend and I were the guests invited to dine with the Wiggin family.

I had seen you the day before at the Metaphysical College and received your permission to enter the next Primary class (Jan. 10, 1887). During the evening my friend spoke of my journeying from the far South, and waiting months in Boston on the bare hope of a few days' instruction by Mrs. Eddy in Christian Science. She and Mrs. Wiggin seemed inclined to banter me on such enthusiasm, but Mr. Wiggin kindly helped me by advancing many good points in the Science, which were so clearly stated that I was surprised when he told me he was not a Christian Scientist.

Seeing my great interest in the subject, he told me of his acquaintance with you and spoke earnestly and beautifully of you and your work. The exact words I do not recall, but the impression he left with me was

AUTHORSHIP OF SCIENCE AND HEALTH

entirely in accordance with what Mr. Bates has so well written in the above-mentioned letter. Before we left that evening, Mr. Wiggin gave me a pamphlet entitled "Christian Science and the Bible," by "Phare Pleigh," which he said he had written in answer to an unfair criticism of you and your book by some minister in the far West. I have his little book yet. How long must it be before the people find out that you have so identified yourself with the truth by loving it and living it that you are not going to lie about anything nor willingly leave any false impression.

In loving gratitude for your living witness to Truth and Love,
FLORENCE WHITESIDE.

CHATTANOOGA, TENN.,
December 4, 1906.

Beloved Teacher: — My heart has been too full to tell you in words all that your wonderful life and sacrifice means to me. Neither do I now feel at all equal to expressing the crowding thoughts of gratitude and praise to God for giving this age such a Leader and teacher to reveal to us His way. Your crowning triumph over error and sin, which we have so recently witnessed, in blessing those who would destroy you if God did not hold you up by the right hand of His righteousness, should mean to your older students much that they may not have been able to appreciate in times past.

I wonder if you will remember that Mr. Snider and myself boarded in the home of the late Rev. J. Henry Wiggin during the time of our studying in the second class with you — the Normal class in the fall of 1887? We were at that time some eight days in Mr. and Mrs.

Wiggin's home. He often spoke his thoughts freely about you and your work, especially your book Science and Health. Mr. Wiggin had somewhat of a thought of contempt for the unlearned, and he scorned the suggestion that Mr. Quimby had given you any idea for your book, as he said you and your ideas were too much alike for the book to have come from any one but yourself. He often said you were so original and so very decided that no one could be of much service to you, and he often hinted that he thought he could give a clearer nomenclature for Science and Health. I remember telling you of this, and you explained how long you had waited on the Lord to have those very terms revealed to you.

I am very sure that neither Mr. Wiggin nor his estimable wife had any other thought but that you were the author of your book, and were he here to-day he would be too honorable to allow the thought to go out that he had helped you write it. He certainly never gave us the impression that he thought you needed help, for we always thought that Mr. Wiggin regarded you as quite his literary equal, and was gratified and pleased in numbering you among his literary friends. Everything he said conveyed this impression to us — that he regarded you as entirely unique and original. He told us laughingly why he accepted your invitation to sit through your class. He said he wanted to see if there was one woman under the sun who could keep to her text. When we asked him if he found you could do so, he replied "Yes," and said that no man could have done so any better.

Both Mr. and Mrs. Wiggin frequently mentioned

many kindnesses you had shown them, and spoke of one especial day when amidst all your duties you personally called to inquire of his welfare (he had been ill) and to leave luscious hothouse fruit. One thing more, that I think will amuse you: Mr. Wiggin was very much troubled that you had bought your house on Commonwealth Avenue, as he was very sure Back Bay property would never be worth what you then paid for it. He regarded the old part of Boston in which he lived as having a greater future than the new Back Bay.

Years ago I offered my services to you in any capacity in which I could serve you, and my desire has never changed. Command me at any time, in any way, beloved Leader.

With increasing love and gratitude, ever faithfully your student,

CARRIE HARVEY SNIDER.

NEW YORK, N. Y.,
    December 7, 1906.

CHAPTER XIX

[The Christian Science Journal]

A MEMORABLE COINCIDENCE AND HISTORICAL FACTS

WE are glad to publish the following interesting letter and enclosures received from our Leader. That legislatures and courts are thus declaring the liberties of Christian Scientists is most gratifying to our people; not because a favor has been extended, but because their inherent rights are recognized in an official and authoritative manner. It is especially gratifying to them that the declaration of this recognition should be coincident in the Southern and Northern States in which Mrs. Eddy has made her home.

Mrs. Eddy's Letter

Dear Editor: — I send for publication in our periodicals the following deeply interesting letter from Elizabeth Earl Jones of Asheville, N. C., — the State where my husband, Major George W. Glover, passed on and up, the State that so signally honored his memory, where with wet eyes the Free Masons laid on his bier the emblems of a master Mason, and in long procession with tender dirge bore his remains to their last resting-place. Deeply grateful, I recognize the divine hand in turning the hearts of the noble

Southrons of North Carolina legally to protect the practice of Christian Science in that State.

Is it not a memorable coincidence that, in the Court of New Hampshire, my native State, and in the Legislature of North Carolina, they have the same year, in 1903, made it legal to practise Christian Science in these States?

MARY BAKER EDDY.

PLEASANT VIEW, CONCORD, N. H.,
October 16, 1903.

MISS ELIZABETH EARL JONES' LETTER

Beloved Leader: — I know the enclosed article will make your heart glad, as it has made glad the hearts of all the Christian Scientists in North Carolina. This is the result of the work done at last winter's term of our Legislature, when a medical bill was proposed calculated to limit or stop the practice of Christian Science in our State. An amendment was obtained by Miss Mary Hatch Harrison and a few other Scientists who stayed on the field until the last. After the amendment had been passed, an old law, or rather a section of an act in the Legislature regulating taxes, was changed as follows, because the representative men of our dear State did not wish to be "discourteous to the Christian Scientists." The section formerly read, "pretended healers," but was changed to read as follows: "All other professionals who practise the art of healing," *etc.*

We thank our heavenly Father for this dignified legal protection and recognition, and look forward to the day, not far distant, when the laws of every State will dignify the ministry of Christ as taught and practised in Christian Science, and as lived by our dear,

dear Leader, even as God has dignified, blessed, and prospered it, and her.

With devoted love,
ELIZABETH EARL JONES.

105 BAILEY ST., ASHEVILLE, N. C.,
October 11, 1903.

The following article, copied from the *Raleigh* (N. C.) *News and Observer*, is the one referred to in Miss Jones' letter: —

The Christian Science people, greatly pleased at the law affecting them passed by the last Legislature, are apt also to be pleased with the fact that the law recognizes them as healers, and that it gives them a license to heal. This license of five dollars annually, required of physicians, has been required of them, and how this came about in Kinston is told in the *Kinston Free Press* as follows: —

Sheriff Wooten issued licenses yesterday to two Christian Science healers in this city. This is probably the first to be issued to the healers of this sect in the State.

Upon the request of a prominent healer of the church, the section of the machinery act of the Legislature covering it was shown, whereupon application for license was made and obtained.

The section, after enumerating the different professions for which a license must be obtained to carry them on in this State, further says, "and all other professionals who practise the art of healing for pay, shall pay a license fee of five dollars."

This was construed to include the healers of the Christian Science church, and license was accordingly taken out.

The idea prevails that the last General Assembly of North Carolina relieved the healers of this sect from paying this fee, but this is not so. The board only excused them from a medical examination before a board of medical examiners.

Mrs. Eddy's reference to the death of her husband, Major George W. Glover, gives especial interest to the following letter from Newbern, N. C., which appeared in the *Wilmington* (N. C.) *Dispatch*, October 24, 1903. Mrs. Eddy has in her possession photographed copies of the notice of her husband's death and of her brother's letter, taken from the *Wilmington* (N. C.) *Chronicle* as they appear in that paper in the issues of July 3 and August 21, 1844, respectively. The photographs are verified by the certificate of a notary public and were presented to Mrs. Eddy by Miss Harrison.

MISS MARY HATCH HARRISON'S LETTER

To the Editor: — At no better time than now, when the whole country is recognizing the steady progress of Christian Science and admitting its interest in the movement, as shown by the fair attitude of the press everywhere, could we ask you to give your readers the following communication. It will put before them some interesting facts concerning Mrs. Mary Baker Eddy, and some incidents of her life in North and South Carolina which might not have been known but for a criticism of this good woman which was published in your paper in August, 1901.

I presume we should not be surprised that a noteworthy follower of our Lord should be maligned, since the great Master himself was scandalized, and he prophesied that his followers would be so treated. The calumniator who informed you in this instance locates Mrs. Eddy in Wilmington in 1843, thus contradicting his own statement, since Mrs. Eddy was not then a resident of Wilmington. A local Christian Scientist of your city, whose womanhood and Christianity are appreciated by all, assisted by a Mason of good standing there and a Christian Scientist of Charleston, S. C., carefully investigated the points concerning Major Glover's history which are questioned by this critic, and has found Mrs. Eddy's statements, relating to her husband (who she states was of Charleston, S. C., not of Wilmington, but who died there while on business in 1844, not in 1843, as claimed in your issue) are sustained by Masonic records in each place as well as by Wilmington newspapers of that year. In "Retrospection and Introspection" (p. 19) Mrs. Eddy says of this circumstance: —

"My husband was a Free Mason, being a member in St. Andrew's Lodge, No. 10, and of Union Chapter, No. 3, of Royal Arch Masons. He was highly esteemed and sincerely lamented by a large circle of friends and acquaintances, whose kindness and sympathy helped to support me in this terrible bereavement. A month later I returned to New Hampshire, where, at the end of four months, my babe was born. Colonel Glover's tender devotion to his young bride was remarked by all observers. With his parting breath he gave pathetic directions to his brother

Masons about accompanying her on her sad journey to the North. Here it is but justice to record, they performed their obligations most faithfully."

Such watchful solicitude as Mrs. Eddy received at the hands of Wilmington's best citizens, among whom she remembers the Rev. Mr. Reperton, a Baptist clergyman, and the Governor of the State, who accompanied her to the train on her departure, indicates her irreproachable standing in your city at that time.

The following letter of thanks, copied from the *Wilmington Chronicle* of August 21, 1844, testifies to the love and respect entertained for Mrs. Eddy by Wilmington's best men, whose Southern chivalry would have scorned to extend such unrestrained hospitality to an unworthy woman as quickly as it would have published the assailant of a good woman: —

A CARD

Through the columns of your paper, will you permit me, in behalf of the relatives and friends of the late Major George W. Glover of Wilmington and his bereaved lady, to return our thanks and express the feeling of gratitude we owe and cherish towards those friends of the deceased who so kindly attended him during his last sickness, and who still extended their care and sympathy to the lone, feeble, and bereaved widow after his decease. Much has often been said of the high feeling of honor and the noble generosity of heart which characterized the people of the South, yet when we listen to Mrs. Glover (my sister) whilst recounting the kind attention paid to the deceased during his late illness, the sympathy extended to her after his death, and the assistance volunteered to restore her to her friends at a distance of more than a thousand miles, the power of language would be but beggared by an attempt at expressing the feelings of a swelling bosom. The silent gush of grateful tears alone can tell the emotions of the thankful heart, — words are indeed but a meagre tribute for so noble an effort in behalf of the unfortunate, yet it is all we can award: will our friends at Wilmington accept it as a tribute of grateful hearts? Many thanks are due Mr. Cooke, who engaged to accompany her only to New York, but did not desert her or remit his kind attention until he saw her in the fond embrace of her friends.

Your friend and obedient servant,
(Signed) GEORGE S. BAKER.

SANBORNTON BRIDGE, N. H.,
August 12, 1844.

The paper containing this card is now in the Young Men's Christian Association at Wilmington.

The facts regarding Major Glover's membership in St. Andrew's Lodge, No. 10, were brought to light in a most interesting way. A Christian Scientist in Charleston was requested to look up the records of this lodge, as we had full confidence that it would corroborate Mrs. Eddy's claims. After frequent searchings and much interviewing with Masonic authorities, it was learned that the lodge was no longer in existence, and that during the Civil War many Masonic records were transferred to Columbia, where they were burned; but on repeated search a roll of papers recording the death of George Washington Glover in 1844 and giving best praises to his honorable record and Christian character was found;

and said record, with the seal of the Grand Secretary, is now in the possession of the chairman of the Christian Science publication committee.

In the records of St. John's Lodge, Wilmington, as found by one of your own citizens, a Mason, it is shown that on the twenty-eighth day of June, 1844, a special meeting was convened for the purpose of paying the last tribute of respect to Brother George W. Glover, who died on the night of the twenty-seventh. The minutes record this further proceeding: —

"A procession was formed, which moved to the residence of the deceased, and from thence to the Episcopal burying-ground, where the body was interred with the usual ceremonies. The procession then returned to the lodge, which was closed in due form."

It has never been claimed by Mrs. Eddy nor by any Christian Scientists that Major Glover's remains were carried North.

The *Wilmington Chronicle* of July 3, 1844, records that this good man, then known as Major George W. Glover, died on Thursday night, the twenty-seventh of June. The *Chronicle* states: "His end was calm and peaceful, and to those friends who attended him during his illness he gave the repeated assurance of his willingness to die, and of his full reliance for salvation on the merits of a crucified Redeemer. His remains were interred with Masonic honors. He has left an amiable wife, to whom he had been united but the brief space of six months, to lament this irreparable loss."

From the *Chronicle*, dated September 25, 1844, we copy the following: "We are assured that reports of unusual sickness in Wilmington are in circulation." This periodical then forthwith strives to give the impression that the rumor is not true. It is reasonable to infer from newspaper reports of that date that some insidious disease was raging at that time.

The allegation that copies of Mrs. Eddy's book, "Retrospection and Introspection," are few, and that efforts are being made to buy them up because she has contradicted herself, is without foundation. They are advertised in every weekly issue of the *Christian Science Sentinel*, and still contain the original account of her husband's demise at Wilmington.

May it not be, since this critic places certain circumstances in 1843, which records show really existed in 1844, that the woman whom he had in mind is some other one?

We can state Mrs. Eddy's teaching on the unreality of evil in no better terms than to quote her own words. Nothing could be further from her meaning than that evil could be indulged in while being called unreal. She declares in her Message to The Mother Church [1901]: "To assume there is no reality in sin, and yet commit sin, is sin itself, that clings fast to iniquity. The Publican's wail won his humble desire, while the Pharisee's self-righteousness crucified Jesus."

MARY HATCH HARRISON.

MAJOR GLOVER'S RECORD AS A MASON

Of further interest in this matter is the following extract from an editorial obituary which appeared in 1845 in the *Freemason's Monthly Magazine*, published by the late Charles W. Moore, Grand Secretary of the Grand Lodge of Massachusetts: —

Died at Wilmington, N. C., on the 27th June last, Major George W. Glover, formerly of Concord, N. H.

Brother Glover resided in Charleston, S. C., and was made a Mason in "St. Andrew's Lodge, No. 10." He was soon exalted to the degree of a Royal Arch Mason in "Union Chapter, No. 3," and retained his membership in both till his decease. He was devotedly attached to Masonry, faithful as a member and officer of the Lodge and Chapter, and beloved by his brothers and companions, who mourn his early death.

Additional facts regarding Major Glover, his illness and death, are that he was for a number of years a resident of Charleston, S. C., where he erected a fine dwelling-house, the drawings and specifications of which were kept by his widow for many years after his death. While at Wilmington, N. C., in June, 1844, Mr. Glover was attacked with yellow fever of the worst type, and at the end of nine days he passed away. This was the second case of the dread disease in that city, and in the hope of allaying the excitement which was fast arising, the authorities gave the cause of death as bilious fever, but they refused permission to take the remains to Charleston.

On the third day of her husband's illness, Mrs. Glover (now Mrs. Eddy) sent for the distinguished physician who attended cases of this terrible disease as an expert (Dr. McRee we think it was), and was told by him that he could not conceal the fact that the case was one of yellow fever in its worst form, and nothing could save the life of her husband. In these nine days and nights of agony the young wife prayed incessantly for her husband's recovery, and was told by the expert physician that but for her prayers the patient would have died on the seventh day.

The disease spread so rapidly that Mrs. Glover (Mrs. Eddy) was afraid to have her brother, George S. Baker, come to her after her husband's death, to take her back to the North. Although he desired to go to her assistance, she declined on this ground, and entrusted herself to the care of her husband's Masonic brethren, who faithfully performed their obligation to her. She makes grateful acknowledgment of this in her book, "Retrospection and Introspection." In this book (p. 20) she also states, "After returning to the paternal roof I lost all my husband's property, except what money I had brought with me; and remained with my parents until after my mother's decease." Mr. Glover had made no will previous to his last illness, and then the seizure of disease was so sudden and so violent that he was unable to make a will.

These letters and extracts are of absorbing interest to Christian Scientists as amplification of the facts given by Mrs. Eddy in "Retrospection and Introspection."

CHAPTER XX

GENERAL MISCELLANY

[*Boston Herald*, Sunday, May 15, 1898]

THE UNITED STATES TO GREAT BRITAIN

HAIL, brother! fling thy banner
    To the billows and the breeze;
We proffer thee warm welcome
    With our hand, though not our knees.

Lord of the main and manor!
    Thy palm, in ancient day,
Didst rock the country's cradle
    That wakes thy laureate's lay.

The hoar fight is forgotten;
    Our eagle, like the dove,
Returns to bless a bridal
    Betokened from above.

List, brother! angels whisper
    To Judah's sceptred race, —
"Thou of the self-same spirit,
    Allied by nations' grace,

"Wouldst cheer the hosts of heaven;
    For Anglo-Israel, lo!
Is marching under orders;
    His hand averts the blow."

Brave Britain, blest America!
Unite your battle-plan;
Victorious, all who live it, —
The love for God and man.

To the Public

The following views of the Rev. Mary Baker Eddy upon the subject of the Trinity, are known to us to be those uniformly held and expressed by her. A reference to her writings will fully corroborate this statement. — EDITOR *Sentinel*.

The contents of the last lecture of our dear brother, on the subject "The Unknown God Made Known," were unknown to me till after the lecture was delivered in Boston, April 5.

The members of the Board of Lectureship are not allowed to consult me relative to their subjects or the handling thereof, owing to my busy life, and they seek a higher source for wisdom and guidance. The talented author of this lecture has a heart full of love towards God and man. For once he may have overlooked the construction that people unfamiliar with his broad views and loving nature might put on his comparisons and ready humor. But all Christian Scientists deeply recognize the oneness of Jesus — that he stands alone in word and deed, the visible discoverer, founder, demonstrator, and great Teacher of Christianity, whose sandals none may unloose.

The Board of Lectureship is absolutely inclined to be, and is instructed to be, charitable towards all, and hating none. The purpose of its members is to subserve the interest of mankind, and to cement the bonds of Christian brotherhood, whose every link leads upward in the chain of being. The cardinal points of Christian Science cannot be lost sight of, namely — one God, supreme, infinite, and one Christ Jesus.

The Board of Lectureship is specially requested to be wise in discoursing on the great subject of Christian Science.

MARY BAKER EDDY.

Fast Day in New Hampshire, 1899

Along the lines of progressive Christendom, New Hampshire's advancement is marked. Already Massachusetts has exchanged Fast Day, and all that it formerly signified, for Patriots' Day, and the observance of the holiday illustrates the joy, grace, and glory of liberty. We read in Holy Writ that the disciples of St. John the Baptist said to the great Master, "Why do we and the Pharisees fast oft, but thy disciples fast not?" And he answered them in substance: My disciples rejoice in their present Christianity and have no cause to mourn; only those who have not the Christ, Truth, within them should wear sackcloth.

Jesus said to his disciples, "This kind goeth not out but by prayer and fasting," but he did not appoint a fast. Merely to abstain from eating was not sufficient to meet his demand. The animus of his saying was: Silence appetites, passion, and all that wars against Spirit and spiritual power. The fact that he healed the sick man without the observance of a material fast confirms this conclusion. Jesus attended feasts, but we have no record of his observing appointed fasts.

St. Paul's days for prayer were every day and every hour. He said, "Pray without ceasing." He classed the usage of special days and seasons for religious observances and precedents as belonging not to the Christian era, but to traditions, old-wives' fables, and endless genealogies.

The enlightenment, the erudition, the progress of religion and medicine in New Hampshire, are in excess of other States, as witness her schools, her churches, and her frown on class legislation. In many of the States in our Union a simple board of health, clad in a little brief authority, has arrogated to itself the prerogative of making laws for the State on the practice of medicine! But this attempt is shorn of some of its shamelessness by the courts immediately annulling such bills and plucking their plumes through constitutional interpretations. Not the tradition of the elders, nor a paltering, timid, or dastardly policy, is pursued by the leaders of our rock-ribbed State.

That the Governor of New Hampshire has suggested to his constituents to recur to a religious observance which virtually belongs to the past, should tend to enhance their confidence in his intention to rule righteously the affairs of state. However, Jesus' example in this, as in all else, suffices for the Christian era. The dark days of our forefathers and their implorations for peace and plenty have passed, and are succeeded by our time of abundance, even the full beneficence of the laws of the universe which man's diligence has utilized. Institutions of learning and progressive religion light their fires in every home.

I have one innate joy, and love to breathe it to the breeze as God's courtesy. A native of New Hampshire, a child of the Republic, a Daughter of the Revolution, I thank God that He has emblazoned on the escutcheon of this State, engraven on her granite rocks, and lifted to her giant hills the ensign of religious liberty — "Freedom to worship God."

Spring Greeting

Beloved brethren all over our land and in every land, accept your Leader's Spring greeting, while

> The bird of hope is singing
> A lightsome lay, a cooing call,
> And in her heart is beating
> A love for all —
> "'Tis peace not power I seek,
> 'Tis meet that man be meek."

[*New York Herald*, May 1, 1901]

[Extract]

Mrs. Eddy Talks

Christian Science has been so much to the fore of late that unusual public interest centres in the personality of Mrs. Mary Baker Eddy, the Founder of the cult. The granting of interviews is not usual, hence it was a special favor that Mrs. Eddy received the *Herald* correspondent.

It had been raining all day and was damp without, so the change from the misty air outside to the pleasant warmth within the ample, richly furnished house was agreeable. Seated in the large parlor, I became aware of a white-haired lady slowly descending the stairs. She entered with a gracious smile, walking uprightly and with light step, and after a kindly greeting took a seat on a sofa. It was Mrs. Eddy. There was no mistaking that. Older in years, white-haired and frailer, but Mrs. Eddy herself. The likeness to the portraits of twenty years ago, so often seen in reproductions, was unmistakable. There is no mistaking certain lines that depend upon the osseous structure; there is no mistaking the eyes — those eyes the shade of which is so hard to catch, whether blue-gray or grayish brown, and which are always bright. And when I say frail, let it not be understood that I mean weak, for weak she was not. When we were snugly seated in the other and smaller parlor across the hall, which serves as a library, Mrs. Eddy sat back to be questioned.

"The continuity of The Church of Christ, Scientist," she said, in her clear voice, "is assured. It is growing wonderfully. It will embrace all the churches, one by one, because in it alone is the simplicity of the oneness of God; the oneness of Christ and the perfecting of man stated scientifically."

"How will it be governed after all now concerned in its government shall have passed on?"

"It will evolve scientifically. Its essence is evangelical. Its government will develop as it progresses."

"Will there be a hierarchy, or will it be directed by a single earthly ruler?"

"In time its present rules of service and present rulership will advance nearer perfection."

It was plain that the answers to questions would be in Mrs. Eddy's own spirit. She has a rapt way of talking, looking large-eyed into space, and works around a question in her own way, reaching an answer often unexpectedly after a prolonged exordium. She explained: "No present change is contemplated in the rulership. You would ask, perhaps, whether my successor will be a woman or a man. I can answer that. It will be a man."

"Can you name the man?"

"I cannot answer that now."

Here, then, was the definite statement that Mrs. Eddy's immediate successor would, like herself, be the ruler.

NOT A POPE OR A CHRIST

"I have been called a pope, but surely I have sought no such distinction. I have simply taught as I learned while healing the sick. It was in 1866 that the light of the Science came first to me. In 1875 I wrote my book. It brought down a shower of abuse upon my head, but it won converts from the first. I followed it up, teaching and organizing, and trust in me grew. I was the mother, but of course the term pope is used figuratively.

"A position of authority," she went on, "became necessary. Rules were necessary, and I made a code of by-laws, but each one was the fruit of experience and the result of prayer. Entrusting their enforcement to others, I found at one time that they had five churches under discipline. I intervened. Dissensions are dangerous in an infant church. I wrote to each church in tenderness, in exhortation, and in rebuke, and so brought all back to union and love again. If that is to be a pope, then you can judge for yourself. I have even been spoken of as a Christ, but to my understanding of Christ that is impossible. If we say that the sun stands for God, then all his rays collectively stand for Christ, and each separate ray for men and women. God the Father is greater than Christ, but Christ is 'one with the Father,' and so the mystery is scientifically explained. There can be but one Christ."

"And the soul of man?"

"It is not the spirit of God, inhabiting clay and then withdrawn from it, but God preserving individuality and personality to the end. I hold it absurd to say that when a man dies, the man will be at once better than he was before death. How can it be? The individuality of him must make gradual approaches to Soul's perfection."

"Do you reject utterly the bacteria theory of the propagation of disease?"

"Oh," with a prolonged inflection, "entirely. If I harbored that idea about a disease, I should think myself in danger of catching it."

ABOUT INFECTIOUS DISEASES

"Then as to the laws — the health laws of the States on the question of infectious and contagious diseases. How does Christian Science stand as to them?"

"I say, 'Render to Caesar the things that are Caesar's.' We cannot force perfection on the world. Were vaccination of any avail, I should tremble for mankind; but, knowing it is not, and that the fear of catching smallpox is more dangerous than any material infection, I say: Where vaccination is compulsory, let your children be vaccinated, and see that your mind is in such a state that by your prayers vaccination will do the children no harm. So long as Christian Scientists obey the laws, I do not suppose their mental reservations will be thought to matter much. But every thought tells, and Christian Science will overthrow false knowledge in the end."

"What is your attitude to science in general? Do you oppose it?"

"Not," with a smile, "if it is really science."

"Well, electricity, engineering, the telephone, the steam engine — are these too material for Christian Science?"

"No; only false science — healing by drugs. I was a sickly child. I was dosed with drugs until they had no effect on me. The doctors said I would live if the drugs could be made to act on me. Then homœopathy came like blessed relief to me, but I found that when I prescribed pellets without any medication they acted just the same and healed the sick. How could I believe in a science of drugs?"

"But surgery?"

"The work done by the surgeon is the last healing that will be vouchsafed to us, or rather attained by us, as we near a state of spiritual perfection. At present I am conservative about advice on surgical cases."

"But the pursuit of modern material inventions?"

"Oh, we cannot oppose them. They all tend to newer, finer, more etherealized ways of living. They seek the finer essences. They light the way to the Church of Christ. We use them, we make them our figures of speech. They are preparing the way for us."

We talked on many subjects, some only of which are here touched upon, and her views, strictly and always from the standpoint of Christian Science, were continually surprising. She talks as one who has lived with her subject for a lifetime, — an ordinary lifetime; and so far from being puzzled by any question, welcomes it as another opportunity for presenting another view of her religion.

Those who have been anticipating nature and declaring Mrs. Eddy non-existent may learn authoritatively from the *Herald* that she is in the flesh and in health. Soon after I reached Concord on my return from Pleasant View, Mrs. Eddy's carriage drove into town and made several turns about the court-house before returning. She was inside, and as she passed me the same expression of looking forward, thinking, thinking, was on her face.

CONCORD, N. H.,
   Tuesday, April 30, 1901.

Mrs. Eddy's Successor

In a recent interview which appeared in the columns of the *New York Herald*, the Rev. Mary Baker Eddy, Discoverer and Founder of Christian Science, stated that her successor would be a man. Various conjectures having arisen as to whether she had in mind any particular person when the statement was made, Mrs. Eddy gave the following to the Associated Press, May 16, 1901: —

"I did say that a man would be my future successor. By this I did not mean any man to-day on earth.

"Science and Health makes it plain to all Christian Scientists that the manhood and womanhood of God have already been revealed in a degree through Christ Jesus and Christian Science, His two witnesses. What remains to lead on the centuries and reveal my successor, is man in the image and likeness of the Father-Mother God, man the generic term for mankind."

Gift of a Loving-cup

The Executive Members of The Mother Church of Christ, Scientist, will please accept my heartfelt acknowledgment of their beautiful gift to me, a loving-cup, presented July 16, 1903. The exquisite design of boughs encircling this cup, illustrated by Keats' touching couplet,

> Ah happy, happy boughs, that cannot shed
> Your leaves, nor ever bid the Spring adieu!

would almost suggest that nature had reproduced her primal presence, bough, bird, and song, to salute me. The twelve beautiful pearls that crown this cup call to mind the number of our great Master's first disciples, and the parable of the priceless pearl which purchases our field of labor in exchange for all else.

I shall treasure my loving-cup with all its sweet associations.

[Special contribution to "Bohemia." A symposium.]

Fundamental Christian Science

Most thinkers concede that Science is the law of God; that matter is not a law-maker; that man is not the author of Science, and that a phenomenon is chimerical, unless it be the manifestation of a fixed Principle whose noumenon is God and whose phenomenon is Science.

My discovery that mankind is absolutely healed of so-called disease and injuries by other than drugs, surgery, hygiene, electricity, magnetism, or will-power, induced a deep research, which proved conclusively that all effect must be the offspring of a universal cause. I sought this cause, not within but *ab extra*, and I found it was God made manifest in the flesh, and understood through divine Science. Then I was healed, and the greatest of all questions was solved sufficiently to give a reason for the hope that was within me.

The religious departure from divine Science sprang from the belief that the man Jesus, rather than his divine Principle, God, saves man, and that *materia medica* heals him. The writer's departure from such a religion was based upon her discovery that neither man nor *materia medica*, but God, heals and saves mankind.

Here, however, was no stopping-place, since Science demanded a rational proof that the divine Mind heals the sick and saves the sinner. God unfolded the way, the demonstration thereof was made, and the certainty of its value to the race firmly established. I had found unmistakably an actual, unfailing causation, enshrined in the divine Principle and in the laws of man and the universe, which, never producing an opposite effect, demonstrated Christianity and proved itself Science, for it healed the sick and reformed the sinner on a demonstrable Principle and given rule. The human demonstrator of this Science may mistake, but the Science remains the law of God — infallible, eternal. Divine Life, Truth, Love is the basic Principle of all Science, it solves the problem of being; and nothing that worketh ill can enter into the solution of God's problems.

FUNDAMENTAL CHRISTIAN SCIENCE 349

God is Mind, and divine Mind was first chronologically, is first potentially, and is the healer to whom all things are possible. A scientific state of health is a consciousness of health, holiness, immortality — a consciousness gained through Christ, Truth; while disease is a mental state or error that Truth destroys. It is self-evident that matter, or the body, cannot cause disease, since disease is in a sense susceptible of both ease and dis-ease, and matter is not sensible. Kant, Locke, Berkeley, Tyndall, and Spencer afford little aid in understanding divine metaphysics or its therapeutics. Christian Science is a divine largess, a gift of God — understood by and divinely natural to him who sits at the feet of Jesus clothed in truth, who is putting off the hypothesis of matter because he is conscious of the allness of God — "looking unto Jesus the author and finisher of our faith." Thus the great Way-shower, invested with glory, is understood, and his words and works illustrate "the way, the truth, and the life."

Divine modes or manifestations are natural, beyond the so-called natural sciences and human philosophy, because they are spiritual, and coexist with the God of nature in absolute Science. The laws of God, or divine Mind, obtain not in material phenomena, or phenomenal evil, which is lawless and traceable to mortal mind — human will divorced from Science.

Inductive or deductive reasoning is correct only as it is spiritual, induced by love and deduced from God, Spirit; only as it makes manifest the infinite nature, including all law and supplying all the needs of man. Wholly hypothetical, inductive reasoning reckons creation as its own creator, seeks cause in effect, and from atom

and dust draws its conclusions of Deity and man, law and
gospel, leaving science at the beck of material phenomena,
or leaving it out of the question. To begin with the
divine noumenon, Mind, and to end with the phenomenon, matter, is minus divine logic and plus human hypothesis, with its effects, sin, disease, and death. It was
in this dilemma that revelation, uplifting human reason,
came to the writer's rescue, when calmly and rationally,
though faintly, she spiritually discerned the divine idea
of the cosmos and Science of man.

WHITHER?

Father, did'st not Thou the dark wave treading
Lift from despair the struggler with the sea?
And heed'st Thou not the scalding tear man's shedding,
And know'st Thou not the pathway glad and free?

This weight of anguish which they blindly bind
On earth, this bitter searing to the core of love;
This crushing out of health and peace, mankind —
Thou all, Thou infinite — dost doom above.

Oft mortal sense is darkened unto death
(The Stygian shadow of a world of glee);
The old foundations of an early faith
Sunk from beneath man, whither shall he flee?

To Love divine, whose kindling mighty rays
Brighten the horoscope of crumbling creeds,
Dawn Truth delightful, crowned with endless days,
And Science ripe in prayer, in word, and deeds.

A Letter from our Leader

With our Leader's kind permission, the *Sentinel* is privileged to publish her letter of recent date, addressed to Mr. John C. Higdon of St. Louis, Mo. This letter is especially interesting on account of its beautiful tribute to Free Masonry.

Beloved Student: — Your interesting letter was handed to me duly. This is my earliest moment in which to answer it.

"Know Thyself," the title of your gem quoted, is indeed a divine command, for the *morale* of Free Masonry is above ethics — it touches the hem of his garment who spake divinely.

It was truly Masonic, tender, grand in you to remember me as the widow of a Mason. May you and I and all mankind meet in that hour of Soul where are no partings, no pain.

Lovingly yours in Christ,
MARY BAKER EDDY.

PLEASANT VIEW, CONCORD, N. H.,
February 9, 1906.

Take Notice

I have not read Gerhardt C. Mars' book, "The Interpretation of Life," therefore I have not endorsed it, and any assertions to the contrary are false. Christian Scientists are not concerned with philosophy; divine Science is all they need, or can have in reality.

MARY BAKER EDDY.

BOX G, BROOKLINE, MASS.,
June 24, 1908.

RECOGNITION OF BLESSINGS

Reverend Mary Baker Eddy,
   Chestnut Hill, Mass.

Beloved Leader: — Informally assembled, we, the ushers of your church, desire to express our recognition of the blessings that have come to us through the peculiar privileges we enjoy in this church work. We are prompted to acknowledge our debt of gratitude to you for your life of spirituality, with its years of tender ministry, yet we know that the real gratitude is what is proved in better lives.

It is our earnest prayer that we may so reflect in our thoughts and acts the teachings of Christian Science that our daily living may be a fitting testimony of the efficacy of our Cause in the regeneration of mankind.

THE USHERS OF THE MOTHER CHURCH.

Boston, Mass., October 9, 1908.

MRS. EDDY'S REPLY

Beloved Ushers of The Mother Church of Christ, Scientist: — I thank you not only for your tender letter to me, but for ushering into our church the hearers and the doers of God's Word.

MARY BAKER EDDY.

Box G, Brookline, Mass.,
   October 12, 1908.

MRS. EDDY'S THANKS

Beloved Christian Scientists: — Accept my thanks for your successful plans for the first issue of *The Christian Science Monitor*. My desire is that every Christian

Scientist, and as many others as possible, subscribe for and read our daily newspaper.

MARY BAKER EDDY.

Box G, Brookline, Mass.,
November 16, 1908.

[Extract from the leading Editorial in Vol. 1, No. 1, of *The Christian Science Monitor*, November 25, 1908]

SOMETHING IN A NAME

I have given the name to all the Christian Science periodicals. The first was *The Christian Science Journal*, designed to put on record the divine Science of Truth; the second I entitled *Sentinel*, intended to hold guard over Truth, Life, and Love; the third, *Der Herold der Christian Science*, to proclaim the universal activity and availability of Truth; the next I named *Monitor*, to spread undivided the Science that operates unspent. The object of the *Monitor* is to injure no man, but to bless all mankind.

MARY BAKER EDDY.

ARTICLE XXII., SECTION 17

MRS. EDDY'S ROOM. — SECTION 17. The room in The Mother Church formerly known as "Mother's Room," shall hereafter be closed to visitors.

There is nothing in this room now of any special interest. "Let the dead bury their dead," and the spiritual have all place and power.

MARY BAKER EDDY.

To Whom It May Concern

In view of complaints from the field, because of alleged misrepresentations by persons offering Bibles and other books for sale which they claim have been endorsed by me, it is due the field to state that I recommend nothing but what is published or sold by The Christian Science Publishing Society. Christian Scientists are under no obligation to buy books for which my endorsement is claimed.

MARY BAKER EDDY.

BOX G, BROOKLINE, MASS.,
April 28, 1909.

EXTEMPORE
January 1, 1910

I

O blessings infinite!
O glad New Year!
Sweet sign and substance
Of God's presence here.

II

Give us not only angels' songs,
But Science vast, to which belongs
The tongue of angels
And the song of songs.

MARY BAKER EDDY.

[The above lines were written extemporaneously by Mrs. Eddy on New Year's morning. The members of her household were with her at the time, and it was gratifying to them, as it will be to the field, to see in her spiritualized thought and mental vigor a symbol of the glad New Year on which we have just entered. — EDITOR *Sentinel*.]

MEN IN OUR RANKS

A letter from a student in the field says there is a grave need for more men in Christian Science practice.

I have not infrequently hinted at this. However, if the occasion demands it, I will repeat that men are very important factors in our field of labor for Christian Science. The male element is a strong supporting arm to religion as well as to politics, and we need in our ranks of divine energy, the strong, the faithful, the untiring spiritual armament.

MARY BAKER EDDY.

CHESTNUT HILL, MASS.,
    February 7, 1910.

A PÆAN OF PRAISE

"Behind a frowning providence
He hides a shining face."

The Christian Scientists at Mrs. Eddy's home are the happiest group on earth. Their faces shine with the reflection of light and love; their footsteps are not weary; their thoughts are upward; their way is onward, and their light shines. The world is better for this happy group of Christian Scientists; Mrs. Eddy is happier because of them; God is glorified in His reflection of peace, love, joy.

When will mankind awake to know their present ownership of all good, and praise and love the spot where God dwells most conspicuously in His reflection of love and leadership? When will the world waken to the privilege of knowing God, the liberty and glory of His presence, — where

> "He plants His footsteps in the sea
> And rides upon the storm."

MARY BAKER EDDY.

CHESTNUT HILL, MASS.,
April 20, 1910.

A Statement by Mrs. Eddy

Editor Christian Science Sentinel: — In reply to inquiries, will you please state that within the last five years I have given no assurance, no encouragement nor consent to have my picture issued, other than the ones now and heretofore presented in Science and Health.

MARY BAKER EDDY.

CHESTNUT HILL, MASS.,
July 18, 1910.

The Way of Wisdom

No man can serve two masters: for either he will hate the one, and love the other; or else he will hold to the one, and despise the other. Ye cannot serve God and mammon. — MATTHEW 6 : 24.

The infinite is one, and this one is Spirit; Spirit is God, and this God is infinite good.

This simple statement of oneness is the only possible correct version of Christian Science. God being infinite,

He is the only basis of Science; hence materiality is wholly
apart from Christian Science, and is only a "Suffer it to
be so now" until we arrive at the spiritual fulness of God,
Spirit, even the divine idea of Christian Science, —
Christ, born of God, the offspring of Spirit, — wherein
matter has neither part nor portion, because matter is the
absolute opposite of spiritual means, manifestation, and
demonstration. The only incentive of a mistaken sense
is malicious animal magnetism, — the name of all evil, —
and this must be understood.

I have crowned The Mother Church building with the
spiritual modesty of Christian Science, which is its jewel.
When my dear brethren in New York desire to build
higher, — to enlarge their phylacteries and demonstrate
Christian Science to a higher extent, — they must begin
on a wholly spiritual foundation, than which there is no
other, and proportionably estimate their success and
glory of achievement only as they build upon the rock of
Christ, the spiritual foundation. This will open the way,
widely and impartially, to their never-ending success, —
to salvation and eternal Christian Science.

Spirit is infinite; therefore *Spirit is all.* "There is no
matter" is not only the axiom of true Christian Science,
but it is the only basis upon which this Science can be
demonstrated.

A Letter by Mrs. Eddy

Mrs. Augusta E. Stetson, New York City.

Beloved Student: — I have just finished reading your
interesting letter. I thank you for acknowledging me as
your Leader, and I know that every true follower of

Christian Science abides by the definite rules which demonstrate the true following of their Leader; therefore, if you are sincere in your protestations and are doing as you say you are, you will be blessed in your obedience.

The Scriptures say, "Watch and pray, that ye enter not into temptation." You are aware that animal magnetism is the opposite of divine Science, and that this opponent is the means whereby the conflict against Truth is engendered and developed. Beloved! you need to watch and pray that the enemy of good cannot separate you from your Leader and best earthly friend.

You have been duly informed by me that, however much I desire to read all that you send to me, I have not the time to do so. The Christian Science Publishing Society will settle the question whether or not they shall publish your poems. It is part of their duties to relieve me of so much labor.

I thank you for the money you send me which was given you by your students. I shall devote it to a worthy and charitable purpose.

Mr. Adam Dickey is my secretary, through whom all my business is transacted.

Give my best wishes and love to your dear students and church.

Lovingly your teacher and Leader,
MARY BAKER EDDY.

BOX G, BROOKLINE, MASS.,
July 12, 1909.

TAKE NOTICE

I approve the By-laws of The Mother Church, and require the Christian Science Board of Directors to main-

tain them and sustain them. These Directors do not
act contrary to the rules of the Church Manual, neither
do they trouble me with their difficulties with individuals in their own church or with the members of branch
churches.

My province as a Leader — as the Discoverer and
Founder of Christian Science — is not to interfere in
cases of discipline, and I hereby publicly declare that I
am not personally involved in the affairs of the church in
any other way than through my written and published
rules, all of which can be read by the individual who
desires to inform himself of the facts.

MARY BAKER EDDY.

BROOKLINE, MASS.,
October 12, 1909.

A Letter from Mrs. Eddy

In the *Sentinel* of July 31, 1909, there appeared under
the heading "None good but one," a number of quotations from a composite letter, dated July 19, which had
been written to Mrs. Augusta E. Stetson by twenty-four
of her students who then occupied offices in the building
of First Church of Christ, Scientist, of New York, and
were known as "the practitioners." This letter was forwarded to Mrs. Eddy by Mrs. Stetson with the latter's
unqualified approval. Upon receipt of this letter Mrs.
Eddy wrote to Mrs. Stetson as follows: —

My Dear Student: — Awake and arise from this temptation produced by animal magnetism upon yourself,
allowing your students to deify you and me. Treat yourself for it and get your students to help you rise out of it.

It will be your destruction if you do not do this. Answer this letter immediately.

> As ever, lovingly your teacher,
> MARY BAKER EDDY.

BROOKLINE, MASS.,
July 23, 1909.

A Letter by Mrs. Eddy [1]

TO THE BOARD OF TRUSTEES, FIRST CHURCH OF CHRIST, SCIENTIST, NEW YORK CITY.

Beloved Brethren: — In consideration of the present momentous question at issue in First Church of Christ, Scientist, New York City, I am constrained to say, if I can settle this church difficulty amicably by a few words, as many students think I can, I herewith cheerfully subscribe these words of love: —

My beloved brethren in First Church of Christ, Scientist, New York City, I advise you with all my soul to support the Directors of The Mother Church, and unite with those in your church who are supporting The Mother Church Directors. Abide in fellowship with and obedience to The Mother Church, and in this way God will bless and prosper you. This I know, for He has proved it to me for forty years in succession.

> Lovingly yours,
> MARY BAKER EDDY.

BROOKLINE, MASS.,
November 13, 1909.

A Letter by Mrs. Eddy

My Dear Student: — Your favor of the 10th instant is at hand. God is above your teacher, your healer, or any

---

[1] The text here given is that of the original letter as sent by Mrs. Eddy, and published in the *Christian Science Sentinel* of November 20, 1909. This letter was republished in the *Sentinel* of December 4, 1909, at Mrs. Eddy's request, with the words "in Truth" inserted after the word "Abide."

earthly friend. Follow the directions of God as simplified
in Christian Science, and though it be through deserts
He will direct you into the paths of peace.

I do not presume to give you personal instruction as
to your relations with other students. All I say is stated
in Christian Science to be used as a model. Please find
it there, and do not bring your Leader into a personal
conflict.

I have not seen Mrs. Stetson for over a year, and have
not written to her since August 30, 1909.

Sincerely yours,
MARY BAKER EDDY.

BROOKLINE, MASS.,
December 11, 1909.

A Telegram and Mrs. Eddy's Reply

[Telegram]

MRS. MARY BAKER EDDY,
Chestnut Hill, Mass.

Beloved Leader: — We rejoice that our church has promptly made its demonstration by action at its annual meeting in accordance with your desire for a truly democratic and liberal government.

BOARD OF TRUSTEES,
FIRST CHURCH OF CHRIST, SCIENTIST,
NEW YORK, N. Y.,
CHARLES DEAN, *Chairman*,
ARTHUR O. PROBST, *Clerk*.

NEW YORK, N. Y.,
January 19, 1910.

MRS. EDDY'S REPLY

CHARLES A. DEAN, CHAIRMAN BOARD OF TRUSTEES,
FIRST CHURCH OF CHRIST, SCIENTIST, NEW YORK CITY.

Beloved Brethren: — I rejoice with you in the victory of right over wrong, of Truth over error.

MARY BAKER EDDY.

CHESTNUT HILL, MASS.,
January 20, 1910.

A LETTER AND MRS. EDDY'S REPLY

MRS. MARY BAKER EDDY,
Chestnut Hill, Mass.

Revered Leader, Counsellor, and Friend: — The Trustees and Readers of all the Christian Science churches and societies of Greater New York, for the first time gathered in one place with one accord, to confer harmoniously and unitedly in promoting and enlarging the activities of the Cause of Christian Science in this community, as their first act send you their loving greetings.

With hearts filled with gratitude to God, we rejoice in your inspired leadership, in your wise counselling. We revere and cherish your friendship, and assure you that it is our intention to take such action as will unite the churches and societies in this field in the bonds of Christian love and fellowship, thus demonstrating practical Christianity.

Gratefully yours,

FIRST CHURCH OF CHRIST, SCIENTIST,
SECOND CHURCH OF CHRIST, SCIENTIST,

THIRD CHURCH OF CHRIST, SCIENTIST,
FOURTH CHURCH OF CHRIST, SCIENTIST,
FIFTH CHURCH OF CHRIST, SCIENTIST,
SIXTH CHURCH OF CHRIST, SCIENTIST,
FIRST CHURCH OF CHRIST, SCIENTIST, Brooklyn,
FOURTH CHURCH OF CHRIST, SCIENTIST, Brooklyn,
FIRST CHURCH OF CHRIST, SCIENTIST, Staten Island,
CHRISTIAN SCIENCE SOCIETY, Bronx,
CHRISTIAN SCIENCE SOCIETY, Flushing, L. I.,
By the Committee.

NEW YORK, N. Y.,
February 5, 1910.

MRS. EDDY'S REPLY

This proof that sanity and Science govern the Christian Science churches in Greater New York is soul inspiring.
MARY BAKER EDDY.

[*The Christian Science Journal*, July, 1895. Reprinted in *Christian Science Sentinel*, November 13, 1909]

TO THE MEMBERS OF THE CHRISTIAN SCIENTIST ASSOCIATION

My address before the Christian Scientist Association has been misrepresented and evidently misunderstood by some students. The gist of the whole subject was not to malpractise unwittingly. In order to be sure that one is not doing this, he must avoid naming, in his mental treatment, any other individual but the patient whom he is treating, and practise only to heal. Any deviation from this direct rule is more or less dangerous. No mortal is infallible, — hence the Scripture, "Judge no man."

The rule of mental practice in Christian Science is strictly to handle no other mentality but the mind of your patient, and treat this mind to be Christly. Any departure from this golden rule is inadmissible. This mental practice includes and inculcates the commandment, "Thou shalt have no other gods before me." Animal magnetism, hypnotism, *etc.*, are disarmed by the practitioner who excludes from his own consciousness, and that of his patients, all sense of the realism of any other cause or effect save that which cometh from God. And he should teach his students to defend themselves from all evil, and to heal the sick, by recognizing the supremacy and allness of good. This epitomizes what heals all manner of sickness and disease, moral or physical. MARY BAKER EDDY.

[*Christian Science Sentinel*, February 15, 1908]

CONCORD, N. H., TO MRS. EDDY, AND MRS. EDDY'S REPLY

THE ESTEEM IN WHICH MRS. EDDY IS HELD IN CONCORD HAS BEEN OFFICIALLY EXPRESSED IN THE FOLLOWING PREAMBLE AND RESOLUTIONS, WHICH WERE UNANIMOUSLY ADOPTED BY THE BOARD OF ALDERMEN AND COMMON COUNCIL OF THAT CITY AND THUS HAVE BECOME A PART OF CONCORD'S RECORDS.

CONCORD, NEW HAMPSHIRE, TO REV. MARY BAKER G. EDDY.

Whereas, Rev. Mary Baker G. Eddy has decided to make her home in Massachusetts, after a residence of nineteen years in Concord, and

Whereas, her residence here has been the source of so much good to the city, and

Whereas, the most kindly and helpful relations have ever existed between Mrs. Eddy and Concord and Concord people,

Be It Resolved, That the City of Concord, through its Board of Aldermen and Common Council, in joint convention, convey to Mrs. Eddy,

1. Its appreciation of her life in its midst,
2. Its regrets over her departure, and
3. The hope that though absent she will always cherish a loving regard for the city, near which she was born, and for its people, among whom she has lived for so many years.

Be It Resolved, That the Mayor and City Clerk be authorized and instructed to sign and attest this testimonial in behalf of the City Council.

Done this tenth day of February, nineteen hundred and eight.

CHARLES R. CORNING, *Mayor.*
Attest: HENRY E. CHAMBERLAIN, *City Clerk.*

MRS. EDDY'S REPLY

TO THE HONORABLE MAYOR AND CITY COUNCIL,
   CONCORD, N. H.

Gentlemen: — I have not only the pleasure, but the honor of replying to the City Council of Concord, in joint convention assembled, and to Alderman Cressy, for the kindly resolutions passed by your honorable body, and for which I thank you deeply. Lest I should acknowledge more than I deserve of praise, I leave their courteous opinions to their good judgment.

My early days hold rich recollections of associations with your churches and institutions, and memory has a distinct model in granite of the good folk in Concord, which, like the granite of their State, steadfast and enduring, has hinted this quality to other states and nations all over the world.

My home influence, early education, and church experience, have unquestionably ripened into the fruits of my present religious experience, and for this I prize them. May I honor this origin and deserve the continued friendship and esteem of the people in my native State.

Sincerely yours,
MARY BAKER G. EDDY.

BOX G, BROOKLINE, MASS.,
February 13, 1908.